The Serpent P(
&
The Lost Book of Djehuti and the
Wisdom of The Caduceus

Fifth Edition
Expanded

P.O.Box 570459
Miami, Florida, 33257
(305) 378-6253 Fax: (305) 378-6253

First U.S. edition 1996 By Reginald Muata Ashby
Second Edition © 1997 By Reginald Muata Ashby
Third Edition © 2001 By Reginald Muata Ashby
Fourth Edition © 2002 By Reginald Muata Ashby
Fifth Edition © 2003 By Reginald Muata Ashby

The author is available for group lectures and individual counseling. For further information contact the publisher.

Ashby, Muata
The Serpent Power ISBN: 1-884564-19-4

Library of Congress Cataloging in Publication Data

1 Yoga 2 Egyptian Philosophy, 3 Eastern Philosophy, 4 Esoterism,
5 Meditation, 6 Self Help.

Culture - Health - Spirituality
For the 21st Century

Sema
Institute of Yoga

Sema (☥) is an ancient Egyptian word and symbol meaning *union*. The Sema Institute is dedicated to the propagation of the universal teachings of spiritual evolution which relate to the union of humanity and the union of all things within the universe. It is a non-denominational organization which recognizes the unifying principles in all spiritual and religious systems of evolution throughout the world. Our primary goals are to provide the wisdom of ancient spiritual teachings in books, courses and other forms of communication. Secondly, to provide expert instruction and training in the various yogic disciplines including Ancient Egyptian Philosophy, Christian Gnosticism, Indian Philosophy and modern science. Thirdly, to promote world peace and Universal Love.

A primary focus of our tradition is to identify and acknowledge the yogic principles within all religions and to relate them to each other in order to promote their deeper understanding as well as to show the essential unity of purpose and the unity of all living beings and nature within the whole of existence.

The Institute is open to all who believe in the principles of peace, non-violence and spiritual emancipation regardless of sex, race, or creed.

Culture - Health - Spirituality
For the 21st Century

About the Author

Who is Sebai Muata Abhaya Ashby D.D. Ph. D.?

Priest, Author, lecturer, poet, philosopher, musician, publisher, counselor and spiritual preceptor and founder of the Sema Institute-Temple of Aset, Muata Ashby was born in Brooklyn, New York City, and grew up in the Caribbean. His family is from Puerto Rico and Barbados. Displaying an interest in ancient civilizations and the Humanities, Sebai Maa began studies in the area of religion and philosophy and achieved doctorates in these areas while at the same time he began to collect his research into what would later become several books on the subject of the origins of Yoga Philosophy and practice in ancient Africa (Ancient Egypt) and also the origins of Christian Mysticism in Ancient Egypt.

Sebai Maa (Muata Abhaya Ashby) holds a Doctor of Philosophy Degree in Religion, and a Doctor of Divinity Degree in Holistic Health. He is also a Pastoral Counselor and Teacher of Yoga Philosophy and Discipline. Dr. Ashby received his Doctor of Divinity Degree from and is an adjunct faculty member of the American Institute of Holistic Theology. Dr. Ashby is a certified as a PREP Relationship Counselor. Dr. Ashby has been an independent researcher and practitioner of Egyptian Yoga, Indian Yoga, Chinese Yoga, Buddhism and mystical psychology as well as Christian Mysticism. Dr. Ashby has engaged in Post Graduate research in advanced Jnana, Bhakti and Kundalini Yogas at the Yoga Research Foundation. He has extensively studied mystical religious traditions from around the world and is an accomplished lecturer, musician, artist, poet, screenwriter, playwright and author of over 25 books on Kamitan yoga and spiritual philosophy. He is an Ordained Minister and Spiritual Counselor and also the founder the Sema Institute, a non-profit organization dedicated to spreading the wisdom of Yoga and the Ancient Egyptian mystical traditions. Further, he is the spiritual leader and head priest of the Per Aset or Temple of Aset, based in Miami, Florida. Thus, as a scholar, Dr. Muata Ashby is a teacher, lecturer and researcher. However, as a spiritual leader, his title is *Sebai,* which means Spiritual Preceptor.

Sebai Dr. Ashby began his research into the spiritual philosophy of Ancient Africa (Egypt) and India and noticed correlations in the culture and arts of the two countries. This was the catalyst for a successful book series on the subject called "Egyptian Yoga". Now he has created a series of musical compositions which explore this unique area of music from ancient Egypt and its connection to world music.

Table of Contents

About the Author 4

Preface 8

Who Were the Ancient Egyptians and why Should we Learn About Them? 8
Where is Egypt? 10

ABOUT THE ANCIENT EGYPTIANS: 14

Author's Foreword 15

Introduction to Egyptian Yoga 22

The Term "Egyptian Yoga" and The Philosophy Behind It 25
The Yogic Postures in Ancient Egypt 37

Chapter 2 48

What is Serpent Power Yoga? 48

History of The Yoga of Life Force Development for Spiritual Enlightenment in Ancient Egypt 49
The Serpent Power Yoga Philosophy and Iconography in Ancient Egypt... 49
History of the Serpent Power in Ancient Egypt 49

The Serpent Power Path 66
Teachings of the Serpent Power teaching in Kamitan (Ancient Egyptian) Iconography and Myth 72

Part II: The Lost Book of Djehuti and the Wisdom of The Caduceus 75

The Ancient Egyptian Story of the Lost Book of Djehuti. 76
The Education of Ancient Egyptian Initiates 82
Where is the highest Wisdom to be found and how can the Highest Spiritual Consciousness be Attained? 86

Chapter 3: The Serpent Power Discipline of Ancient Kamit 98

Stage 1 - Cleansing of the Physical, Subtle and Causal Bodies 98
Mysticism of the Color Green 111
"Si i(e) mettu wadj" or " mettu swaj" for short 113
The Forces of Chaos 116

Chapter 4: The Philosophy of the Life Force and the Process fo Spiritual Evolution 117

Chapter 5: Cultivation of the Serpent Power 128
The Body-Mind-Soul Relationship 132
Working With The Psycho-spiritual Energy Centers 133

The Movement of the Serpent Power According to the Ancient Egyptian Scripture 134

The Ancient Egyptian Temple Architecture and the Serpent Power 137

More Examples of the Kamitan Caduceus: 141

Understanding the Principles of the Energy Centers 144

The Movement of the Serpent Power 163

How to Make the Serpent Power Move 171

Vibration, Hekau, Life Force and the Serpent Power 175

The Ancient Egyptian Concept of Vibration 175

Poles of Vibration **178**

Poles of vibration: *178*

Music and Color **179**

Color and Spiritual Evolution **180**

Precautions **182**

Chapter 6: Meditations and Exercises For Serpent Power Cultivation and Spiritual Transcendence *183*

Index *197*

Bibliography .... Error! Bookmark not defined.

OTHER BOOKS BY MUATA ASHBY .... Error! Bookmark not defined.

Self-Publish For Profit, Spiritual Fulfillment and Service to Humanity .... Error! Bookmark not defined.

Music Based on the Prt M Hru and other Kamitic Texts *216*

DEDICATION

To

Arti (Arati)

The Two Goddesses who illumine the universe and cause Creation to exist, the two beautiful ladies who rise up, enlighten and edify the mind and show the way to supreme peace, unlimited bliss and contentment of the Divine.

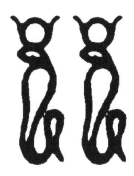

Preface

Who Were the Ancient Egyptians and why Should we Learn About Them?

The Ancient Egyptian religion (*Shetaut Neter*), language and symbols provide the first "historical" record of Mystical Philosophy and Religious literature. Egyptian Mysticism is what has been commonly referred to by Egyptologists as Egyptian "Religion" or "Myth," but to think of it as just another set of stories or allegories about a long lost civilization is to completely miss the greater teaching it has to offer. Mystical spirituality, in all of its forms and disciplines of spiritual development, was practiced in Ancient Egypt (Kamit) earlier than anywhere else in history. This unique perspective from the highest philosophical system which developed in Africa over seven thousand years ago provides a new way to look at life, religion, the discipline of psychology and the way to spiritual development leading to spiritual Enlightenment. Ancient Egyptian myth, when understood as a system of *Sema (Smai) Tawi* (Egyptian Yoga), that is, a system which promotes the union of the individual soul with the Universal Soul or Supreme Consciousness, gives every individual insight into their own divine nature, and also a deeper insight into all religions, mystical and Yoga systems.

Next, let us answer the question of "Why should we learn about the Ancient Egyptians? Of what benefit will it be to us today, in the here and now?" Ancient Egyptian culture and philosophy is crucial to the understanding of world history and spirituality. One of the misconceptions which is still promoted and prevalent in modern times is that Egypt is not a part of, or located on, the continent of Africa. Rather, it is espoused that Egypt is in the Middle East. This information is incorrect, as Egypt is where it has always been located, though in history it extended beyond its current margins, in the northeast corner of the African Continent. Further, it is widely believed by others that even though Egypt may be in Africa, that it was not an African country, and still others may agree that it was an African country, but not originally founded and populated by "black" African people (like present day Algeria, which is in Africa but populated by Middle Easterners -Arabs). These errors must be redressed in order for humanity to move forward. Truth must be promoted and in this case, it is crucial that this particular truth be brought forth into our human sphere of knowledge, as it offers a chance to humanity for achieving some level of peace and harmony as a world community. Also it will promote the redemption of African culture and thereby uplift African society and thereby the world. Africa provides a common ground, literally and figuratively, for humanity to come together, if we so choose, as both the physical origins of modern day humans is rooted in African soil, and also the spiritual roots of all religions and spiritual traditions can be traced there as well. Most of the wars that have occurred in human history after the close of Ancient Egyptian history have been due to religious differences, especially between orthodox aspects of the three major world religions, Christianity, Islam and Judaism, and the various subgroups of religions to which they each have given rise. Yet, all of these religions, and as we shall see, all spiritual traditions of the world, have their birthplace in Kamit. They are as if children and grandchildren of the Kamitan tradition. Imagine what happens in a simple human family when the children and grandchildren enter into conflicts and feuds. In the history of the U.S.A., there is a well-established example of the effects of this in the story of the Hatfields and the McCoys, a family feud that lasted for generations. Also,

consider the United States' civil war. From this viewpoint, it is easy to understand why the world is in the shape it is in today. In the case of the world religions, they are not directly fighting to claim the cultural inheritance and prestige of their Kamitan ancestors, although their traditions utilize many of the symbols or concepts of the Kamitan tradition in limited ways. Rather, for the most part they have shunned their ancestry and the history of their "roots" in favor of each trying to legitimize themselves as the only "true" religion, without regards to the culture and land of origin which forms the very nucleus (core, nidus) of all current traditions. Not only have they shunned their ancestry, but in many ways also disparage it. Consequently, although they all claim to have some aspects of commonality (Muslims accept Jesus, but only as a prophet, and Jews and Christians have the Old Testament in common, etc.), they are inherently unable to unite, as ultimately, each tradition believes and espouses that it is the only one true religion and has the only one true God.

The current state of human relations in the world has been likened to a family of dysfunctional people. One of the causes cited for this disfunctionality is the misunderstanding of human origins and relationships which leads to the adoption of bogus concepts such as racism, religious sectarianism, superiority complexes, inhumanity, violence and war. The world community needs to have the knowledge of its African human and spiritual origins so that Africa can take its rightful place as the "parent" of all humanity. In this way the error by which most people live will be resolved in the understanding that we are all of one family, one "race". It is also important for people who identify themselves as being of African descent to know and understand their deepest "roots" beyond the most current history of enslavement and all the negative racist ramifications it spawned (i.e. Africans are inferior, stupid, etc.). Most people of African ancestry have had to live with, and to some degree accept, denigrating and deprecating conditions, in order to survive. Thus, those who identify themselves as being ethnically of African origins can, through espousing and accepting the truth with respect to world history, become esteemed members of the world community.

The study of Kamitan Spirituality is also of particular importance for people who follow African Religion, Christianity, Hinduism and Buddhism, as they too share directly in the Kamitan legacy. This knowledge will allow them to understand the depth of their own culture and spiritual tradition, as well as aid in the restoration of positive interactions with people of African descent in India, the Diaspora, and Africa itself.

Where is Egypt?

Figure 1: Egypt is located in the north-eastern corner of the African Continent.

Figure 2: Below left: A map of North East Africa showing the location of the land of *Ta-Meri* or *Kamit*, also known as Ancient Egypt and South of it is located the land which in modern times is called Sudan.

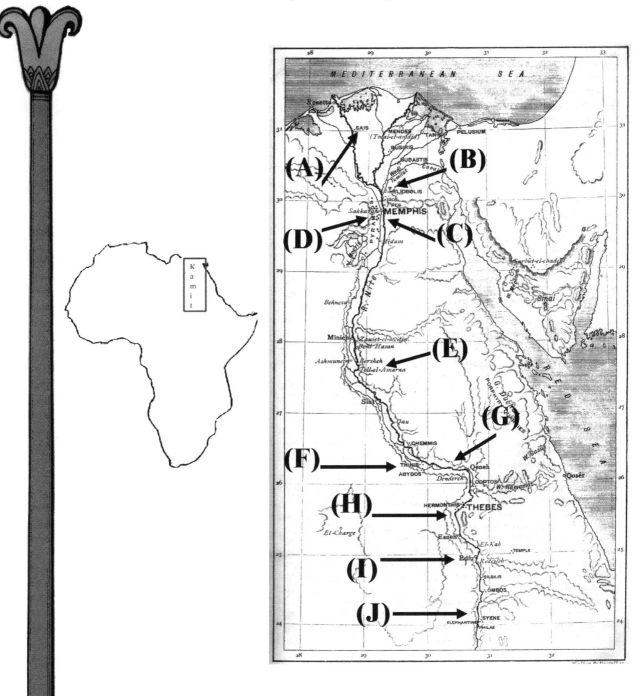

Figure 3: Above right- The Land of Ancient Egypt-Nile Valley

The cities wherein the theology of the Trinity of Amun-Ra-Ptah was developed were: A- Sais (temple of Net), B- Anu (Heliopolis- temple of Ra), C-Men-nefer or Hetkaptah (Memphis, temple of Ptah), and D- Sakkara (Pyramid Texts), E- Akhet-Aton (City of Akhnaton, temple of Aton), F- Abdu (temple of Asar), G- Denderah (temple of Hetheru), H- Waset (Thebes, temple of Amun), I- Edfu (temple of Heru), J- Philae (temple of Aset). The cities wherein the theology of the Trinity of Asar-Aset-Heru was developed were Anu, Abydos, Philae, Denderah and Edfu.

The Two Lands of Egypt

In Chapter 4[1] and Chapter 17[2] of the Ancient Egyptian mystical text, the *Prt m Hru, The Ancient Egyptian Book of Enlightenment*, more commonly known as the *Book of the Dead,* the term "Sema (Smai) Tawi" is used. It means "Union of the two lands of Egypt." The two lands refers to the two main districts of the country, North and South, and, in a mystical sense they refer to the gods Heru (the north) and Set (the south land), who are elsewhere referred to as the spiritual Higher Self and lower self of a human being, respectively. Thus, the term Sema Tawi is compatible with the Indian Sanskrit term "Yoga," which also means union of the Higher Self and lower self as well as other terms used by other systems of mystical spirituality (Enlightenment, Kingdom of Heaven, Liberation, etc.).

Diodorus Siculus (Greek Historian) writes in the time of Augustus (first century B.C.):

"Now the Ethiopians, as historians relate, were the first of all men and the proofs of this statement, they say, are manifest. For that they did not come into their land as immigrants from abroad, but were the natives of it and so justly bear the name of autochthones (sprung from the soil itself) is, they maintain, conceded by practically all men..."

"They also say that the Egyptians are colonists sent out by the Ethiopians, Asar having been the leader of the colony. For, speaking generally, what is now Egypt, they maintain, was not land, but sea, when in the beginning the universe was being formed; afterwards, however, as the Nile during the times of its inundation carried down the mud from Ethiopia, land was gradually built up from the deposit...And the larger parts of the customs of the Egyptians are, they hold, Ethiopian, the colonists still preserving their ancient manners. For instance, the belief that their kings are Gods, the very special attention which they pay to their burials, and many other matters of a similar nature, are Ethiopian practices, while the shapes of their statues and the forms of their letters are Ethiopian; for of the two kinds of writing which the Egyptians have, that which is known as popular (demotic) is learned by everyone, while that which is called sacred (hieratic), is understood only by the priests of the Egyptians, who learnt it from their Fathers as one of the things which are not divulged, but among the Ethiopians, everyone uses these forms of letters. Furthermore, the orders of the priests, they maintain, have much the same position among both peoples; for all are clean who are engaged in the service of the gods, keeping themselves shaven, like the Ethiopian priests, and having the same dress and form of staff, which is shaped like a plough and is carried by their kings who wear high felt hats which end in a knob in the top and are circled by the serpents which they call asps; and this symbol appears to carry the thought that it will be the lot who shall dare to attack the king to encounter death-carrying stings. Many other things are told

---

[1] Commonly referred to as Chapter 17
[2] Commonly referred to as Chapter 176

by them concerning their own antiquity and the colony which they sent out that became the Egyptians, but about this there is no special need of our writing anything."

Figure 4: Below- the Ancient Egyptian Hor-m-Akhet (Sphinx).

The archeological and geological evidence surrounding the great Sphinx in Giza, Egypt, Africa, shows that it was created no later than 10,000 B.C.E. to 7,000 B.C.E. This gives us the understanding that Kamit, Ancient Egypt, produced the earliest known artifacts, which denotes civilization. Thus, the Kamitan or Ancient Egyptian civilization is the oldest known civilization in our history.

⋆KMT is commonly known as Ancient Egypt. It is the land area on the north-eastern corner of the continent of Africa that is now currently occupied by a mostly Arabs and Muslim population. The culture and religion of Ancient Egypt is different from the modern day inhabitants of the land and they are not the descendants of the original peoples of Ancient Egypt.

ABOUT THE ANCIENT EGYPTIANS:

"Our people originated at the base of the mountain of the Moon, at the origin of the Nile river."†

"They also say that the Egyptians are colonists sent out by the Ethiopians, Asar having been the leader of the colony."

-Diodorus Siculus

"When therefore, you hear the myths of the Egyptians concerning the Gods - wanderings and dismemberings and many such passions, think none of these things spoken as they really are in state and action. For they do not call Hermes "Dog" as a proper name, but they associate the watching and waking from sleep of the animal who by Knowing and not Knowing determines friend from foe with the most Logos-like of the Gods."

-Plutarch

"The Egyptians and Nubians have thick lips, broad noses, woolly hair and burnt skin...
...And the Indian tribes I have mentioned, their skins are all of the same color, much like the Ethiopians... their country is a long way from Persia towards the south..."

- Herodotus

"The riches of Egypt are for the foreigners therein."

-Anonymous Arabic proverb.

"Truly at weaving wiles the Egyptians are clever."

-Anonymous

The Ethiopians and Egyptians are very black."

- Aristotle

"Compared with the Egyptians, the Greeks are childish mathematicians."

- Plato

"And upon his return to Greece, they gathered around and asked, "tell us about this great land of the Blacks called Ethiopia." And Herodotus said, "There are two great Ethiopian nations, one in Sind (India) and the other in Egypt."

- Recorded by Diodorus (Greek historian 100 B.C.)

Author's Foreword

Who Were the Ancient Egyptians and What is Yoga Philosophy?

The Ancient Egyptian religion (*Shetaut Neter*), language and symbols provide the first "historical" record of Yoga Philosophy and Religious literature. Egyptian Yoga is what has been commonly referred to by Egyptologists as Egyptian "Religion" or "Mythology," but to think of it as just another set of stories or allegories about a long lost civilization is to completely miss the greatest secret of human existence. Yoga, in all of its forms and disciplines of spiritual development, was practiced in Egypt earlier than anywhere else in history. This unique perspective from the highest philosophical system which developed in Africa over seven thousand years ago provides a new way to look at life, religion, the discipline of psychology and the way to spiritual development leading to spiritual Enlightenment. Egyptian mythology, when understood as a system of Yoga (union of the individual soul with the Universal Soul or Supreme Consciousness), gives every individual insight into their own divine nature and also a deeper insight into all religions and Yoga systems.

Diodorus Siculus (Greek Historian) writes in the time of Augustus (first century B.C.):

"Now the Ethiopians, as historians relate, were the first of all men and the proofs of this statement, they say, are manifest. For that they did not come into their land as immigrants from abroad but were the natives of it and so justly bear the name of autochthones (sprung from the soil itself), is, they maintain, conceded by practically all men..."

"They also say that the Egyptians are colonists sent out by the Ethiopians, Asar having been the leader of the colony. For, speaking generally, what is now Egypt, they maintain, was not land, but sea, when in the beginning the universe was being formed; afterwards, however, as the Nile during the times of its inundation carried down the mud from Ethiopia, land was gradually built up from the deposit...And the larger parts of the customs of the Egyptians are, they hold, Ethiopian, the colonists still preserving their ancient manners. For instance, the belief that their kings are Gods, the very special attention which they pay to their burials, and many other matters of a similar nature, are Ethiopian practices, while the shapes of their statues and the forms of their letters are Ethiopian; for of the two kinds of writing which the Egyptians have,

that which is known as popular (demotic) is learned by everyone, while that which is called sacred (hieratic), is understood only by the priests of the Egyptians, who learnt it from their Fathers as one of the things which are not divulged, but among the Ethiopians, everyone uses these forms of letters. Furthermore, the orders of the priests, they maintain, have much the same position among both peoples; for all are clean who are engaged in the service of the gods, keeping themselves shaven, like the Ethiopian priests, and having the same dress and form of staff, which is shaped like a plough and is carried by their kings who wear high felt hats which end in a knob in the top and are circled by the serpents which they call asps; and this symbol appears to carry the thought that it will be the lot who shall dare to attack the king to encounter death-carrying stings. Many other things are told by them concerning their own antiquity and the colony which they sent out that became the Egyptians, but about this there is no special need of our writing anything."

The Ancient Egyptian texts state:

> *"Our people originated at the base of the mountain of the Moon, at the origin of the Nile river."*

"KMT" (Qmt)
"Egypt," "Burnt," "Land of Blackness," "Land of the Burnt People."

KMT (Ancient Egypt) is situated close to Lake Victoria in present day Africa. This is the same location where the earliest human remains have been found, in the land currently known as Ethiopia-Tanzania. Recent genetic technology as reported in the new encyclopedias and leading news publications has revealed that all peoples of the world originated in Africa and migrated to other parts of the world prior to the last Ice Age 40,000 years ago. Therefore, as of this time, genetic testing has revealed that all humans are alike. The earliest bone fossils which have been found in many parts of the world were those of the African Grimaldi type. During the Ice Age, it was not possible to communicate or to migrate. Those trapped in specific locations were subject to the regional forces of weather and climate. Less warmer climates required less body pigment, thereby producing lighter pigmented people who now differed from their dark-skinned ancestors. After the Ice Age when travel was possible, these light-skinned people who had lived in the northern, colder regions of harsh weather during the Ice Age period moved back to the warmer climates of their ancestors, and mixed with the people there who had remained dark-skinned, thereby producing the Semitic colored people. "Semite" means mixture of skin color shades.

Therefore, there is only one human race who, due to different climactic and regional exposure, changed to a point where there seemed to be different "types" of people. Differences were noted with respect to skin color, hair texture, customs, languages, and with respect to the essential nature (psychological and emotional makeup) due to the experiences each group had to face and overcome in order to survive.

From a philosophical standpoint, the question as to the origin of humanity is redundant when it is understood that _ALL_ come from one origin which some choose to call the "Big Bang" and others "The Supreme Being."

"Thou makest the color of the skin of one race to be different from that of another, but however many may be the varieties of mankind, it is thou that makes them all to live."

Ancient Egyptian Proverb from _The Hymns of Amun_

"Souls, Heru, son, are of the self-same nature, since they came from the same place where the Creator modeled them; nor male nor female are they. Sex is a thing of bodies not of Souls."

Ancient Egyptian Proverb from _The teachings of Aset to Heru_

Historical evidence proves that Ethiopia-Nubia already had Kingdoms at least 300 years before the first Kingdom-Pharaoh of Egypt.

"Ancient Egypt was a colony of Nubia - Ethiopia. ...Asar having been the leader of the colony..."

"And upon his return to Greece, they gathered around and asked, "tell us about this great land of the Blacks called Ethiopia." And Herodotus said, "There are two great Ethiopian nations, one in Sind (India) and the other in Egypt."

Recorded by Egyptian high priest _Manetho_ (300 B.C.) also Recorded by _Diodorus_ (Greek historian 100 B.C.)

The pyramids themselves however, cannot be dated, but indications are that they existed far back in antiquity. The Pyramid Texts (hieroglyphics inscribed on pyramid walls) and Coffin Texts (hieroglyphics inscribed on coffins) speak authoritatively on the constitution of the human spirit, the vital Life Force along the human spinal cord (known in India as _"Kundalini"_), the immortality of the soul, reincarnation and the law of Cause and Effect (known in India as the Law of Karma).

Kamitan Terms and Ancient Greek Terms

It is important to understand that the names of the Ancient Egyptian divinities which have been used widely in Western literature and by Western scholars are actually Greek interpretations of the Kamitan (Ancient Egyptian) names. In keeping with the spirit of the culture of Kamitan spirituality, in this volume we will use the Kamitan names for the divinities through which we will bring forth the Philosophy of Neterianism (Ancient Egyptian religion and myth). Therefore, the Greek name Osiris will be converted back to the Kamitan (Ancient Egyptian) Asar (Asar), the Greek Isis to Aset (Auset), the Greek Nephthys to Nebthet, Anubis to Anpu or Apuat, Hathor to Hetheru, Thoth or Hermes to Djehuti, etc. (see the table below) Further, the term Ancient Egypt will be used interchangeably with "Kamit," or "Ta-Meri," as these were the terms used by the Ancient Egyptians to refer to their land and culture. The table below provides a listing of the corresponding names of the main Kamitan divinities.

Table 1: Kamitan Names of the main Gods and Goddesses of Ancient Egypt and the Greek translation in common use.

Kamitan (Ancient Egyptian) Names	Greek Names
Amun	Zeus
Ra	Helios
Ptah	Hephastos
Nut	Rhea
Geb	Kronos
Net	Athena
Khonsu	Heracles
Set	Ares or Typhon
Bast	Artemis
Uadjit	Leto
Asar (Asar)	Osiris or Hades
Aset (Auset)	Isis or Demeter
Nebthet	Nephthys
Anpu or Apuat	Anubis
Hetheru	Hathor (Aphrodite)
Heru	Horus or Apollo
Djehuti	Thoth or Hermes
Maat	Astraea or Themis
Sekhmit	Nemesis

What is Yoga Philosophy and Spiritual Practice

Since a complete treatise on the theory and practice of yoga would require several volumes, only a basic outline will be given here.

When we look out upon the world, we are often baffled by the multiplicity which constitutes the human experience. What do we really know about this experience? Many scientific disciplines have developed over the last two hundred years for the purpose of discovering the mysteries of nature, but this search has only engendered new questions about the nature of existence. Yoga is a discipline or way of life designed to promote the physical, mental and spiritual development of the human being. It leads a person to discover the answers to the most important questions of life such as Who am I?, Why am I here? and Where am I going?

The literal meaning of the word YOGA is to *"YOKE"* or to *"LINK"* back. The implication is: to link back to the original source, the original essence, that which transcends all mental and intellectual attempts at comprehension, but which is the essential nature of everything in CREATION. While in the strict or dogmatic sense, Yoga philosophy and practice is a separate discipline from religion, yoga and religion have been linked at many points throughout history. In a manner of speaking, Yoga as a discipline may be seen as a non-sectarian transpersonal science or practice to promote spiritual development and harmony of mind and body thorough mental and physical disciplines including meditation, psycho-physical exercises, and performing action with the correct attitude.

The disciplines of Yoga fall under five major categories. These are: *Yoga of Wisdom, Yoga of Devotional Love, Yoga of Meditation, Tantric Yoga* and *Yoga of Selfless Action.* Within these categories there are subsidiary forms which are part of the main disciplines. The important point to remember is that all aspects of yoga can and should be used in an integral fashion to effect an efficient and harmonized spiritual movement in the practitioner. Therefore, while there may be an area of special emphasis, other elements are bound to become part of the yoga program as needed. For example, while a yogin may place emphasis on the yoga of wisdom, they may also practice devotional yoga and meditation yoga along with the wisdom studies.

While it is true that yogic practices may be found in religion, strictly speaking, yoga is neither a religion or a philosophy. It should be thought of more as a way of life or discipline for promoting greater fullness and experience of life. Yoga was developed at the dawn of history by those who wanted more out of life. These special men and women wanted to discover the true origins of creation and of themselves. Therefore, they set out to explore the vast reaches of consciousness within themselves. They are sometimes referred to as "Seers," "Sages," etc. Awareness or consciousness can only be increased when the mind is in a state of peace and harmony. Thus, the disciplines of meditation (which are part of Yoga), and wisdom (the philosophical teachings for understanding reality as it is) are the primary means to controlling the mind and allowing the individual to mature psychologically and spiritually.

The teachings which were practiced in the Ancient Egyptian temples were the same ones later intellectually defined into a literary form by the Indian Sages of Vedanta and Yoga. This was discussed in my book *Egyptian Yoga: The Philosophy of Enlightenment*. The Indian Mysteries of Yoga and Vedanta represent an unfolding and intellectual exposition of the Egyptian Mysteries. Also, the study of Gnostic Christianity or Christianity before Roman Catholicism will be useful to our study since Christianity originated in Ancient Egypt and was also based on the Ancient Egyptian Mysteries. Therefore, the study of the Egyptian Mysteries, early Christianity and Indian Vedanta-Yoga will provide the most comprehensive teaching on how to practice the disciplines of yoga leading to the attainment of Enlightenment.

The question is how to accomplish these seemingly impossible tasks? How to transform yourself and realize the deepest mysteries of existence? How to discover "who am I?" This is the mission of Yoga Philosophy and the purpose of yogic practices. Yoga does not seek to convert or impose religious beliefs on any one. Ancient Egypt was the source of civilization and the source of religion and Yoga. Therefore, all systems of mystical spirituality can coexist harmoniously within these teachings when they are correctly understood.

The goal of yoga is to promote integration of the mind-body-spirit complex in order to produce optimal health of the human being. This is accomplished through mental and physical exercises which promote the free flow of spiritual energy by reducing mental complexes caused by ignorance. There are two roads which human beings can follow, one of wisdom and the other of ignorance. The path of the masses is generally the path of ignorance which leads them into negative situations, thoughts and deeds. These in turn lead to ill health and sorrow in life. The other road is based on wisdom and it leads to health, true happiness and enlightenment.

Our mission is to extol the wisdom of yoga and mystical spirituality from the Ancient Egyptian perspective and to show the practice of the teachings through our books, videos and audio productions. You may find a complete listing of other books by the author, in the back of this volume.

How to study the wisdom teachings:

There is a specific technique which is prescribed by the scriptures themselves for studying the teachings, proverbs and aphorisms of mystical wisdom. The method is as follows:

The spiritual aspirant should read the desired text thoroughly, taking note of any particular teachings which resonates with him or her.

The aspirant should make a habit of collecting those teachings and reading them over frequently. The scriptures should be read and re-read because the subtle levels of the teachings will be increasingly understood the more the teachings are reviewed.

One useful exercise is to choose some of the most special teachings you would like to focus on and place them in large type or as posters in your living areas so as to be visible to remind you of the teaching.

The aspirant should discuss those teachings with others of like mind when possible because this will help to promote greater understanding and act as an active spiritual practice in which the teachings are kept at the forefront of the mind. In this way, the teachings can become an integral part of everyday life and not reserved for a particular time of day or of the week.

The study of the wisdom teachings should be a continuous process in which the teachings become the predominant factor of life rather than the useless and oftentimes negative and illusory thoughts of those who are ignorant of spiritual truths. This spiritual discipline should be observed until Enlightenment is attained.

May you discover supreme peace in this very lifetime!

MUATA ⊙

Introduction to Egyptian Yoga

Most students of yoga are familiar with the yogic traditions of India consider that the Indian texts such as the Bhagavad Gita, Mahabharata, Patanjali Yoga Sutras, etc. are the primary and original source of Yogic philosophy and teaching. However, upon examination, the teachings currently espoused in all of the major forms of Indian Yoga can be found in Ancient Egyptian scriptures, inscribed in papyrus and on temple walls as well as steles, statues, obelisks and other sources.

What is Yoga?

Yoga is the practice of mental, physical and spiritual disciplines which lead to self-control and self-discovery by purifying the mind, body and spirit, so as to discover the deeper spiritual essence which lies within every human being and object in the universe. In essence, the goal of Yoga practice is to unite or *yoke* one's individual consciousness with Universal or Cosmic consciousness. Therefore, Ancient Egyptian religious practice, especially in terms of the rituals and other practices of the Ancient Egyptian Temple system known as *Shetaut Neter* (the way of the hidden Supreme Being), also known in Ancient times as *Smai Tawi* "Egyptian Yoga," should as well be considered as universal streams of self-knowledge philosophy which influenced and inspired the great religions and philosophers to this day. In this sense, religion, in its purest form, is also a Yoga system, as it seeks to reunite the soul with its true and original source, God. In broad terms, any spiritual movement or discipline that brings one closer to self-knowledge is a "Yogic" movement. The main recognized forms of Yoga disciplines are:

- *Yoga of Wisdom,*
- *Yoga of Devotional Love,*
- *Yoga of Meditation,*
    - *Physical Postures Yoga*
- *Yoga of Selfless Action,*
- *Tantric Yoga*
    - *Serpent Power Yoga*

The diagram below shows the relationship between the Yoga disciplines and the path of mystical religion (religion practiced in its three complete steps: 1st receiving the myth {knowledge}, 2nd practicing the rituals of the myth {following the teachings of the myth} and 3rd entering into a mystical experience {becoming one with the central figure of the myth}).

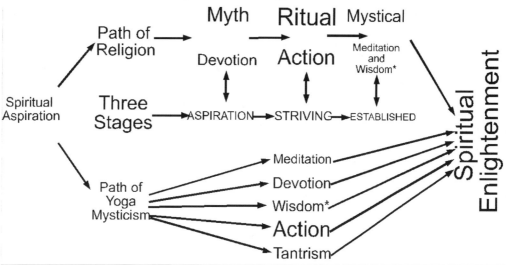

The disciplines of Yoga fall under five major categories. These are: *Yoga of Wisdom, Yoga of Devotional Love, Yoga of Meditation, Tantric Yoga* and *Yoga of Selfless Action*. When these disciplines are practiced in a harmonized manner this practice is called "Integral Yoga." Within these categories there are subsidiary forms which are part of the main disciplines. The emphasis in the Kamitan Asarian (Osirian) Myth is on the Yoga of Wisdom, Yoga of Devotional Love and Yoga of Selfless Action. The important point to remember is that all aspects of Yoga can and should be used in an integral fashion to effect an efficient and harmonized spiritual movement in the practitioner. Therefore, while there may be an area of special emphasis, other elements are bound to become part of the Yoga program as needed. For example, while a Yogin (practitioner of Yoga, aspirant, initiate) may place emphasis on the Yoga of Wisdom, they may also practice Devotional Yoga and Meditation Yoga along with the wisdom studies. So the practice of any discipline that leads to oneness with Supreme Consciousness can be called Yoga. If you study, rationalize and reflect upon the teachings, you are practicing *Yoga of Wisdom*. If you meditate upon the teachings and your Higher Self, you are practicing *Yoga of Meditation*.

Thus, whether or not you refer to it as such, if you practice rituals which identify you with your spiritual nature, you are practicing *Yoga of Ritual Identification* (which is part of the Yoga of Wisdom {Kamitan-Rekh, Indian-Jnana} and the Yoga of Devotional Love {Kamitan-Ushet, Indian-Bhakti} of the Divine). If you develop your physical nature and psychic energy centers, you are practicing *Serpent Power* (Kamitan-*Uraeus* or Indian-*Kundalini*) *Yoga* (which is part of Tantric Yoga). If you practice living according to the teachings of ethical behavior and selflessness, you are practicing *Yoga of Action* (Kamitan-Maat, Indian-Karma) in daily life. If you practice turning your attention towards the Divine by developing love for the Divine, then it is called *Devotional Yoga* or *Yoga of Divine Love*. The practitioner of Yoga is called a Yogin (male practitioner) or Yogini (female practitioner), or the term "Yogi" may be used to refer to either a female or male practitioner in general terms. One who has attained the culmination of Yoga (union with the Divine) is also called a Yogi. In this manner, Yoga has been developed into many disciplines which may be used in an integral fashion to achieve the same goal: Enlightenment. Therefore, the aspirant is to learn about all of the paths of Yoga and choose those elements which best suit {his/her} personality or practice them all in an integral, balanced way.

Enlightenment is the term used to describe the highest level of spiritual awakening. It means attaining such a level of spiritual awareness that one discovers the underlying unity of the entire universe as well as the fact that the source of all creation is the same source from which the innermost Self within every human heart arises.

What is Egyptian Yoga?

The Term "Egyptian Yoga" and The Philosophy Behind It

As previously discussed, Yoga in all of its forms were practiced in Egypt apparently earlier than anywhere else in our history. This point of view is supported by the fact that there is documented scriptural and iconographical evidence of the disciplines of virtuous living, dietary purification, study of the wisdom teachings and their practice in daily life, psychophysical and psycho-spiritual exercises and meditation being practiced in Ancient Egypt, long before the evidence of its existence is detected in India (including the Indus Valley Civilization) or any other early civilization (Sumer, Greece, China, etc.).

The teachings of Yoga are at the heart of *Prt m Hru*. As explained earlier, the word "Yoga" is a Sanskrit term meaning to unite the individual with the Cosmic. The term has been used in certain parts of this book for ease of communication since the word "Yoga" has received wide popularity especially in western countries in recent years. The Ancient Egyptian equivalent term to the Sanskrit word yoga is: *"Smai."* Smai means union, and the following determinative terms give it a spiritual significance, at once equating it with the term "Yoga" as it is used in India. When used in conjunction with the Ancient Egyptian symbol which means land, *"Ta,"* the term "union of the two lands" arises.

In Chapter 4 and Chapter 17 of the *Prt m Hru,* a term "Smai Tawi" is used. It means "Union of the two lands of Egypt," ergo "Egyptian Yoga." The two lands refer to the two main districts of the country (North and South). In ancient times, Egypt was divided into two sections or land areas. These were known as Lower and Upper Egypt. In Ancient Egyptian mystical philosophy, the land of Upper Egypt relates to the divinity Heru (Heru), who represents the Higher Self, and the land of Lower Egypt relates to Set, the divinity of the lower self. So *Smai Taui* means "the union of the two lands" or the "Union of the lower self with the Higher Self. The lower self relates to that which is negative and uncontrolled in the human mind including worldliness, egoism, ignorance, etc. (Set), while the Higher Self relates to that which is above temptations and is good in the human heart as well as in touch with transcendental consciousness (Heru). Thus, we also have the Ancient Egyptian term *Smai Heru-Set,* or the union of Heru and Set. So Smai Taui or Smai Heru-Set are the Ancient Egyptian words which are to be translated as **"Egyptian Yoga."**

Above: the main symbol of Egyptian Yoga: *Sma.* The Ancient Egyptian language and symbols provide the first "historical" record of Yoga Philosophy and Religious literature. The hieroglyph Sma, ⚶ "Sema," represented by the union of two lungs and the trachea, symbolizes that the union of the duality, that is, the Higher Self and lower self, leads to Non-duality, the One, singular consciousness.

The Ancient Egyptians called the disciplines of Yoga in Ancient Egypt by the term *"Smai Tawi."* So what does Smai Tawi mean?

Smai Tawi
(From Chapter 4 of the *Prt m Hru*)

The Ancient Egyptian Symbols of Yoga

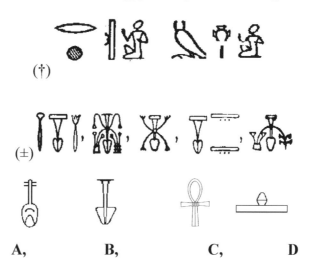

(†)

(±)

A,   B,   C,   D

The theme of the arrangement of the symbols above is based on the idea that in mythological and philosophic forms, Egyptian mythology and philosophy merge with world mythology, philosophy and religion. The hieroglyphic symbols at the very top (†) mean: ***"Know Thyself," "Self knowledge is the basis of all true knowledge"*** and (±) abbreviated forms of ***Smai taui,*** signifies "Egyptian Yoga." The next four below represent the four words in Egyptian Philosophy, which mean ***"YOGA."*** They are: (A) ***"Nefer"*** (B) ***"Sema"*** (C) ***"Ankh"*** and (D) ***"Hetep."***

The Term "Egyptian Yoga" and The Philosophy Behind It

As previously discussed, Yoga in all of its forms were practiced in Egypt apparently earlier than anywhere else in our history. This point of view is supported by the fact that there is documented scriptural and iconographical evidence of the disciplines of virtuous living, dietary purification, study of the wisdom teachings and their practice in daily life, psychophysical and psycho-spiritual exercises and meditation being practiced in Ancient Egypt, long before the evidence of its existence is detected in India (including the Indus Valley Civilization) or any other early civilization (Sumer, Greece, China, etc.).

The teachings of Yoga are at the heart of *Prt m Hru*. As explained earlier, the word "Yoga" is a Sanskrit term meaning to unite the individual with the Cosmic. The term has been used in certain parts of this book for ease of communication since the word "Yoga" has received wide popularity especially in western countries in recent years. The Ancient Egyptian equivalent term to the Sanskrit word yoga is: ***"Smai."*** *Smai* means union, and the following determinative terms give it a spiritual significance, at once equating it with the term "Yoga" as it is used in India. When used in conjunction with the Ancient Egyptian symbol which means land, ***"Ta,"*** the term "union of the two lands" arises.

In Chapter 4 and Chapter 17 of the *Prt m Hru,* a term "Smai Tawi" is used. It means "Union of the two lands of Egypt," ergo "Egyptian Yoga." The two lands refer to the two main districts of the country (North and South). In ancient times, Egypt was divided into two sections or land areas. These were known as Lower and Upper Egypt. In Ancient Egyptian mystical philosophy, the land of Upper Egypt relates to the divinity Heru (Heru), who represents the Higher Self, and the land of Lower Egypt relates to Set, the divinity of the lower self. So ***Smai Taui*** means "the union of the two lands" or the "Union of the lower self with the Higher Self. The lower self relates to that which is negative and uncontrolled in the human mind including worldliness, egoism, ignorance, etc. (Set), while the Higher Self relates to that which is above temptations and is good in the human heart as well as in touch with transcendental consciousness (Heru). Thus, we also have the Ancient Egyptian term ***Smai Heru-Set,*** or the union of Heru and Set. So Smai Taui or Smai Heru-Set are the Ancient Egyptian words which are to be translated as "**Egyptian Yoga.**"

Above: the main symbol of Egyptian Yoga: *Sma.* The Ancient Egyptian language and symbols provide the first "historical" record of Yoga Philosophy and Religious literature. The hieroglyph Sma, "Sema," represented by the union of two lungs and the trachea, symbolizes that the union of the duality, that is, the Higher Self and lower self, leads to Non-duality, the One, singular consciousness.

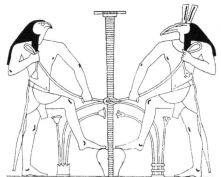

Above left: Smai Heru-Set, Heru and Set join forces to tie up the symbol of Union (Sema –see (B) above). The Sema symbol refers to the Union of Upper Egypt (Lotus) and Lower Egypt (Papyrus) under one ruler, but also at a more subtle level, it refers to the union of one's Higher Self and lower self (Heru and Set), as well as the control of one's breath (Life Force) through the union (control) of the lungs (breathing organs). The character of Heru and Set are an integral part of the Pert Em Heru.

The central and most popular character within Ancient Egyptian Religion of Asar is Heru, who is an incarnation of his father, Asar. Asar is killed by his brother Set who, out of greed and demoniac (Setian) tendency, craved to be the ruler of Egypt. With the help of Djehuti, the God of wisdom, Aset, the great mother and Hetheru, his consort, Heru prevailed in the battle against Set for the rulership of Kemit (Egypt). Heru's struggle symbolizes the struggle of every human being to regain rulership of the Higher Self and to subdue the lower self.

The most ancient writings in our historical period are from the Ancient Egyptians. These writings are referred to as hieroglyphics. The original name given to these writings by the Ancient Egyptians is *Metu Neter,* meaning "the writing of God" or *Neter Metu* or "Divine Speech." These writings were inscribed in temples, coffins and papyruses and contained the teachings in reference to the spiritual nature of the human being and the ways to promote spiritual emancipation, awakening or resurrection. The Ancient Egyptian proverbs presented in this text are translations from the original hieroglyphic scriptures. An example of hieroglyphic text was presented above in the form of the text of Smai Taui or "Egyptian Yoga."

Egyptian Philosophy may be summed up in the following proverbs, which clearly state that the soul is heavenly or divine and that the human being must awaken to the true reality, which is the Spirit, Self.

"Self knowledge is the basis of true knowledge."

"Soul to heaven, body to earth."

"Man is to become God-like through a life of virtue and the cultivation of the spirit
through scientific knowledge, practice and bodily discipline."

"Salvation is accomplished through the efforts of the individual.
There is no mediator between man and {his/her} salvation."

"Salvation is the freeing of the soul from its bodily fetters, becoming a
God through knowledge and wisdom, controlling the forces of the
cosmos instead of being a slave to them, subduing the lower nature and
through awakening the Higher Self, ending the cycle of rebirth
and dwelling with the Neters who direct and control the Great Plan."

Egyptian Yoga is a revolutionary new way to understand and practice Ancient Egyptian Mysticism, the Ancient Egyptian mystical religion (*Shetaut Neter*). Egyptian Yoga is what has been commonly referred to by Egyptologists as Egyptian "Religion" or "Mythology," but to think of it as just another set of stories or allegories about a long lost civilization is to completely miss the greatest secret of human existence. What is Yoga? The literal meaning of the word YOGA is to *"YOKE"* or to *"LINK"* back. The implication is to link back individual consciousness to its original source, the original essence: Universal Consciousness. In a broad sense Yoga is any process which helps one to achieve liberation or freedom from the bondage to human pain and spiritual ignorance. So whenever you engage in any activity with the goal of promoting the discovery of your true Self, be it studying the wisdom teachings, exercise, fasting, meditation, breath control, rituals, chanting, prayer, etc., you are practicing yoga. If the goal is to help you to discover your essential nature as one with God or the Supreme Being or Consciousness, then it is Yoga. Yoga, in all of its forms as the disciplines of spiritual development, as practiced in Ancient Egypt earlier than anywhere else in history. The ancient scriptures describe how Asar, the first mythical king of Ancient Egypt, traveled throughout Asia and Europe establishing civilization and the practice of religion. This partially explains why the teachings of mystical spirituality known as Yoga and Vedanta in India are so similar to the teachings of Shetaut Neter (Ancient Egyptian religion - Egyptian Yoga. This unique perspective from the highest philosophical system which developed in Africa over seven thousand years ago provides a new way to look at life, religion, psychology and the way to spiritual development leading to spiritual Enlightenment. So Egyptian Yoga is not merely a philosophy but a discipline for promoting spiritual evolution in a human being, allowing him or her to discover the ultimate truth, supreme peace and utmost joy which lies within the human heart. These are the true worthwhile goals of life. Anything else is settling for less. It would be like a personality who owns vast riches thinking that he is poor and homeless. Every human being has the potential to discover the greatest treasure of all existence if they apply themselves to the study and practice of the teachings of Yoga with the proper guidance. Sema ($\text{\J}$) is the Ancient Egyptian word and symbol meaning *union or Yoga*. This is the vision of Egyptian Yoga.

The Study of Yoga

When we look out upon the world, we are often baffled by the multiplicity, which constitutes the human experience. What do we really know about this experience? Many scientific disciplines have developed over the last two hundred years for the purpose of discovering the mysteries of nature, but this search has only engendered new questions about the nature of existence. Yoga is a discipline or way of life designed to promote the physical, mental and spiritual development of the human being. It leads a person to discover the answers to the most important questions of life such as, Who am I? Why am I here? Where am I going?

As explained earlier, the literal meaning of the word *Yoga* is to *"Yoke"* or to *"Link"* back, the implication being to link the individual consciousness back to the original source, the original essence, that which transcends all mental and intellectual attempts at comprehension, but which is the essential nature of everything in Creation, termed "Universal Consciousness. While in the strict sense, Yoga may be seen as a separate discipline from religion, yoga and religion have been linked at many points throughout history and continue to be linked even today. In a manner of speaking, Yoga as a discipline may be seen as a non-sectarian transpersonal science or practice to promote spiritual development and harmony of mind and body thorough mental and physical disciplines including meditation, psycho-physical exercises, and performing action with the correct attitude.

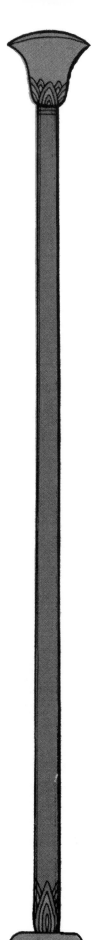

The teachings which were practiced in the Ancient Egyptian temples were the same ones later intellectually defined into a literary form by the Indian Sages of Vedanta and Yoga. This was discussed in our book *Egyptian Yoga: The Philosophy of Enlightenment*. The Indian Mysteries of Yoga and Vedanta may therefore be understood as representing an unfolding exposition of the Egyptian Mysteries.

The question is how to accomplish these seemingly impossible tasks? How to transform yourself and realize the deepest mysteries of existence? How to discover "Who am I?" This is the mission of Yoga Philosophy and the purpose of yogic practices. Yoga does not seek to convert or impose religious beliefs on any one. Ancient Egypt was the source of civilization and the source of religion and Yoga. Therefore, all systems of mystical spirituality can coexist harmoniously within these teachings when they are correctly understood.

The goal of yoga is to promote integration of the mind-body-spirit complex in order to produce optimal health of the human being. This is accomplished through mental and physical exercises which promote the free flow of spiritual energy by reducing mental complexes caused by ignorance. There are two roads which human beings can follow, one of wisdom and the other of ignorance. The path of the masses is generally the path of ignorance which leads them into negative situations, thoughts and deeds. These in turn lead to ill health and sorrow in life. The other road is based on wisdom and it leads to health, true happiness and enlightenment.

The central and most popular character within ancient Egyptian Religion of Asar is Heru who is an incarnation of his father, Asar. Asar is killed by his brother Set who, out of greed and demoniac (Setian) tendency, craves to be the ruler of Egypt. With the help of Djehuti, the God of wisdom, Aset, the great mother and Hetheru, his consort, Heru prevails in the battle against Set for the rulership of Egypt. Heru' struggle symbolizes the struggle of every human being to regain rulership of the Higher Self and to subdue the lower self. With this understanding, the land of Egypt is equivalent to the Kingdom/Queendom concept of Christianity.

The most ancient writings in our historical period are from the ancient Egyptians. These writings are referred to as hieroglyphics. Also, the most ancient civilization known was the ancient Egyptian civilization. The proof of this lies in the ancient Sphinx which is over 12,000 years old. The original name given to these writings by the ancient Egyptians is *Metu Neter,* meaning "the writing of God" or *Neter Metu* or "Divine Speech." These writings were inscribed in temples, coffins and papyruses and contained the teachings in reference to the spiritual nature of the human being and the ways to promote spiritual emancipation, awakening or resurrection. The —Ancient Egyptian Proverbs presented in this text are translations from the original hieroglyphic scriptures. An example of hieroglyphic text is presented on the front cover.

Egyptian Philosophy may be summed up in the following proverbs which clearly state that the soul is heavenly or divine and that the human being must awaken to the true reality which is the spirit Self.

"Self knowledge is the basis of true knowledge."

"Soul to heaven, body to earth."

"Man is to become God-like through a life of virtue and the cultivation of the spirit through scientific knowledge, practice and bodily discipline."

"Salvation is accomplished through the efforts of the individual. There is no mediator between man and his / her salvation."

"Salvation is the freeing of the soul from its bodily fetters, becoming a God through knowledge and wisdom, controlling the forces of the cosmos instead of being a slave to them, subduing the lower nature and through awakening the Higher Self, ending the cycle of rebirth and dwelling with the Neters who direct and control the Great Plan."

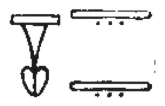

Smai Tawi
(From Chapter 4 of
the *Prt m Hru*)

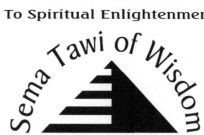

One discipline of Yoga requires special mention here. It is called Wisdom Yoga or the Yoga of Wisdom. In the Temple of Aset (Isis) in Ancient Egypt the Discipline of the Yoga of Wisdom is imparted in three stages:

1-<u>Listening</u> to the wisdom teachings on the nature of reality (creation) and the nature of the Self.
2-<u>Reflecting</u> on those teachings and incorporating them into daily life.
3-<u>Meditating</u> on the meaning of the teachings.

Aset (Isis) was and is recognized as the goddess of wisdom and her temple strongly emphasized and espoused the philosophy of wisdom teaching in order to achieve higher spiritual consciousness. It is important to note here that the teaching which was practiced in the Ancient Egyptian Temple of Aset[3] of **Listening** to, **Reflecting** upon, and **Meditating** upon the teachings is the same process used in Vedanta-Jnana Yoga of India of today. **The Yoga of Wisdom** is a form of Yoga based on insight into the nature of worldly existence and the transcendental Self, thereby transforming one's consciousness through development of the wisdom faculty. Thus, we have here a correlation between Ancient Egypt that matches exactly in its basic factor respects.

THE THREE-FOLD PROCESS OF WISDOM YOGA IN EGYPT:

According to the teachings of *the Ancient Temple of Aset* the Yoga of Wisdom, entails the process of three steps:

Discipline of Wisdom Yoga in Ancient Egypt
1-<u>Listening</u> to the wisdom teachings on the nature of reality (creation) and the nature of the Self.
2-<u>Reflecting</u> on those teachings and incorporating them into daily life.
3-<u>Meditating</u> on the meaning of the teachings.

---

[3] See the book *The Wisdom of Aset* by Dr. Muata Ashby

Figure 5: The image of goddess Aset (Isis) suckling the young king is the quintecential symbol of initiation in Ancient Egypt.

Temple of Aset
GENERAL DISCIPLINE

Fill the ears, listen attentively- Meh mestchert.

Listening

1- Listening to Wisdom teachings. Having achieved the qualifications of an aspirant, there is a desire to listen to the teachings from a Spiritual Preceptor. There is increasing intellectual understanding of the scriptures and the meaning of truth versus untruth, real versus unreal, temporal versus eternal. The glories of God are expounded and the mystical philosophy behind the myth is given at this stage.

MAUI

"to think, to ponder, to fix attention, concentration"

Reflection

2- Reflection on those teachings that have been listened to and living according to the disciplines enjoined by the teachings is to be practiced until the wisdom teaching is fully understood. Reflection implies discovering, intellectually at first, the oneness behind the multiplicity of the world by engaging in intense inquiry into the nature of one's true Self. Chanting the hekau and divine singing *Hesi,* are also used here.

"Devote yourself to adore God's name."
—Ancient Egyptian Proverb

 *uaa* "Meditation"

Meditation

3- Meditation in Wisdom Yoga is the process of reflection that leads to a state in which the mind is continuously introspective. It means expansion of consciousness culminating in revelation of and identification with the Absolute Self.

Note: It is important to note here that the same teaching which was practiced in ancient Egypt of **Listening** to, **Reflecting** upon, and **Meditating** upon the teachings is the same process used in Vedanta-Jnana Yoga (from India) of today.

To Spiritual Enlightenment

Sema Tawi of Right Action

GENERAL DISCIPLINE
In all Temples especially
The Temple of Heru and Edfu

Scripture: Prt M Hru and special scriptures including the Berlin Papyrus and other papyri.

1- Learn Ethics and Law of Cause and Effect-Practice right action
(42 Precepts of Maat)
to purify gross impurities of the personality
Control Body, Speech, Thoughts

2- Practice cultivation of the higher virtues
(selfless-service)
to purify mind and intellect from subtle impurities

3- Devotion to the Divine
See maatian actions as offerings to the Divine

4- Meditation
See oneself as one with Maat, i.e. United with the cosmic order which is the Transcendental Supreme Self.

Plate 1: The Offering of Maat-Symbolizing the Ultimate act of Righteousness (Temple of Seti I)

Sema Tawi of Divine Love

GENERAL DISCIPLINE
In all Temples

Scripture: Prt M Hru and Temple Inscriptions.

<u>Discipline of Devotion</u>

1– Listening to the myth
    Get to know the Divinity
    Empathize
    Romantisize

2-Ritual about the myth
    Offerings to Divinity – propitiation
    act like divinity
    Chant the name of the Divinity
    Sing praises of the Divinity
    COMMUNE with the Divinity

3– Mysticism
    Melting of the heart
    Dissolve into Divinity

    IDENTIFY-with the Divinity

In the Kamitan teaching of Devotional love:

God is termed *Merri,* "Beloved One"

Love and Be Loved
"That person is beloved by the Lord." PMH, Ch 4

Offering Oneself to God-Surrender to God- Become One with God

Figure 6: The Dua Pose- Upraised arms with palms facing out towards the Divine Image

Sema Tawi of Meditation

Posture-Sitting With Hands on Thighs

It is well known and commonly accepted that meditation has been practiced in India from ancient times. Therefore, there is no need to site specific references to support that contention. Here we will concentrate on the evidence supporting the existence of the philosophy of meditation in Ancient Egypt.

The Paths of Meditation Practiced in Ancient Egypt

System of Meditation: **Glorious Light System**
Location where it was practiced in ancient times: **Temple of Seti I, City of Waset (Thebes)** [4]

System of Meditation: **Wisdom System**
Location where it was practiced in ancient times: **Temple of Aset – Philae Island, Aswan**

System of Meditation: **Serpent Power System**
Location where it was practiced in ancient times: **Temple of Asar- City of Abdu**

System of Meditation: **Devotional Meditation**
Location where it was practiced in ancient times: **IN ALL TEMPLES- GENERAL DISCIPLINE**

Basic Instructions for the Glorious Light Meditation System- Given in the Tomb of Seti I. (1350 B.C.E.)

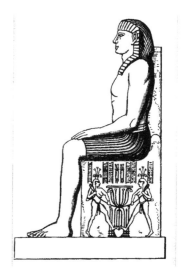

Formal meditation in Yoga consists of four basic elements: Posture, Sound (chant-words of power), Visualization, Rhythmic Breathing (calm, steady breath). The instructions, translated from the original hieroglyphic text contain the basic elements for formal meditation.

(1)-Posture and Focus of Attention
      iuf iri-f ahau maq b-phr nty   hau iu
   body do   make stand, within the Sundisk (circle of
                        Ra)

---

[4] For More details see the book ***The Glorious Light Meditation System of Ancient Egypt*** by Dr. Muata Ashby.

This means that the aspirant should remain established as if in the center of a circle with a dot in the middle.

(2)- **Words of power-chant**[5]

Nuk Hekau (I am the word* itself)
Nuk Ra Akhu (I am Ra's Glorious Shinning** Spirit)
Nuk Ba Ra (I am the soul of Ra)
Nuk Hekau (I am the God who creates*** through sound)
`
(3)- **Visualization**

Iuf   mi Ra heru mestu-f   n-shry   chet
"My body is like Ra's on the day of his birth

   This teaching is what in Indian Vedanta Philosophy is referred to as Ahamgraha Upashama – or visualizing and meditating upon oneself as being one with God. This teaching is the main focus of the Prt m Hru (Book of Enlightenment) text of Ancient Egypt. It is considered as the highest form of meditation practice amongst Indian mystics.[6]

Plate 2: Basic Instructions for the Glorious Light Meditation System- Given in the Tomb of Seti I. (c. 1350 B.C.E.)

   As we have seen, the practice of meditation in Ancient Egypt and its instruction to the masses and not just to the priests and priestesses, can be traced to at least 800 years earlier. If the instructions given by sage Seti I and those given by sage Patanjali are compared, many similarities appear.

---

[5] The term "Words of Power" relates to chants and or recitations given for meditation practice. They were used in a similar way to the Hindu "Mantras."
[6] Statement made by Swami Jyotirmayananda in class with his disciples.

The Yogic Postures in Ancient Egypt

Since their introduction to the West, the exercise system of India known as "Hatha Yoga" has gained much popularity. The disciplines related to the yogic postures and movements were developed in India around the 10th century A.C.E. by a sage named Goraksha.[7] Up to this time, the main practice was simply to adopt the cross-legged meditation posture known as the lotus for the purpose of practicing meditation. The most popular manual on Hatha Yoga is the ***Hatha Yoga-Pradipika ("Light on the Forceful Yoga).*** It was authored by Svatmarama Yogin in mid. 14th century A.C.E.[8]

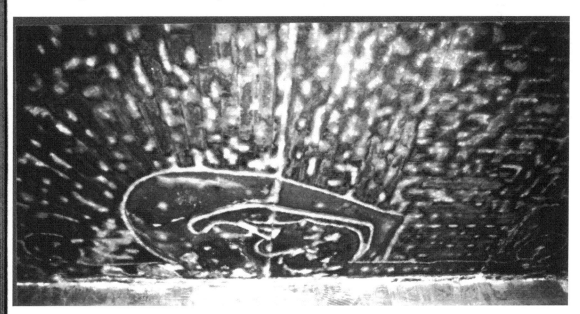

Plate 3: Above- The god Geb in the plough posture engraved on the ceiling of the antechamber to the Asarian Resurrection room of the Temple of Hetheru in Egypt. (photo taken by Ashby). Below: Illustration of the posture engraved on the ceiling.

---

[7] Yoga Journal, {The New Yoga} January/February 2000
[8] ***Hatha-Yoga-Pradipika,*** <u>*The Shambhala Encyclopedia of Yoga*</u> by Georg Feuerstein, Ph. D.

Prior to the emergence of the discipline of the physical movements in India just before 1000 A.C.E.,[9] a series of virtually identical postures to those which were practiced in India can be found in various Ancient Egyptian papyruses and inscribed on the walls and ceilings of the temples. The Ancient Egyptian practice can be dated from 10,000 B.C.E to 300 B.C.E and earlier. Examples: Temple of Hetheru (800-300 B.C.E.), Temple of Heru (800-300 B.C.E.), Tomb of Queen Nefertari (reigned 1,279-1,212 B.C.E.), and various other temples and papyruses from the New Kingdom Era (c. 1,580 B.C.E). In Ancient Egypt the practice of the postures, called *Tjef Sema Paut Neteru* which means "Movements to promote union with the gods and goddesses" or simply *Sema Paut* (Union with the gods and goddesses), were part of the ritual aspect of the spiritual myth, which when practiced, served to harmonize the energies and promote the physical health of the body and direct the mind in a meditative capacity to discover and cultivate divine consciousness. These disciplines are part of a larger process called Sema or *Smai Tawi* (Egyptian Yoga). By acting and moving like the gods and goddesses one can essentially discover their character, energy and divine agency within one's consciousness, and thereby also become one of their retinue, that is, one with the Divine Self. In modern times, most practitioners of Indian Hatha Yoga see it primarily as a means to attain physical health only. However, even the practice in India had an origin in myth and a mythic component which is today largely ignored by modern practitioners.

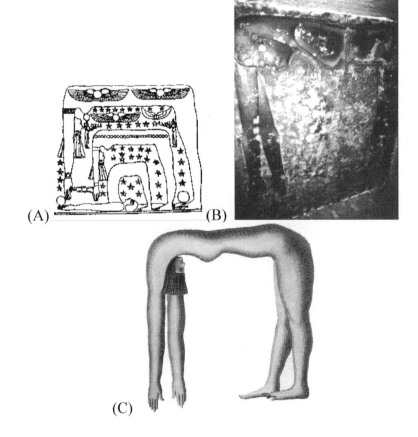

(A)   (B)

(C)

[9] *The Shambhala Encyclopedia of Yoga* by Georg Feuerstein, Ph. D.

Figure 7: Above left: The Kamitan goddess Nut and god Geb and the higher planes of existence. Above center and right: The goddess Nut performs the forward bend posture.

The figure above (left) depicts another conceptualization of the Netherworld, which is at the same time the body of Nut in a forward bend yoga exercise posture. The innermost goddess symbolizes the lower heaven where the moon traverses, the physical realm. The middle one symbolizes the course of the sun in its Astral journey. This shows a differentiation between the physical heavens and the Astral plane, as well as time and physical space and Astral time and space, i.e., the concept of different dimensions and levels of consciousness. The outermost symbolizes the causal plane.

Plate 4: Below- The Egyptian Gods and Goddesses act out the Creation through their movements: Forward bend -Nut, Spinal twist -Geb, Journey of Ra – Ra in his boat, and the squatting and standing motions of Nun and Shu.

Figure 8: The varied postures found in the Kamitan papyruses and temple inscriptions.

Figure 9: The practice of the postures is shown in the sequence below.

To Spiritual Enlightenment

20th Century A.C.E.

1. **Ananda Yoga** (Swami Kriyananda)
2. **Anusara Yoga** (John Friend)
3. **Ashtanga Yoga** (K. Pattabhi)
4. **Ashtanga Yoga** (Pattabhi Jois)
5. **Bikram Yoga** (Bikram Choudhury)
6. **Integral Yoga** (Swami Satchidananda b.
7. **Iyengar Yoga** (B.K.S. Iyengar)
8. **Kripalu Yoga** (Amrit Desai)
9. **Kundalini Yoga** (Yogi Bhajan)
10. **Sivananda Yoga** (Swami Vishnu-devananda)
11. **Svaroopa Yoga** (Rama Berch)

Women first admitted to Hatha Yoga practice

1893 A.C.E.	**World Parliament of Religions – Vedanta Introduced to the West**
1750 A.C.E.	**Shiva Samhita – Hatha Yoga text –melds Vedanta with Hatha**
1539 A.C.E.	**Birth of Sikhism**
1350 A.C.E.	**Hatha Yoga Pradipika text -India**
1000 A.C.E.	**Goraksha – Siddha Yogis First Indian Hatha Yoga Practice**
600 A.C.E.	**Birth of Islam**
Year 0	**Birth of Jesus – Christianity**
300 B.C.E.	**Arat, Geb, Nut Egyptian Yoga Postures – Late Period**
1,680 B.C.E.	**Geb, Nut, Ra, Asar, Aset, Sobek Egyptian Yoga Postures – New Kingdom**
2,000 B.C.E.	**Indus Valley – Kundalini – Serpent Power-Lotus Pose**
3,600 B.C.E.	**Nefertem Egyptian Yoga Posture – Old-Middle Kingdom Period**
10,000 B.C.E.	**Serpent Power-Horemakhet Egyptian Yoga Posture – Ancient Egyptian**

Sema Tawi of Tantrism

Tantric influence, however, is not limited to India alone, and there is evidence that the precepts of tantrism traveled to various parts of the world, especially Nepal, Tibet, China, Japan and parts of South-East Asia; its influence has also been evident in Mediterranean cultures such as those of Egypt and Crete.[10]
-Ajit Mookerjee (Indian Scholar-Author –from the book *The Tantric Way*)

Tantra Yoga is purported to be the oldest system of Yoga. Tantra Yoga is a system of Yoga which seeks to promote the re-union between the individual and the Absolute Reality, through the worship of nature and ultimately the Cosmos as an expression of the Absolute. Since nature is an expression of GOD, it gives clues as to the underlying reality that sustains it and the way to achieve wisdom, i.e. transcendence of it. The most obvious and important teaching that nature holds is the idea that creation is made up of pairs of opposites: Up-down, here-there, you-me, us-them, hot-cold, male-female, Ying-Yang, etc. The interaction, of these two complementary opposites, we call life and movement.

Insight (wisdom) into the true nature of reality gives us a clue as to the way to realize the oneness of creation within ourselves. By re-uniting the male and female principles in our own bodies and minds, we may reach the oneness that underlies our apparent manifestation as a man or woman. Thus, the term Tantra means to create a bridge between the opposites and in so doing the opposites dissolve, leaving unitary and transcendental consciousness. The union of the male and female principles may be effected by two individuals who worship GOD through GOD's manifestation in each other or by an individual who seeks union with GOD through uniting with his or her male or female spiritual partner. All men and women have both female and male principles within themselves.

In the Egyptian philosophical system, all Neteru or God principles emanate from the one GOD. When these principles are created, they are depicted as having a *__male and female__* principle. All objects and life forms appear in creation as either male or female, but underlying this apparent duality, there is a unity which is rooted in the pure consciousness of oneness, the consciousness of GOD, which underlies and supports all things. To realize this oneness consciously deep inside is the supreme goal.

In Tantrism, sexual symbolism is used frequently because these are the most powerful images denoting the opposites of Creation and the urge to unify and become whole, for sexuality is the urge for unity and self-discovery albeit limited

---

[10] *The Tantric Way* by Ajit Mookerjee and Madhu Khanna

to physical intercourse by most people. If this force is understood, harnessed and sublimated it will lead to unity of the highest order that is unity with the Divine Self.

Figure 10: Above- the Kamitan God Geb and the Kamitan Goddess Nut separate after the sexual union that gave birth to the gods and goddesses and Creation. Below: three depictions of the god Asar in tantric union with Aset.

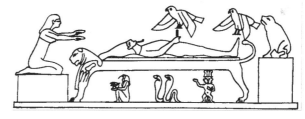

Figure 11: Above-The virgin birth of Heru (The resurrection of Asar - higher, Heru consciousness). Isis in the winged form hovers over the reconstructed penis of dead Asar. Note: Asar uses right hand.

Figure 12: Drawing found in an Ancient Egyptian Building of The Conception of Heru[11]

Isis (representing the physical body-creation) and the dead body of Asar (representing the spirit, that essence which vivifies matter) are shown in symbolic immaculate union (compare to the "Kali Position" on the following page) begetting Heru, symbolizing to the immaculate conception which takes place at the birth of the spiritual life in every human: the birth of the soul (Ba) in a human is the birth of Heru.

-From a Stele at the British Museum 1372. 13th Dyn.

Figure 13: Above- the god Shiva and his consort Shakti

The "Kali position" (above) features **Shiva and Shakti (Kundalini-Prakriti)** in divine union (India). As with Asar and Isis of Egypt, Shiva is the passive, male aspect who "gives" the life essence (spirit) and creative impetus and Shakti is energy, creation, the active aspect of GOD. Thus Creation is akin to the idea of GOD making love with him/herself. Shiva and Shakti are the true essence of the human being, composed of spirit and matter (body). In the active aspect, the female is in the "active" position while the male is in the "passive" position. In Kamitan philosophy, the god Geb is the earth and the goddess Nut is the sky. Just as the earth is sedentary and the sky is dynamic so too are the divinities depicted in this way in Southern (African) and Eastern (India) iconography.

Figure 14: Above- Buddha and his consort.

---

[11] *Sexual Life in Ancient Egypt* by Lise Manniche

Above: Tibetan Buddhist representation of The Dharmakaya, the cosmic father-mother. expressing the idea of the Supreme Being as a union of both male and female principals.

Notice that the female divinities are always on the top position. This is classic in Eastern and Kamitan mysticism. It is a recognition that the spirit (male aspect) is sedentary while matter, the female aspect, is in perpetual motion and the two complement and complete each other.

Figure 15: Below left- The Triune ithyphallic form of Asar[12]

Figure 16: Below right- the Trilinga (Triune ithyphallic form) of Shiva.[13]

Figure 17: Below far right- the multi-armed (all-pervasive) dancing Shiva-whose dance sustains the Creation.

[12] For more details see the book *Egyptian Yoga Volume 1*
[13] For more details see the book *Egyptian Yoga Volume 1*

Figure 18: Below- left Ashokan[14] pillar with lion capital-Kamitan pillar with lion capitals. Center: Ancient Egyptian pillar with lion capitals. Far right: the Ethiopian divinity Apedemak, displaying the same leonine trinity concept and the multi-armed motif.

The trinity symbolically relates the nature of the Divine, who is the source and sustenance of the three worlds (physical, astral and causal), the three states of consciousness (conscious, subconscious and unconscious), the three modes of nature (dull, agitated and lucid), the three aspects of human experience (seer, seen and sight), as well as the three stages of initiation (ignorance, aspiration and enlightenment). This triad idea is common to Neterianism, Hinduism and Christianity.

The idea of the multi-armed divinity is common in Indian Iconography. However, the depiction above from Ethiopia spiritual iconography shows that it was present in Africa as well.

Figure 19: Below (A)- Line art drawing of the Hindu Lingam-Yoni (Phallus-Vulva) of India and the Crowns of Ancient Egypt.

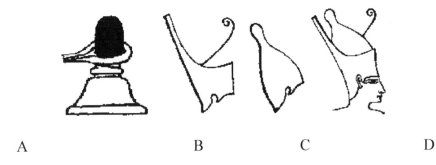

A   B   C   D

Above left, (A)- Line art drawing of the Hindu Lingam-Yoni (Phallus-Vulva) of India symbolizes the unity of the male and female essence into one non-dualistic whole. Figures B-D display the Tantric symbolism embedded in the Ancient Egyptian Pharaonic Crowns. The Red Crown of Lower Egypt, known as the *deshret* crown (B), represents the female principle. The white Crown of Upper Egypt, known as the *hedjet* crown (C), represents the male principle. The Crown of Upper and Lower Egypt together, known as the *Wereret* crown (D), represent the male principle going into the female- symbolizing unity, balance, and

---

[14] Constructed in the period of the Indian King Asoka (Ashoka) who adopted Buddhism.

transcendence of duality, i.e. it signifies the attainment of transcendental consciousness as well as rulership over the lower nature and the Higher.   As, no crowns of have survived from ancient times and no references to it have been discovered in the extant records from Ancient Egypt, Egyptologists have speculated on the nature and symbolism of the Pharaonic crowns from the beginning of modern Egyptology up to the present. The understanding of the crowns in light of tantric symbolism has eluded western Egyptologists partly because of the refusal to admit the possibility that there is tantric, yogic, or mystical symbolism and metaphor in Kamitan culture. Therefore, it should be no surprise that the tantric symbolism of the crowns was first noticed in modern times by the Indian scholar Sudhansu Kumar Ray in 1956.[15]

---

[15] Ray, Kumar Sudhansu, *Prehistoric India and Ancient Egypt* 1956

Chapter 2

Sema Tawi of Serpent Power

What is Serpent Power Yoga?

Serpent Power Yoga is a specific discipline of philosophy, psychology, and life force cultivation and manipulation that allows a human being to discover and harness subtle energies within themselves and their environment. This is done to promote the reconnection of that energy with its ancient source which is the transcendental Self. When the inner life force energy is caused to move it carries with it the conscience of a human being to deeper planes of reality, thereby enlightening that individual. This form of yogic discipline requires great purity of heart (mind) and purity of body as well. This discipline is the oldest known form of spiritual discipline and it is found inscribed on the Great Sphinx in Kamit (Egypt), Africa.

The Serpent Power discipline is one aspect of the overall philosophy of Smai Tawi or "Egyptian Yoga.

History of The Yoga of Life Force Development for Spiritual Enlightenment in Ancient Egypt

The Serpent Power Yoga Philosophy and Iconography in Ancient Egypt

History of the Serpent Power in Ancient Egypt

The Serpent Power teaching, known as Kundalini Yoga in India, was understood and practiced in Ancient Egypt. It is the teaching related to understanding the psychology of the human soul and personality as it relates to spiritual evolution. It is tied to the science of the Psycho-spiritual energy centers and the three main conduits of the Life Force energy, known as Sekhem in Ancient Egypt.[16]

late 5: Frontal Close Up View of the Great Sphinx

The Serpent Power teaching, known as Kundalini Yoga in India, was understood and practiced in Ancient Egypt. It is the teaching related to understanding the psychology of the human soul and personality as it relates to spiritual evolution. It is tied to the science of the Psycho-spiritual energy centers and the three main conduits of the Life Force energy, known as Sekhem in Ancient Egypt.[17] The origins of the Serpent Power teaching in Ancient Egypt go

---

[16] For a more detailed study see the book *The Serpent Power* – by Dr. Muata Ashby
[17] For a more detailed study see the book *The Serpent Power* – by Dr. Muata Ashby

back to the inception of Ancient Egyptian civilization. This is proven by the fact that the oldest Ancient Egyptian monument bears the emblem of the serpent power tradition. The Ancient Egypt Great Sphinx once had a massive head of a cobra perched on its forehead. It is now in the British Museum. However, we know that the positioning of the serpent symbol relates to the serpent power teaching because a scripture describing the serpent power movement and how it leads a human being to spiritual evolution was discovered among various papyri related to the rituals of the temple. (translation by Muata Ashby)

Plate 6: Cobra of the Great Sphinx now in the British Museum

The Pharaonic headdress tradition visible in Ancient Egyptian culture from the headdress of the Sphinx in the predynastic era to the early Christian era establishes a Serpent Power tradition and the tradition of the Pharaonic system of government in Egypt of at least 10,400 years.

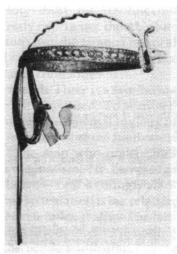

Above left: The funerary mask of King Tutankhamon showing the convergence of the two goddesses (Uatchet and Nekhebet) at the forehead. New Kingdom Period

Above right: The diadem worn by the mummy of Tutankhamun literally depicts the movement of the serpent power as described in the serpent power text (page 46). The two serpents move up the back and go to the sides of the head and then move up across the brain to meet at the point between the eyebrows.

The forehead region is the sixth center of psycho-spiritual consciousness. The vulture and the serpent are the symbols of the serpent goddesses. One

symbolizing the death and consumption of life (lower aspect-vulture) and the other symbolizing the higher aspect-(cobra).

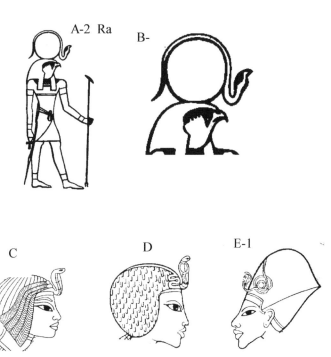

A-1

A-2 Ra

B-

C

D

E-1

There are many parallels between the Arat Shekhem (Serpent Power) system of Ancient Egypt and the Kundalini Yoga system that developed much later in India. These are some examples.

Figure 20: Below -Stele of *Paneb*. Dyn. 19. From Dier el-Medina (Waset Egypt) He worships the serpent goddess *Mertseger* (She who loves silence) in order ot propitiate her favor in the development of transcendental awareness.[18]

Figure 21: Below –An Indian yoga practitioner touches his body in the areas corresponding to the Chakras in order to focus the mantras (words of power) and develop the Kundalini (Serpent Power). From Rajasthan, 1858, gauche on paper.[19]

---

[18] Dictionary of Ancient Egypt. Ian Shaw and Paul Nicholson
[19] Kundalini, Ajit Mookergee

Figure 22: Below- Deity with worshipers and Serpents Indus Valley, Ancient India. Recognized as possibly the oldest known depiction of Yoga in India, this image incorporates the philosophy later known as Kundalini Yoga.

Figure 23: The Serpent goddesses Aset (Isis) and Nebethet (Nephthys) worship Asar (Asar), Ancient Egypt, Africa. The Hawk above symbolizes raising consciousness. The two goddesses represent the serpent power in Kamitan mysticism from the earliest period of Ancient Egyptian history.

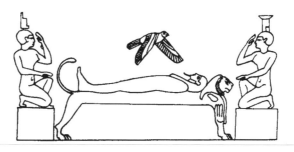

Figure 24: Below- The Serpent goddesses Aset (Isis) and Nebethet (Nephthys) depicted as the dual serpents with are in reality manifestations of the one singular essence.

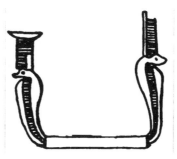

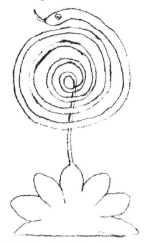

Goddess Kundalini of India rising out of the Lotus.

In India, the revered ancient Sage Shankaracarya in the book "Vivekacudamani" stated:

"The Self is within, and the self is without, the Self is before and the Self is behind, the Self is in the south, and the Self is in the north, the Self likewise is <u>Above and Below</u>... The embodied consciousness is none other than the Universal Consciousness."

Figure 25: Below- Left-The Ancient Egyptian Papyrus Greenfield (British Museum).

Figure 26: Papyrus Qenna (Leyden Museum), displaying the rings signifying the serpentine path of the Life Force from the Spirit above to the heart below, and the levels of spiritual consciousness (the Chakras or Psycho-spiritual consciousness centers)

The Energy Centers of the Subtle Body

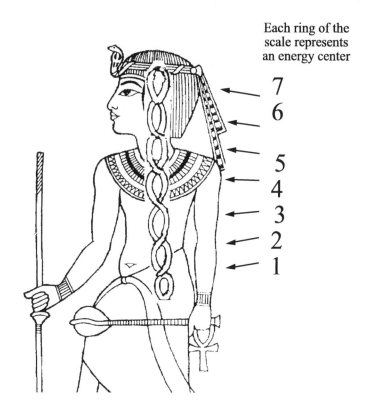

Each ring of the scale represents an energy center

7
6
5
4
3
2
1

Above- Ancient Egyptian artistic representation displaying the "chains" (intertwining serpents) of the *Arat Shekhem* (Serpent Power) and the *Sefech Ba Ra* (seven Life Force energy centers) based on the Greenfield Papyrus.

The secret iconography holds the keys to understanding the origins and nature of the life force energy. First of all note that all of the goddesses are serpents. This is confirmed by the determinative at the end of each name. Next the female leonine symbolism is used with the goddess of Creation, Tefnut. This energy manifests in its grocer state in the form of Sekhmet through her power of Sekhem (Shekhem). This power manifests in its dual forms (Sekhemti). This dual nature of the goddess is also the same one which works in the Maati Hall through the Maati goddesses., who are also known as the Iarrti, the goddesses Aset (Isis) and Nebthet (Nephthys). Thus, the two goddesses who are the inseparable companions of Asar in the inner shrine are none other than the same two serpent goddesses who proceed from the same and singular essence. This same leonine energy, the Lion Power, manifests in the most powerful icon of the Serpent Power in Kamitic (Ancient Egyptian) Iconography, the Horemakhet (Sphinx). Thus, the supreme attainment is symbolized as a raising of the leonine life force from the lower nature to the point between the eyebrows, i.e., the third eye.

The Kamitic System of
Energy-Consciousness Centers
Sefekh Ba Ra / Sefekh Uadjit

Union with the Cosmic Self
Transcendental awareness
Self-control
Universal love
Power and control over others
Sexuality and Creativity
Fear and survival

MEDITATIVE PRINCIPLE

7-I am The Self.
6-Spirit and matter have the same source.
5-I have the power to control my own destiny.
4-I love and care for others and not just myself.
3-I will understand my potential to serve others.
2-I will control and harness my Sexuality and Create positive thoughts, feelings and impressions.
1-I am sustained and provided for by the Self.

The Seven Souls of Ra / The Seven Serpents

If we look back in history we discover that the mythic association between the Kamites and the Nubians in predynastic times is supported by the earliest writings of Ancient Egypt. Firstly, the god Bes, who is usually referred to as a "Sudani" (Nubian) god, is also equated by the Ancient Egyptian scripture and iconography with the divinity Heru. The following image shows this link most succinctly.

In anthropology, pigmies are known as members of any of various peoples, especially of equatorial Africa and parts of southeast Asia, having an average height less than 5 feet (127 centimeters). In the ancient period, the pigmies of Nubia were renowned for knowing "the dance of the God" and for being jovial but forthright people. In this vain they were renowned musicians and lovers of play and festivity but also leaders in wars of righteousness and protectors of children. These are all attributes of Bes. Bes also appears in the Pyramid Texts along with the other gods and goddesses of Kamit. The Pyramid Texts are the earliest known extensive writings about the myth and philosophy of Kamit (Ancient Egypt). Therefore, any divinity which is mentioned in those texts, emerges with at least the same importance of the other Kamitan gods and goddesses depending on the interrelationships provided in the text itself.

Notice the following image of the Ancient Egyptian god Bas who is in the form of Neberdjer, the "all-encompassing divinity." He stands on a serpent who bites its own tail and who encircles seven animals. These animals represent, like the animals in the Indian Kundalini Yoga system, the form of the energy which manifests through the psycho-spiritual energy centers.

The Ancient Egyptian God Bas

The Serpent of Evil and the Sacred Cat of Ra

From ancient times the serpent has been seen as the very embodiment of evil. No doubt this is because of its power to inflict pain and death. This aspect was most heavily popularized by the evil serpent in the Christian Bible. However, mystical teaching reveals that this serpent of "darkness" is indeed the same energy of the Serpent Power. However, since it is not controlled and guided by wisdom it manifests in the form of sinfulness and the negative aspects of the mind (anger, hatred, greed, lust, selfishness, etc.). So it is important to understand that the battle is within yourself. You must strive to oppose negativity and to promote what is positive, righteous and good. This will allow you to succeed in sublimating the Serpent Power. The cat is considered to be a sacred animal because it exemplifies the energy in nature which is inimical to the serpent of evil. The cat, Mau, is seen as an aspect of the goddess Hathor, who is herself the Udjat Eye as well as Arat, the fiery serpent of Ra that burns up evil (ignorance and with it the negative aspects of the mind). Also, the cat is related to the lioness, Sekhmet. This is why there are many scenes in the Ancient Egyptian Book of Coming Forth By Day which depict the spiritual aspirant or the cat doing battle with a serpent fiend. Thus, the cat principles (agility, fierceness, poise, strength and determination) are important to the Serpent Power. A spiritual aspirant should develop these in order to face the negative aspects of the mind.

Note that the serpent is not called a "devil." It represents "darkness" (ignorance) and the cat represents "light," will power, strength and the wisdom of spiritual enlightenment.

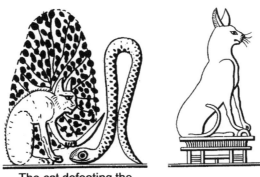

The cat defeating the
serpent of darkness.

The cat defeating the
serpent of darkness.

Below: From the tomb of Pharaoh Tutankhamon, a visual exposition of the idea expressed by the God Djehuti-Hermes: "As above, so below", as two serpents enclose the cosmic form of man (the universe). That which is above (spirit) is eternal, that which is below (matter) is also eternal. The serpent of the earth and the serpent of the sky encircle the lower as well as the higher self. The lower self and the higher self are complementary halves of the whole if brought into harmony. The serpent biting its own tail is reminiscent of the god Bes and it can be seen in many other parts of Africa, representing eternity and self-consumption (nature regenerates itself by consuming itself.)

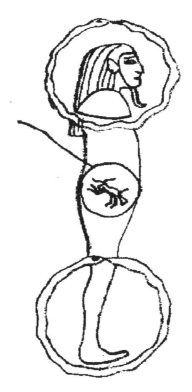

The center area at the base of the spine is highlighted with a line and by the ram-headed hawk positioned with arms raised (in adoration "Ka") toward the sacral region of the spine - the root energy center (chakra).

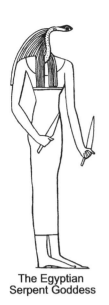

Images of the Serpent Power in Ancient Egypt

Urt-ḥekau, the Cobra-goddess

The Egyptian Serpent Goddess

The modern Caduceus

Arat: The Serpent Power also known as Goddess Isis.

Djehuti wielding the Caduceus composed of the Two Uraeus goddesses, Uatchit and Nekhebet (Isis and Nephthys).

At left: The serpent goddess Nehebka, who assisted Anubis in reconstituting the body of Osiris.

At left:
Netjer Ankh, "The God of Life" who helps the spiritual aspirants on their journey through the netherworld" (Duat).
The Duat or underworld is the realm of illusion and darkness. In order to discover peace and joy (Osiris) it is necessary to successfully traverse the Duat.

Above: Anpu (Anpu) in the aspect of warrior who fights against the enemies of Asar (serpent of darkness and ignorance).

Abovet: From the Theban tombs of Ancient Egypt, the serpent power is like a vehicle through which the consciousness rides to heavenly levels.

Above: The hieroglyph of the "Vertebrae".

Bottom right: From the *"Egyptian Book of Coming Forth By Day,"* This episode is known as "The Slaughter." The soul of Ankhwahibre does battle with Apopis who is sitting atop the vertebrae (Back - Djed Pillar of Osiris) implying that Apopis seeks control of the spiritual energy present in the spiritual subtle channels of the back.

The initiate does battle by invoking the fire of wisdom and therefore asserts the absolute reality he has discovered in himself: ***"I am Ra, continually praised...I*** *am he in whom is the sacred eye.."* (See eye of Ra).   The "Back" is where unbounded spiritual energy (Buto-Uraeus) resides. The initiate is admonished to "develop the fire of the back."

Below- A-The Serpent goddesses Aset (Isis) and Nebethet (Nephthys) depicted as the dual serpents which B- are in reality manifestations of the one singular essence.

(A)

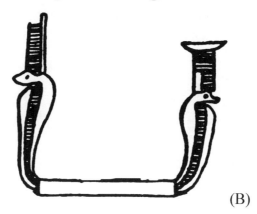

(B)

Below- The Ancient Egyptian god Asar is depicted as the Djed Pillar and at his feet the serpent goddesses Aset (Isis) and nebethet (Nephthys) arise. This is one of the forms of the caduceus, the two intertwining serpents and the single central shaft.

When the serpents are harmonized, the life force energy rises up the central shaft and enlightens the mind -producing higher consciousness.

THE SERPENT POWER IN OTHER PARTS OF AFRICA

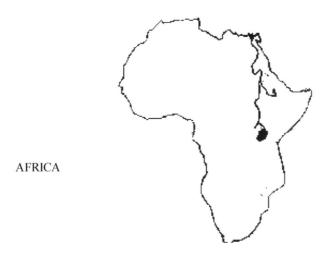

AFRICA

The !Kung People of Africa

The knowledge of the *"Life Force"* inherent in the human body which was known as *Arat* in Ancient Egypt, *Kundalini* in India, *Chi* in China, and *Qi or Ki in Japan,* existed in various traditions around the world. The *!Kung Nation of Africa* who reside in the *Kalahari Desert* are one of the societies referred to as *"Bushmen."* They possess the knowledge of the inner Life Force, and from ancient times, practiced the disciplines to arouse it for the purpose of attaining spiritual evolution.

The *!Kung* practitioners describe the classical Life Force arousal which begins at the pelvic region, moves up the back and rises to the brain, there causing ecstatic and mystical experiences which allow the practitioners to attain expanded states of consciousness known to them as: *!Kia**. This experience allows them to better serve their society. As in other nations of Africa, the *!Kung* begin by engaging in hours long rituals of dancing similar to the modern day Sufi sect known as The Whirling Dervishes. Intense rituals or any prolonged activity can assist the mind in entering into altered states of consciousness. The goal is to arouse *n/um* (Life Force) which is said to reside in the pit of the stomach (Energy Center #3), and when *"warmed"* (aroused), rises from the base of the spine. As with other accounts from around the world, the initial onset of the arousal may be painless or may be attended by the painful movement of energy (not unlike the birth of a child) with such a force that it may challenge the sanity of the individual. This occurrence can understandably cause intense fear which when overcome, allows the release of the soul into new realms of consciousness (the *!Kia State)*.

The state of *!Kia* is equal to the state of *Sihu* (religious ecstasy) of Ancient Egypt, *Samadhi* in Indian Yoga and *Satori* in Zen Meditation.

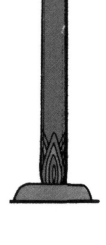

Below: A two dimensional schematic drawing of the subtle human constitution and its relationship to the Self or Soul.

The Self, in every individual, emanates the Life Force energy which creates and sustains the three bodies: Causal, Astral and Physical.

The Causal Body consists of the unconscious mind with the sum total of karmic impressions which impel an individual to have desires and aspirations. It is the plane where the veil of ignorance sustains the illusion of separation from the Self and the notion of egoism and individuality.

The Astral Body is composed of the mind and senses.

The Physical Body is the gross, visible manifestation of the Life Force energy through increasingly more dense (condensed) subtle matter.

The Life Force (serpent power) energy originates from the Self in the process of creation and returns to the Self in the process of dissolution. Therefore, Serpent Power Yoga is the process of causing the energy to become internalized and to return to its source rather than being externalized in the realm of time and space (the three bodies).

When the Serpent Power is cultivated and directed through the physical and astral bodies, its journey ends when it pierces through the causal body and reveals the Self to the individual. When this occurs, the causal, astral and physical bodies as if dissolve since the consciousness of unity with the Divine has replaced the consciousness of being an individual human ego-personality.

The Serpent Power Path

"Develop the life giving fire; few know how to use it and fewer how to master it."

"Master the fire of the back."

Ancient Egyptian Proverbs

Arat Shekhem means "the Ancient Egyptian discipline of the Serpent Power" or simply "Serpent Power."

There are five major types of Yoga under which all other forms may be classified. These are, Yoga of Wisdom, Yoga of Action, Yoga of Devotion, Yoga of Meditation, and Yoga of Sublimation of the Sexual energy and Internal Life Force. All of these yogas should be practiced in an integral fashion for optimum results in the personal spiritual discipline of the aspirant even though one may be emphasized over the others.

This Volume will introduce the concept of the Life Force energy and its relation to human consciousness and the process of psycho-spiritual evolution. In all of the different Yogas there is a common thread which binds and unites them all. This thread is human consciousness. Human consciousness evolves over a period of many lifetimes through the process of reincarnation and transmigration of the soul, gradually rising to the higher levels of consciousness until it finally reaches awareness of the highest wisdom of its true Self.

It is important to understand that as a spiritual aspirant your goal is to raise your level of spiritual consciousness. To this end you are to use a blend of the different yogas. Each form of yoga serves to create a process by which you can raise the Life Force energy which you are trying to develop. If you are practicing Yoga of Wisdom, your consciousness will be raised through your study and understanding of the teachings. If you are practicing Yoga of Action, by your performance of actions in a selfless manner which will lead you to attain mental peace. This mental peace will allow the energy of your soul to flow in an unobstructed manner, thereby you moving towards its destined goal: the higher Self. If you are practicing Yoga of Devotion, your consciousness will be raised through directing your mind towards the Divine by attuning your emotions and feelings toward expressing love for and surrender to the Divine Self. If you are practicing Yoga of Meditation, your consciousness will be raised by calming the waves which disturb the ocean of your consciousness. When this occurs you will experience the transcendental nature of your deeper Self. If you are practicing Yoga of Sublimation of the Sexual Energy and Internal Life Force you will use the energies of the body by controlling and harnessing them. Once controlled, these constitute a formidable force to destroy the ignorance and other human faults which obstruct the soul from full expression in an individual. This last form of yoga underlies all the other forms. When the other forms are properly

practiced, the internal Life Force is automatically balanced and raised. Therefore, regardless of which form of yoga you choose to concentrate on you need to have a full understanding of the Life Force energy and the process of its evolution.

The Concept of Sekhem (Shekem)

The concept of Sekhem or Life Force Energy is related to the most ancient Ancient Egyptian Creation Myth wherein the power emerges from the Supreme Spirit, Ra, the Creator, in the form of a lioness goddess, who is at the same time, the power emanating from the sun. The name of the goddess is Sekhemit and she is also known as Hetheru.

The following diagrams provide insight into the evolution of the Sekhem from the subtle aspect as Tefnut to the dual aspect goddesses Aset and Nebthet in accordance with the Kamitan scriptures.

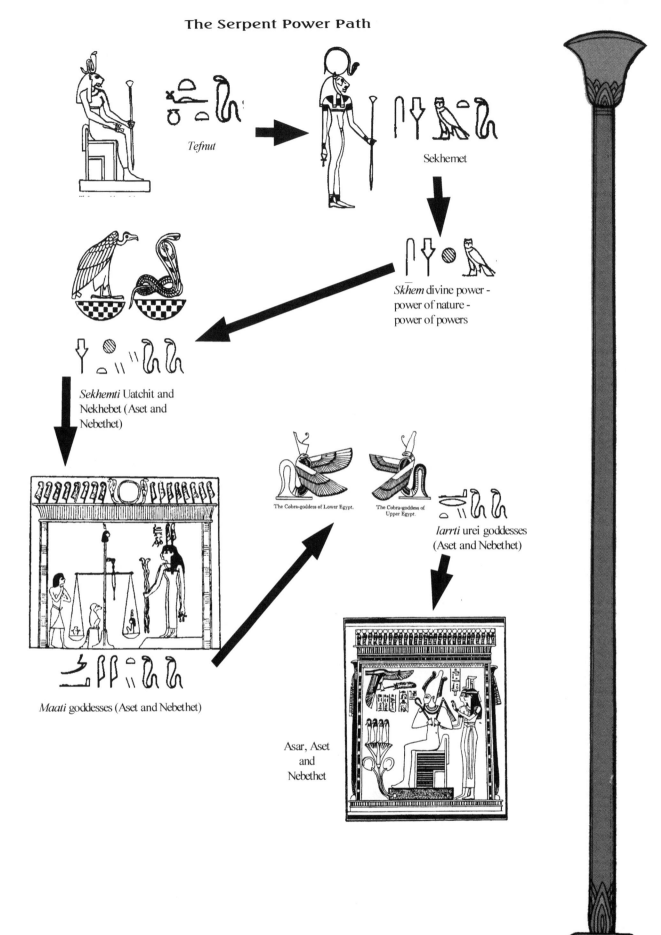

Tefnut

Sekhemet

Skhem divine power -
power of nature -
power of powers

Sekhemti Uatchit and
Nekhebet (Aset and
Nebethet)

The Cobra-goddess of Lower Egypt.

The Cobra-goddess of Upper Egypt.

Iarrti urei goddesses
(Aset and Nebethet)

Maati goddesses (Aset and Nebethet)

Asar, Aset
and
Nebethet

The Ancient History of The Serpent Power Cont.

The ancient history of the Serpent Power begins with Ancient Egypt. The evidence for this come from the Ancient Egyptian Sphinx which has now been dated to 10,000 B.C.E. or older. Next the iconography of Indus Valley reliefs depict the practice of the serpent power technology. Next it appears in China and the rest of the world.

The Bible contains some vague references to *"seven demons"* that were *"cast out of"* Mary Magdalene, *"Jacobs Ladder,"* the seven seals that are to be opened, and the *"Tree of Life."*

The Ancient Egyptian *Greenfield Papyrus* and the Egyptian *Book of Coming Forth By Day* of Kenna, which are both treatises of the Asarian Resurrection religion of Ancient Egypt, contain important teachings in reference to what is today known as Kundalini Yoga in India. We explored both of these in the book *Egyptian Yoga: The Philosophy of Enlightenment* and here we will discuss some more advanced theory related to the Serpent Power and the first level of Serpent Power Yoga meditation. There is an audio tape meditation series which follows along with this section. If you are interested in the audio workshop and meditation music contact the publisher or book distributor.

The subject of life force energy and the sublimation of sexual energy into spiritual energy existed many thousands of years in Egypt prior to its development in modern India under the name *Kundalini Yoga*. It later appears in many parts of the world but it did not find extensive documentation until the Sages of India composed the voluminous scriptures in relation to Kundalini Yoga.

As in the Indian Chakra System, the Egyptian Seven Powers are related to the seven energy centers of the subtle body. They are not visible to the ordinary eye. They are located in the same space as the physical spinal column though not in the same plane as the physical body. They are linked to the awakening of one's spiritual powers and consciousness. As one progresses on the spiritual path of evolution, while either purposely employing a yogic spiritual discipline (study and application of spiritual and philosophic scriptures, reflection and meditation) or learning through the process of trial and error, these centers will automatically open, allowing one to experience increasing communion with the Higher Self: GOD. The process of raising one's spiritual power may be aided by specific exercises such as concentration, proper breathing, meditation on the meanings of the spiritual symbols and surrendering to the will of the Higher Self (GOD). These techniques allow one to transform one's waking personality so that one may discover their innermost Self: GOD. This should be done under the guidance of a qualified teacher (spiritual master, guru, etc.).

The energy centers of the subtle body are likened to a tree which the aspirant climbs through personality integration, which leads him/her to intuitional realization of the transcendental self. In the process of creation, the creative energy manifests in the form of six planes of consciousness. This is the realm of phenomenal reality including physical, astral and mental existence. Most people function on the level of the first three energy-consciousness levels. The goal of this Yoga (Serpent Power) is to unite the six phenomenal consciousness centers with the seventh or transcendental realm of consciousness, the Absolute. This Absolute is what various religions refer to by different names such as the Kingdom of Heaven, Asar, Krishna, Brahman, the Tao, God, Higher Self, Goddess, Christ, Buddha, etc.

Kundalini energy, known as Prana, chi, and Ra-Sekhem, flows throughout thousands of *Nadis* or energy channels. If any of the energy channels are blocked or over-sensitized, a dis-balance can arise, causing illness in the mind and physical body. There are three most important channels through which the Serpent Power flows. In India these are known as: *Sushumna, Ida and Pingala* - These are represented by the Egyptian Caduceus of Djehuti which is composed of a staff which has two serpents wrapped around it. During the ceremonies connected to the mysteries of the Uraeus serpent Goddess *Uatchet* (Udjat), the priest addresses the initiate:

From the temple of Seti I: The God Djehuti wields the

Caduceus and gives life to Seti

From the earliest times of the dynastic period (5,000 B.C.E. to 600 A.D.), the ancient Egyptian texts speak of "rejoining the two lands." The double Uraeus also symbolizes this separation between upper and lower Egypt. There is also a deeper mystical implication to this symbol. The double Uraeus, representing the serpents of the caduceus (wand) of Djehuti, is leading us to understand that we must re-unite the two levels of our consciousness (lower self and higher self).

AESCULAPIUS is the Greek god of medicine, **Asclepius** in Latin. **Aesculapius** is often depicted in art holding a *staff with a serpent coiled around it.* The serpent, which was sacred to him, symbolized renewal of youth, because it casts off its skin. It is also akin to the caduceus of Djehuti, which relates to the Serpent Power Energy.

In ancient Greek myth, Aesculapius was the son of the Greek divinities Apollo and Coronis. The centaur brought him up and taught him the art of healing. His daughter Hygeia personified health, and his daughter Panacea, healing. Two of his sons appear in Homer's 'Iliad' as physicians in the Greek army. Their supposed descendants, called **Asclepiadae,** formed a large order of priest-physicians. The sacred secrets of medicine belonged only to them and were passed on from father to son.

The **Asclepiadae** practiced their art in magnificent temples of health, called **Asclepieia.** The temples were actually sanatoriums equipped with gymnasiums, baths, and even theaters. The patient was first put to sleep. His dream, interpreted by the priests, was supposed to furnish directions for treatment. All cures were recorded as miracles.

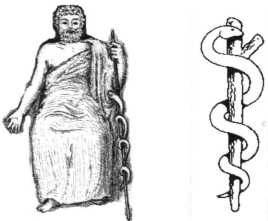

Plate 7: Aesculapius, the Greek god of medicine. Right- Caduceus of Aesculapius.

Teachings of the Serpent Power teaching in Kamitan (Ancient Egyptian) Iconography and Myth

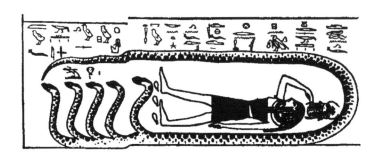

Above: The Serpent Power is the force which engenders Creation - The god Khepri causes the primordial serpent god *Asha Hrau* (many faced one-i.e. manifold heads) to churn the primeval ocean and thereby cause *Dech* or vibrations and these cause matter to take shape. (From Theban Tomb-Ancient Egypt)

Below: Illustration of a panel that was found in the Djozer pyramid (below) in Sakkara Ancient Egypt. It details how the serpent power consolidates in the sun and its rays, passing through Ra-Heru (hawk head) shine on the mummified body in order to revive it. This panel intimates the purpose of the pyramid itself, to act as a focal point for harnessing the Life Force energy and to promote the movement of the serpent power and thereby assist the process of spiritual enlightenment. This is of course a great and powerful mystery only to be practiced by initiates.

The panel from the Djozer pyramid relates to the vignette above from the Per m Hru (Book of the Dead) chapter 154. This chapter relates to the renewal of the body through solar Life Force energy. The sun protrudes out from the sky and releases three rays that enliven the body, not allowing it to perish, I.e. the astral body revives and the personality moves on the path to meet the spirit (Ra). After paying homage to the divinity, there is a declaration of virtue and therefore worthiness of not being allowed to perish. Thus, the Divine is induced to revive the body and not allow it to perish in the netherworld.

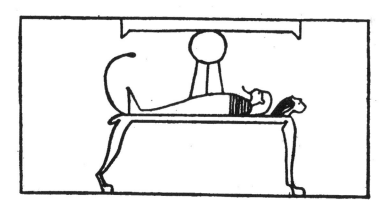

Below-The body receives cosmic energy from the stars while the soul (hawk with the head of a person) looks on. (From an Ancient Egyptian relief.)

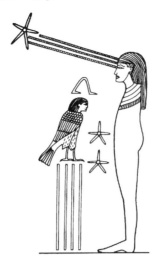

Below: Queen Ty, the mother of King Akhnaton, receives the life force from the rays of the Aton (sundisk)

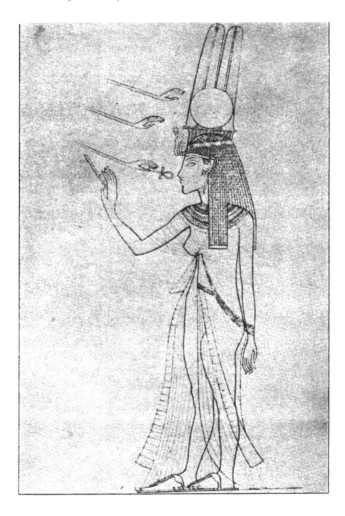

Part II: The Lost Book of Djehuti and the Wisdom of The Caduceus

The Ancient Egyptian Story of the Lost Book of Djehuti.

Who is Djehuti?

Djehuti is the god whom the ancient Greeks later called Hermes. Djehuti, represented as a man's body with an Ibis-head (see below), is the divinity to which the Medu Neter (hieroglyphic legends) ascribe the creation of hieroglyphic scripture, and with it, the wisdom teachings of Ancient Egypt. He also presided over the judgment scene where the soul's deeds are weighed against the feather of Maat.

Forms of Djehuti

Djehuti is the symbol of right reason, the link to the Higher Self. When the determination to pursue the Divine arises, the struggle becomes a holy war against ignorance and illusion within one's consciousness.

He is also known by the Ancient Egyptians as *"Djehuti Lord of Divine Words"* and the more well-known title Djehuti three times Great. He was known to the practitioners in the Greco-Roman period of Ancient Egypt as Hermes the "Thrice Greatest," as he is lord of the three worlds. The Romans called him "Mercury."

The Crescent Moon Symbol of Djehuti

(A)   (B)   (C)

Figure 27: Left- A- symbol of Djehuti. B- the god Djehuti. C- The Ancient Egyptian god Khonsu. B & C: The Ancient Egyptian Gods Djehuti (symbol of intellect) and Khonsu (reflection of consciousness in time and space) with their Crescent Moon symbolisms.

The symbol of the crescent moon is of special importance to the Kamitans and the Hindus. As a symbol of the reflection of the sun, the moon symbolizes the reflection of Divine Consciousness which every human being can achieve as they turn towards the source of light, the Divine Self, as symbolized by the sun. The moon does not produce its own luminescence. It depends on the sun. In the same manner, the human mind, that is, human consciousness or soul, is not self-sustaining. It owes not only its existence, but also its continued survival to the presence of the sun, i.e. the Spirit.

The crescent moon symbolizes waxing or increasing spiritual knowledge, increasing purity of intellect and the development of intuitional wisdom. This is accomplished through all of the means available that the sages have prescribed for the practice of the yogic disciplines: Devotion, Study of the wisdom teachings, Right action and Meditation.

Sebai Djehuti

Djehuti is the god of learning, writing, mathematics and language. Djehuti is referred to as Thoth by the Greeks. In Ancient Egyptian mythology, he is the scribe of the gods. He appears as the record keeper of the dead in the *Books of Coming Forth By Day*. He is the patron of learning and of the arts. He is the inventor of writing, and in the specific theology related to him, he is also seen as the Creator of the universe. Djehuti is depicted as a man with the head of a baboon or an ibis bird. He also bears pen and ink, and sometimes also the lunar disk and crescent.

Above: Djehuti is the transporter of the WORD of God (Ra). He brings the magic (spiritual power) of the Supreme Being (Ra) which will heal Horus.

The ibis is a wading bird related to the stork and the heron. The choice of the ibis indicates a unique feature or quality which spiritual learning requires. This quality is related to the *wading* nature of the ibis. Wading means *walking in or through a substance, as water, that offers resistance, impedes or makes movement difficult*. Djehuti represents intellect, the mind and its capacity to cut (wade)

through the myriad of thoughts and concepts (water-ocean of consciousness) in order to get to the truth.

The crescent moon symbol of Djehuti is a figure of the moon in its first quarter. It has concave[20] and convex[21] edges terminating in points. The crescent moon symbol signifies growing or increasing understanding, reason and spiritual wisdom. Therefore, Djehuti is the embodiment of knowledge. This is one of the reasons why he is said to have created writing. He is also the messenger of Ra who brings the special words of power to Aset in the Ausarian Resurrection Story in order for Aset to resurrect Heru. In this aspect the symbolizes the Spiritual Preceptor who brings the wisdom of the Divine Self to the aspirant so the aspirant can resurrect his\her spiritual aspiration.

Above: Djehuti in the form of a baboon sitting atop the pillar of Osiris.

The universe is understood to be like an ocean of matter through which Ra sails on his barque in order to sustain Creation. Djehuti is Ra's mind, the cosmic mind, with which Ra moves through the ocean of Creation. Thus, the universe is known as an ocean of consciousness called Nu or Nun. The spirit (Ra) uses the Cosmic Mind (Djehuti) to create the objects and varied forms of Creation and maintain order in Creation. Therefore, matter (Creation) is in reality consciousness (Primeval Ocean) which has taken on forms (physical objects) in accordance with the will of the Cosmic Mind. The Cosmic Mind also brings forth learning and knowledge to Creation through the arts, sciences and language. Nothing is invented by human beings. Everything that is created by civilization comes from the Cosmic Mind, and not from any individual human being. To believe otherwise would be egoistic thought. The more a person is in tune with the Cosmic Mind the more knowledge he or she can obtain and the more inner peace and fulfillment a person can experience. The farther away a person gets from the Cosmic mind through negative actions, ignorance and delusion, the less able a person is to discover goodness, inner peace, knowledge, happiness and health in life.

Djehuti is the quintessential image of the Sebai (Spiritual Preceptor) in this story. The word "Sebai" is a Kamitan term meaning "Spiritual Preceptor," a teacher of spiritual truths. A Spiritual Preceptor is a Sage who shows others the way to understand the higher reality beyond the ordinary phenomenal universe. He or she shows others how to discover their true identity and realize their oneness with the Divine. In essence, they are spiritual guides.

---

[20] Curved like the inner surface of a sphere.
[21] Curved outward, as the exterior of a sphere.)

In the beginning, the Spiritual Preceptor must help the individual to somehow turn the anguish and pain experienced as a result of interaction with the world into a desire to rise above it. To this end, a series of techniques and disciplines have been developed over thousands of years. Some of these methods are myths, parables, mental disciplines, meditation and physical culture (Yoga exercises and development of the internal Life Force). The teacher needs to help the seeker to restructure and channel those energies which arise from disappointment and frustration into a healthy dispassion for the illusoriness of the world and its entanglements. The teacher shows the way to develop spiritual aspiration and self-effort directed at sustaining a viable personal spiritual program or *Sheti*.

In Ancient Egyptian Mythology there are two great Spiritual Preceptors. Djehuti is one of them. He is the wonderful teacher of Hetheru.[22] The other one is Aset. In the Shetaut Asar or The Story of Asar, Aset and Heru otherwise known as the Ausarian Resurrection,[23] Aset is the teacher to her son Heru. She trains him in the arts, sciences and the mystical philosophy of Creation and the nature of the Divine Self. She enables Heru to receive the Divine Vision which she obtained from Ra in the Story of Ra and Aset.

A Spiritual Preceptor is not only a person who has attained a high level of internal self-discovery and purity, but also a person who is well versed in the scriptural writings and has knowledge of parables and myths along with their mystical implications. He or she also knows the practices which lead a person to spiritual evolution (Yoga disciplines).

If the teaching is given directly it may be misunderstood or even repudiated altogether due to the state of mind of the individual. Hence, the student must be properly initiated into the teaching and the proper relationship must be established between teacher and student.

The teacher offers humility and honesty with a beguiling wit, cheerfulness and an uplifting outlook. This is symbolized by the divine food Djehuti offered Hetheru. The teacher brings divine food in the form of wisdom teachings which uplift the mind by relieving the burden of pain and sorrow which weighs down the soul of a human being due to ignorance and negativity. The divine food is the taste of divine glory. It is a glimpse of the goal which a disciple must aspire to experience in its fullness. However, this fullness is experienced in degrees as the teacher gives the spiritual teaching and as it is assimilated by the student.

The student must learn to respect and trust the teacher. Also, the student must allow the teaching to penetrate deeply within the heart. It is only then that the teaching will have a transformative effect. In the myth of Hetheru and Djehuti, Hetheru allowed Djehuti's words to penetrate her cold, anguished heart. Then she began to remember her past glory. This is the process of divine memory wherein she began to regain the remembrance of her true identity. The pain of seeing her current level of existence in comparison with her past glory brought her to tears. Also, she felt the pain of realizing that she was missing out on the boundless divine love of her father, Ra. This is the common emotional experience of a spiritual aspirant when understanding as to their true predicament begins to dawn. "What have I done to come down from the heights of divinity to the limited state

---

[22] See the book *Glorious Light Meditation* by Muata Ashby
[23] See the book *Resurrecting Osiris* by Muata Ashby

of human life and mortal existence? How wretched am I? How degraded am I?" These are the kinds of questions asked by a spiritual aspirant before he / she begins to understand the meaning of the spiritual teachings. This form of thinking leads to a resolution to regain one's true glory and to rise up from the degradation of ignorance, "May I find a teacher who can guide me on the path to self-discovery and enlightenment at once!" Thus, Hetheru, came to respect Djehuti. She accepted his offering, listened to his teaching and later trusted him with her life. As one begins to reflect on the teaching, intuitional understanding opens up the opportunity to view the beauty and experience the infinite compassion of the Self. Then there are no more questions, only a keen desire to experience this elevated state more and more. An aspirant might say at this point, "I have glimpsed a wondrous bliss within. Let me fully discover it and abide in it."

Above: left-Djehuti restoring to Heru the Udjat (Uatchit) Eye, 𓂀, which Set (egoism) had blinded.

Above: right- Djehuti restoring to Hetheru the Udjat (Uatchit) Eye, 𓂀, which had become blinded by ignorance.

Djehuti is the spiritual preceptor of two important Kamitan Divinities, Hetheru and Heru. He fixes their faulty vision, i.e., he enlightens their intellect in the myth of the Divine Cow (also known as the Story of Hetheru and Djehuti) and the myth of the Asarian Resurrection. The picture above-left is from the latter myth, where Djehuti repairs the higher vision of Heru, that was damaged by Set, the ego consciousness. In this manner, the aspirant should allow {himself/herself} to be enlightened by the teaching. In this manner the Serpent Power becomes effective and powerful.

The Education of Ancient Egyptian Initiates

Clement of Alexandria (150? A.C.E.- 220? A.C.E.) was an early Christian church father who attempted to harmonize the Christian teaching with the Greek Gnostic and Egyptian in the Egyptian city of Alexandria. The Orthodox Roman church rejected these attempts and the reaction was the opposite of harmonization – a distinctly separate Christian teaching. His writings were important because they provide insights into the Ancient Egyptian, Gnostic and Christian teachings of his time.

Clement described a procession of Ancient Egyptian priests and their gradations. He also described their curriculum which was composed of studies of among other things the "42 Books of Hermes." These included studies in

- Music and Hymns
- Astronomy
- Geography
- Embalming
- Medical science
- Architecture
- Farming
- Engineering
- Reading and writing
- Geometry
- Myths
- Parables
- Wisdom texts
- Book of the Dead texts
- Esoteric philosophy
- Etc.

The priests and priestesses conducted all of the tasks required for managing the society and therefore, they had a need to preserve and pass on a wide variety of skills and knowledge from generation to generation. This system is what allowed Ancient Egyptian culture to prosper for thousands of years, well beyond the longevity of any other culture in history. During the Greco-Roman period in Ancient Egyptian history, many writings that were in hieroglyphic (Ancient Egyptian) text were transcribed into Greek and later Latin. These were studied by

European intellectuals 1500 years later, preserved and translated into many languages during the renaissance period.

The renaissance period in Europe was a humanistic revival of classical art, architecture, literature, and learning that originated in Italy in the 14th century and later spread throughout Europe through the 16th century. It marked the transition from medieval to modern times. Italian scholars of the 14th century began a fresh study of Greek and Latin authors, called the "new learning." Medieval scholars studied the classics to bolster Christian theology.[24] During this period, the European intellectuals took an interest in Humanism and the writings of the Greek classical and Hermetic periods when the ancient Greeks had adopted the philosophy of Djehuti of Ancient Egypt. It was thought, based on the writings of Clement of Alexandria and others, that Djehuti had written 42 books. Many writings from Ancient Egypt have survived the passage of time and the onslaught of invaders and pillagers in Egypt. All of these treat some area which Clement has described, especially the texts of the Books of the Dead. However, most scholars continue to entertain the notion that there are somewhere hidden some writings of Djehuti which are signed by him and are exactly 42 in number.

Resurrection, spiritual Enlightenment- *Nehast*

When we take into account that, according to the entire literature of the Ancient Egyptian tradition it is said to have proceeded from Djehuti, and when we realize that we have writings to cover all of the subject areas mentioned by Clement, it becomes clear that we at least have the essence of the teachings of Djehuti, if we do not have them in their entirety. Nonetheless, the writings continue to be a mystery to most people because of the unreasonable expectations. Also, as for other esoteric manuscripts, there are several chapters of the *Pert m Heru* that are classified by the texts themselves as the highest mysteries. So why does the search continue? Because the keys to unlocking the mysteries is unknown to those who are not qualified to understand the mystical language of the myth and philosophy of the hieroglyphic scripture. There is an important and overlooked story which contains the key to the whereabouts of Djehuti's most important and powerful writings, the solution to the mysteries of nature and the mysteries of God, i.e. the goal of all mysticism, to discover the ultimate and absolute questions of life, Nehast; this is what the Buddhists call "Enlightenment," the Hindus call "Moksha" (liberation), the Gnostics call "Resurrection," and what the Hermeticists call "The Supreme Wisdom," etc.

In the Hermetic parable called "Virgin of the World," which is based on the Ancient Egyptian epic "The Asarian Resurrection,"[25] where Heru is taught the

---

[24] Random House Encyclopedia Copyright (C) 1983,1990 by Random House Inc.
[25] *Resurrecting Asar* by Muata Ashby

wisdom of life (initiated into the mysteries) by his mother Aset, she reveals the secret whereabouts of the books of Djehuti and the means by which they will be revealed. (underlined portions by Ashby)

> 3. *"Such was all-knowing Djehuti, who saw all things, and seeing understood, and understanding had the power both to disclose and to give explanation.* <u>*For what he knew, he engraved on stone; yet though he engraved them onto stone he hid them mostly, keeping sure silence though in speech, that every younger age of cosmic time might seek for them.*</u> *And thus, with charge unto his kinsmen of the gods to keep sure watch, he mounted to the stars."*

4. Hermes, however, made explanation to surrounding [space], how that not even to his son (because of the yet newness of his youth) had he been able to hand on the Perfect Vision. But when the Sun did rise for me, and <u>with all-seeing eyes I gazed upon the hidden [mysteries] of that New Dawn, and contemplated them, slowly there came to me-but it was sure-conviction that the sacred symbols (hieroglyphs – Medu Neter) of cosmic elements were hid away by the secrets of Osiris.</u>

> 5. *"Hermes (Djehuti) returned to Heaven and invoked a spell on them, and spoke these words:* <u>*'O holy books, who have been made by my immortal hands,*</u> *by incorruption's magic Hekau (words of power) . . . free from decay throughout eternity, remain untouched and incorrupt from time!* <u>*Become un-seeable, un-findable, for every one whose foot shall tread the plains*</u> *of this land,* <u>*until old Heaven does bring forth the proper instruments for you, whom the Creator shall call souls.' "*</u>

"Thus, O my son Heru, Djehuti brought the teachings of wisdom which were given to him by the God of All, and they are hidden in nature until the time when those who are ready to seek for their essential nature, those with true aspiration, seek with honesty and reverence."[26]

From the preceding verses we learn:

- ❑ In verse #3 we learn that the secret teachings are hidden, "engraved in stone."
- ❑ In verse #4 Aset explains that she reached a level of evolution which allowed the mysteries to be revealed to her.
- ❑ In verse #5 we are told that Djehuti himself decreed that even though the teachings are inscribed in stone and thus available for all to see, they should remain hidden, i.e. unknowable, until, that is, the proper heavenly instruments are brought to those who are called "souls" by the Creator.
- ❑ In succeeding verses we learn that the qualifications for souls are virtue, living by love and necessity. These constitute nobility.

[26] *Virgin of the World (I)* translated by G.R.S. Mead

Heru, later in the text asks more questions, the answers to which reveal the secret nature of the hieroglyphs and what knowledge they contain. Aset explains that she and Asar incarnated on earth as avatars of Ra and that they were taught the wisdom by Djehuti (k) and that they inscribed the knowledge that was useful to mortals (used to create civilization) and kept the rest themselves (e). They were sent to earth to teach human beings, show them how to keep the balance between things below and thing above (l), to civilize them and when the time comes that the ordinary human being is ready, i.e. comes to the gods and goddesses (stretched forth his hands unto the Gods) as initiates, priests and priestesses practicing their rituals (holy rites) and teachings (m), they (Aset and Asar) will impart to them the higher mysteries, the understanding of the text. (underlined portions by Ashby)

36. And Heru thereon said:

God the Monarch, the universal Orderer and Architect, sent for a little while thy mighty sire Asar, and the mightiest Goddess Aset, that they might help the world, for all things needed them.

a. 'Tis they (Asar and Aset) who filled life full of life.

b. 'Tis they who caused the savagery of mutual slaughtering of men to cease.

c. 'Tis they who hallowed precincts to the Gods their ancestors and spots for holy rites.

d. 'Tis they who gave to men laws, food, and shelter.

e. 'Tis they who will, says Hermes, <u>learn to know the secrets of my records all, and will make separation of them; and some they will keep for themselves, while those that are best suited for the benefit of mortal men, they will engrave on tablet and on obelisk.</u>

f. 'Tis they who were the first to set up courts of law; and filled the world with justice and fair rule.

g. 'Tis they who were the authors of good pledges and of faith, and brought the mighty witness of an oath into men's lives.

h. 'Tis they who taught men how to wrap up those who ceased to live, as they should be. (mummification)

i. 'Tis they who searched into the cruelty of death, and learned that though the spirit which goes out longs to return into men's bodies, yet if it ever fail to have the power of getting back again, then loss of life results.

j. 'Tis they who learned from Hermes that surrounding space was filled with daemons, and graved on hidden stones [the hidden teaching].

k. 'Tis they alone who, taught by Hermes in God's hidden codes, became the authors of the arts, and sciences, and all pursuits which men do practice, and givers of their laws.

l. 'Tis they who, taught by Hermes that the things below have been disposed by God to be in sympathy with things above, established on the earth the sacred rites o'er which the mysteries in Heaven preside.

m. 'Tis they who, knowing the destructibility of [mortal] frames, devised the grade of prophets, in all things perfected, in order that no prophet who stretched forth his hands unto the Gods, should be in ignorance of anything, that magic and philosophy should feed the soul, and medicine preserve the body when it suffered pain. [27]

Where is the highest Wisdom to be found and how can the Highest Spiritual Consciousness be Attained?

Thus we are to understand that Asar and Aset were instructed by Djehuti, who left the earth and presides over the world from heaven. Also, this means that the hidden teaching is to be found in the mysteries rites of the two divinities, Asar and Aset, i.e. the mysticism contained in the myth and rituals of these divinities. The secret teachings of Asar are contained in the Asarian Resurrection myth, the sacred rites of the temple of Asar, his iconography and the Prt M Hru texts.[28] The secret teachings of Aset are contained in the myth of Aset and Ra, its scripture, her iconography and the sacred rites of the temple of Aset.[29] All of these are available but the keys to understanding them has been missed by most seekers and scholars.

All of these revelations require that the aspirant go beyond the scripture itself after becoming "Noble," that is purified by virtuous living and pious devotion to the divine (studying the scripture and practicing the sacred rites). Those who do not follow these instructions will never be able to understand the teachings by intellectual pursuit alone. Hence, virtue, and piety are requirements for revelation of the higher mysteries because the revelation occurs not in the scripture itself nor in the mind. It is a transcending of the physical, mortal, worldly self. This is

---

[27] *Virgin og the World (I)* translated by G.R.S. Mead
[28] *Resurrecting Asar* by Muata Ashby
[29] *Mysteries of Aset* by Muata Ashby

called intuitional wisdom. So the book is an instructional manual, a road the soul's journey to the Higher Self (God). Only those who are virtuous a have practiced the rites can fully grasp and understand this teaching. Wh do they are ready to proceed to pierce through the veil of ignorance.

The first key is to understand the purpose of the scriptures, to lead a soul, to discover its true nature. Most seekers and scholars look on the scripture as primitive magic or as unintelligible words whose meaning was known only by its creators. This important key, the key of mysticism, allows us to look at the text in a different way, as texts that reveal the nature of self as originating in the Supreme Spirit, how the soul came into being and how it discovers its essential nature. Then the practice of the regulations of virtue are important, followed by formal, rituals, the sacred rites. These purify the heart, rendering the physical constitution ("watery encasements") subtle so as to release the soul from its bondage. Those who remain at an intellectual level, and or do not practice the teachings of virtue and the rituals related to the myths of Asar or Aset, treating the scriptures as mere words to be read but not practiced or treated mystically, seeking to retain worldly values and desires, will remain at the level of intellectualism and speculation.

"As above, so below; as below, so above."

-Djehuti

So far there have been two paths given to reveal the secrets of the hieroglyphic texts ("hidden teaching carved in stone"), the path of Asar (Mystical Identification-I Am That) and the path of Aset (Mystical Wisdom-Who am I?). The third path that makes this spiritual movement possible, the revelation of the "hidden teaching carved in stone" is through Djehuti himself. Remember that the teaching is hidden but no qualified seeker should be "in ignorance of anything, that magic and philosophy should feed the soul." Magic is the practice of the holy rites, rituals and virtuous living. Philosophy is the study of the teachings of the myths and texts which becomes subtler as the aspirant purifies {him/her} self and goes deeper within. The secret teachings of Djehuti are contained in the myth of the Book of Djehuti, the sacred rites of the temple of Djehuti, his iconography and the text of the myth itself. This is the path of Wisdom and Life Force Cultivation, i.e. the Serpent Power. The Serpent Power is that force which operates in all paths. Here it is highlighted and used to effectively and quickly lead the initiate to higher spiritual realization, the revelation that transcends all scriptures and secrets. A summary of this myth is presented below.

The Book of Djehuti

The Book of Djehuti[30]

1. THE MIGHTY KING User.maat.ra (Ramases the Great) had a son named Setna Kha.em.uast who vas a great scribe, and very learned in all the ancient writings. And he heard that the magic book of Djehuti, by which a man may enchant heaven and earth, and know the language of all birds and beasts, was buried in the cemetery of Memphis. And he went to search for it with his brother An.he.hor.eru; and when they found the tomb of the king's son, Na.nefer.ka.ptah, son of the king of Upper and Lower Egypt, Mer.neb.ptah, Setna opened it and went in.

    Gloss: Naneferkaptah was a prince and seeker after spiritual truth. Another prince, Setna, a prince and scribe, also sought to know the great mysteries of Creation and the Divine.

2. Now in the tomb was Na.nefer.ka.ptah, and with him was the *ka* of his wife Ahura; for though she was buried at Koptos, her *ka* dwelt at Memphis with her husband, whom she loved. And Setna saw them seated before their offerings, and the book lay between them. And Na.nefer.ka.ptah said to Setna, "Who are you that break into my tomb in this way?" He said, "I am Setna, son of the great King User.maat.ra, living for ever, and I come for that book which I see between you." And Na.nefer.ka.ptah said, "It cannot be given to you." Then said Setna, "But I will carry it away by force."

Naneferkaptah demands the book from Ahura and Naneferkaptah

Gloss: Setna found out that the book was in the tomb of Naneferkaptah. Naneferkaptah and his with Ahura told Setna that it was not wise to try to take the book but he impulsively demanded it from them.

---

[30] This tale of Setna only exists in one copy, a demotic papyrus in the Ghizeh Museum. The demotic was published in facsimile by Mariette in 1871, among "Les Papyrus du Musee de Boulaq" and it has been translated by Brugsch, Revillout, Maspero, and Hess. The last version-"Der Demotische Roman von Stne Ha-m-us, von J. J. Hess" -being a full study of the text with discussion and glossary, has been followed here; while the interpretation of Maspero has also been kept in view in the rendering of obscure passages. This presentation was edited by Muata Ashby. XIXTH DYNASTY, PTOLEMAIC PERIOD WRITING

3. Then Ahura said to Setna, "Do not take this book; for it will bring trouble on you, as it has upon us. Listen to what we have suffered for it."

Ahura's Tale

4. 'We were the two children of the King Mer.neb.ptah, and he loved us very much, for he had no others: and Naneferkaptah was in his palace as heir over all the land.'

Gloss: In order to reason with Setna, Ahura tells him the story of how Naneferkaptah pursued it and how it destroyed their family.

5. "And when my brother Na.nefenka.ptah went to the cemetery of Memphis, he did nothing on earth but read the writings that are in the catacombs of the kings, and the tablets of the 'House of life,' and the inscriptions that are seen on the monuments, and he worked hard on the writings.

Naneferkaptah passes the time reading all the hieroglyphic inscriptions.

6. And there was a priest there called Nesi-ptah; and as Na.nefer.ka.ptah went into a temple to pray, it happened that he went behind this priest, and was reading the inscriptions that were on the chapels of the gods. And the priest mocked him and laughed. So Na.nefer.ka.ptah said to him:

Gloss: She told him how Naneferkaptah was also a seeker and a scribe as well as a prince and how he read the tomb inscriptions wherever they were in search of the highest wisdom.

7. "Why are you laughing at me?' And he replied, 'I was not laughing at you, or if I happened to do so, it was at your reading writings that are worthless. If you wish so much to read writings, come to me, and I will bring you to the place where the book is which Djehuti himself wrote with his own hand, and which will bring you to the gods. When you read but two pages in this you will enchant the heaven, the earth, the abyss, the mountains, and the sea; you shall know what the birds of the sky and the crawling things are saying; you shall see the fishes of the deep, for a divine power is there to bring them up out of the depth. And when you read the second page, if you are in the world of ghosts, YOU will become again in the shape you were in on earth. You will see the sun shining in the sky, with all the gods, and the full moon.'"

Naneferkaptah pays the priest

8. "And Na.nefer.ka.ptah said, 'By the life of the king! Tell me of anything you want done and I'll do it for you, if you will only send me where this book is.' And the priest answered Na.nefer.ka.ptah, 'If you want to go to the place where the book is, you must give me a hundred pieces of silver for my funeral, and provide that they shall bury me as a rich priest.' So Na.nefer.ka.ptah called his lad and told him to give the priest a hundred pieces of silver; and he made them do as he wished, even everything that he asked for.

Gloss: Ahura tells Setna how a priest laughed at Naneferkaptah's efforts and told him about the book of Djehuti which contained the highest wisdom about nature and the Divine which was written by Djehuti himself and not by intermediary scribes.

9. Then the priest said to Na.nefenka.ptah, 'This book is in the middle of the river at Koptos, in an iron box; in the iron box is a bronze box; in the bronze

box is a sycamore box; in the sycamore box is an ivory and ebony. In the ivory and ebony box is a silver box in the silver box is a golden box, and in that is the book. It is twisted all round with snakes and scorpions and all the other crawling things around the box in which the book is; and there is a deathless snake by the box.'

Gloss: Naneferkaptah was immediately taken with the idea of pursuing the book regardless of the dangers.

10. And when the priest told Na.nefer.ka.ptah, he did not know where on earth he was, he was so much delighted.

Gloss: Naneferkaptah was so intent on discovering the book and the prospect of attaining its wisdom that he entered into a trance or ecstasy just from hearing the words of the priest.

11. "And when he came from the temple he told me all that had happened to him. And he said, 'I shall go to Koptos, for I must fetch this book; I will not stay any longer in the north.' And I said, 'Let me dissuade you, for you prepare sorrow and you will bring me into trouble in the Thebaid.' And I laid my hand on Na.nefer.ka.ptah, to keep him from going to Koptos, but he would not listen to me; and he went to the king, and told the king all that the priest had said. The king asked him 'What is it that you want?' and he replied, 'Let them give me the royal boat with its belongings, for I will go to the south with Ahura and her little boy Mer-ab, and fetch this book without delay.' So they gave him the royal boat with its belongings, and we went with him to the haven, and sailed from there up to Koptos.

12. "Then the priests of Aset of Koptos, and the high priest of Aset, came down to us without waiting, to meet Na.nefenka.ptah, and their wives also came to me. We went into the temple of Aset and Heru.pa.khart (Heru the child); and Na.nefer.ka.ptah brought an ox, a goose, and some wine, and made a food-offering and a drink-offering before Aset of Koptos and Heru.pa.khart (Heru the child). They brought us to a very fine house, with all good things; and Na.nefer.ka.ptah spent four days there and feasted with the priests of Aset of Koptos, and the wives of the priests of Aset also made holiday with me.

Gloss: On his way, Naneferkaptah met with priests and made offerings to the temple of Aset.

13. And the morning of the fifth day came; and Na.nefer.ka.ptah called a priest to him, and made a magic cabin that was full of men and tackle. He put the spell upon it, and put life in it, and gave them breath, and sank it in the water. He filled the royal boat with sand, and took leave of me, and sailed from the heaven: and I sat by the river at Koptos that I might see what would become of him. And he said, 'Workmen, work for me, even at the place where the book is.' And they toiled by night and by day; and when they had reached it in three days, he threw the sand out, and made a shoal in the river.

Gloss: The final three days of the journey to find the book are without sleep or rest. This tradition of the three days follows the Asarian Resurrection teachings

14. And then he found on it entwined serpents and scorpions and all kinds of crawling things around the box in which the book was; and by it he found a deathless snake around the box. And he laid the spell upon the entwined serpents and scorpions and all kinds of crawling things which were around the box, that they should not come out.

Gloss: Naneferkaptah finds the place where the book is and finds it there, covered by crawling creatures, symbols of the lower nature and uncontrolled thoughts.

15. And he went to the deathless snake, and fought with him, and killed him; but he came to life again, and took a new form. He then fought again with him a second time; but he came to life again, and took a third form. He then cut him in two parts, and put sand between the parts, that he should not appear again.

Naneferkaptah battles the "deathless snake."

GLOSS

Naneferkaptah used words of power to subdue the serpents and scorpions entwined around the box but these were useless against the deathless snake. The serpents and scorpions are the restless thoughts of the mind that can be controlled by a steady and regular practice of chanting the special words of power. However the "deathless snake" represents the egoism that every aspirant must face in order to release the power of the Serpent Power. This serpent cannot be defeated by words or illusions. Aspirants may think they have transcended the ego and yet it comes back to life to cause them misery in life. This is why it comes back to life. It can only be defeated by placing a permanent separation between its parts, that is, between the ego and the Self. One must understand one's higher nature as separate from the ego.

16. "Na.nefer.ka.ptah then went to the place where he found the box.
   16.1. He uncovered a box of <u>iron,</u> and opened it;
   16.2. he found then a box of <u>bronze</u>, and opened that;
   16.3. then he found a box of <u>sycamore wood</u>, and opened that; again,
   16.4. he found a box of <u>ivory</u> and in it an
   16.5. <u>ebony</u> box, and opened that; yet,
   16.6. he found a box of <u>silver</u>, and opened that; and
   16.7. then he found a box of <u>gold</u>; he opened that, and found the book in it.

Gloss 1: Naneferkaptah discovers that there are a total of seven boxes, one within the next in a successive fashion. The seven boxes represent the seven succeeding levels of consciousness, i.e., the Life Force Energy nters of the astral body, the same teaching of the Greenfield and Qenna papyri.

Gloss 2: Naneferkaptah succeeds in opening all the boxes, i.e. awakening all the energy centers and allowing the Serpent Power to flow freely. Reading the two Hekau allowed him to discover the mystery behind Nature and the Divine.

17. He took the book from the golden box, and read a page of Hekau (words of power) from it.

    17.1. He enchanted the heaven and the earth, the abyss, the mountains, and the sea; he knew what the birds of the sky, the fish of the deep, and the beasts of the hills all said.

    17.2. He read another page of the Hekau (words of power), and saw the sun shining in the sky, with all the gods, the full moon, and the stars in their shapes; he saw the fishes of the deep, for a divine power was present that brought them up from the water.

    17.3. He then read the spell upon the workmen that he had made, and taken from the heaven, and said to them, 'Work for me, back to the place from which I came.' And they toiled night and day, and so he came back to the place where I sat by the river of Koptos; I had not drunk nor eaten anything, and had done nothing on earth, but sat like one who is gone to the grave.

Gloss: Ahura also read the book, proving that women as well as men were equal participants in the mystery system (religion) of the temple in Ancient Egypt.

18. "I then told Na.nefer.ka.ptah that I wished to see this book, for which we had taken so much trouble.

    18.1. He gave the book into my hands; and when I read a page of the Hekau (words of power) in it I also enchanted heaven and earth, the abyss, the mountains, and the sea; I also knew what the birds of the sky the fishes of the deep, and the beasts of the hills all said.

    18.2. I read another page of the Hekau (words of power), and I saw the sun shining in the sky with all the gods, the full moon, and the stars in their shapes; I saw the fishes of the deep, for a divine power was present that brought them up from the water.

    18.3. As I could not write, I asked Na.nefer.ka.ptah, who was a good writer, and a very learned one; he called for a new piece of papyrus, and wrote on it all that was in the book before him. He dipped it in beer, and washed it off in the liquid; for he knew that if it were washed Off, and he drank it, he would know all that there was in the writing.

Gloss: The mysteries of Nature and the Divine are also the same as "Heaven and Earth" or the "Above and Below," i.e. the secrets of the spirit and the secrets of matter. There was one problem though, Naneferkaptah and Ahura had not sought the permission of Djehuti to read the book, i.e., they were not qualified aspirants.

19. 'We returned back to Koptos the same day, and made a feast before Aset of Koptos and Heru.pa.khart (Heru the child). We then went to the haven and sailed, and went northward of Koptos.

20. And as we went on Djehuti discovered all that Na.nefer.ka.ptah had done with the book; and Djehuti hastened to tell Ra and said, 'Now know that my book and my revelation are with Na.nefenka.ptah, son of the King Mer.neb.ptah. He has forced himself into my place, and robbed it, and seized my box with the writings, and killed my guards who protected it.' And Ra replied to him, 'He is before you, take him and all his kin.' He sent a power from heaven with the command, 'Do not let Na.nefer.ka.ptah return safe to Memphis with -all his kin.' And after this hour, the little boy Mer-ab, going out from the awning of the royal boat, fell into the river: he called on Ra, and everybody who was on the bank raised a cry. Na.nefer.ka.ptah went out of the cabin, and read the spell over him; he brought his body up because a divine power brought him to the surface. He read another spell over him, and made him tell of all that happened to him, and of what Djehuti had said before Ra.

21. "We turned back with him to Koptos. We brought him to the Good House, we fetched the people to him, and made one embalm him; and we buried him in his coffin in the cemetery of Koptos like a great and noble person.

Naneferkaptah reading the words of power.

Gloss: It is important to understand that the words of power are not just word-spells but wisdom teachings for understanding the nature of Self and Creation. This is the essential goal of all the teachings.

22. "And Na.nefer.ka.ptah, my brother, said, 'Let us go down, let us not delay, for the king has not yet heard of what has happened to him, and his heart will be sad about it.' So we went to the haven, we sailed, and did not stay to the north of Koptos. When we were come to the place where the little boy Mer-ab had fallen in the water, I went out from the awning of the royal boat, and I fell into the river. They called Na.nefenka.ptah, and he came out from the cabin of the royal boat; he read a spell over me, and brought my body up, because a divine

power brought me to the surface. He drew me out, and read the spell over me, and made me tell him of all that had happened to me, and of what Djehuti had said before Ra. Then be turned back with me to Koptos, he brought me to the Good House, he fetched the people to me, and made one embalm me, as great and noble people are buried, and laid me in the tomb where Mer-ab my young child was.

23. "He turned to the heavens, and sailed down, and delayed not in the north of Koptos. When he was come to the place where we fell into the river, he said to his heart, 'Shall I not better turn back again to Koptos, that I may lie by them? For, if not, when I go down to Memphis, and the king asks after his children, what shall I say to him? Can I tell him, "I have taken your children to the Thebaid, and killed them, while I remained alive, and I have come to Memphis still alive"?' Then he made them bring him a linen cloth of striped byssus; he made a band, and bound the book firmly, and tied it upon him. Na.nefer.ka.ptah then went out of the awning of the royal boat and fell into the river. He cried on Ra; and all those who were on the bank made an outcry, saying, 'Great woe! Sad woe! Is he lost, that good scribe and able man that has no equal?'"

Naneferkaptah, feeling regret and anguish over his error, throws himself overboard also and dies.

24. "The royal boat went on, without any one on earth knowing where Na.nefer.ka.ptah was. It went on to Memphis, and they told all this to the king. Then the king went down to the royal boat in mourning, and all the soldiers and high priests and priests of Ptah were in mourning, and all the officials and courtiers. And when he saw Na.nefenka.ptah, who was in the inner cabin of the royal boat-from his rank of high scribe-he lifted him up. And they saw the book by him; and the king said, 'Let one hide this book that is with him.' And the officers of the king, the priests of Ptah, and the high priest of Ptah, said to the king, 'Our Lord, may the king live as long as the sun! Na.nefer.ka.ptah was a good scribe, and a very skilful man.' And the king had him laid in his Good

House to the sixteenth day, and then had him wrapped to the thirty-fifth day, and then laid him out to the seventieth day, and then had him put in his grave in his resting-place.

Setna Reads
the Book of
Djehuti

25. Thus, it is important to understand that there are certain kinds of wisdom that are not for all human beings because they are not worthy (ready) to hear the teaching. Arrogance and power may allow them to gain access to certain materials and levels of consciousness but they are not ready to understand what they will experience and therefore they cannot integrate it properly into their lives. Consequently they self-destruct and those around them also suffer, because of their shortsightedness, greed and egoism, which can be so subtle that even those in positions of power or even in the royalty, can be unrighteous or harbor unrighteous thoughts that may seem to them as reasonable and true. However, the final and ultimate authority over all of this is Djehuti himself, who symbolizes the intellect aspect of personality. One's own intellect rejects the wisdom teaching and leads one to misery due to the subtle impurities of the mind that cause flaws in the thought process and cloud the reasoning capacity. Even though Naneferkaptah and Setna were warned they ignored this and pressed on anyway. Aspirants should learn humility and patience while gaining purity of heart. Then they should approach an authentic preceptor who will guide them in the proper way and show them the mysteries at the appropriate time and place.

GLOSS

Naneferkaptah was placed in the tomb where Setna found him and the soul of Ahura and his son joined him there. This is part one of the story. Part two tells of how Setna paid no heed to their warnings and took the book, read it and his life was almost completely destroyed. So the power of the Book of Djehuti should only be sought by qualified aspirants. It is the highest wisdom which is not found on temple walls but on the very essential nature of the innermost being. The words point to the higher wisdom which every initiate must discover inside themselves, i.e. the illusoriness of the ego consciousness and understanding the underlying essence of Nature and God as being one in Creation as well as the innermost truth of one's very self. The Serpent Power path to this level of spiritual consciousness can only be approached by qualified (purified) and well instructed aspirants.

Chapter 3: The Serpent Power Discipline of Ancient Kamit

Stage 1 – Cleansing of the Physical, Subtle and Causal Bodies

"Ab"
{purity, to purify the aspirant (priest or priestess)}

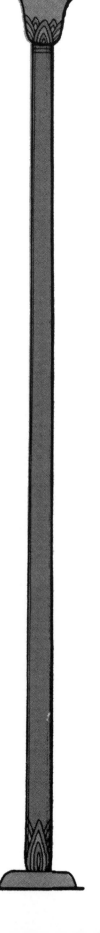

INTRODUCTION

There are two stages of practice in the Yoga of life force energy development. The first stage of practice is the cleansing stage. Here the concentration is on cleansing the mind and body and on balancing the energy flow of the body. The mind is purified by practicing the wisdom teachings, selfless service and meditation. The body is purified by purifying the diet and regular practice of physical exercises which include various breathing techniques such as alternate nostril breathing which harmonize and balance the Life Force energy. In order for your consciousness to unfold your mind needs to be cleansed of gross impurities such as anger, hate, greed, selfishness, etc., and the physical body needs to be cleansed of mind altering chemicals and elements of lower vibratory rate which will agitate the mind making it more susceptible to becoming preoccupied with the desires of the body and other worldly concerns.

After the cleansing stage of Kundalini Yoga wherein the elements of the body are cleansed (*bhuta shudhi*), and the subtle energy channels of the body are cleansed (*nadi shudhi*), which may take months, years or lifetimes, the attention turns to the three main channels wherein spiritual realization unfolds. This is accomplished by manipulating the energy in the subtle mental planes and directing it towards the Divine. (This is the subject of the second audio tape in this series.)

The Psychic Energy Centers in the spiritual or etheric body are distributed throughout the spine going up from the base of the spine to the Crown of the head: <u>*The Uraeus.*</u> Each one of these centers are called *Chakras* or vortexes of spinning energy. In Egyptian symbolism they are depicted as circles or links in a chain in the karmic scales of the initiate. In Indian symbolism they are portrayed as a *padmas* or Lotuses, symbolizing psycho-spiritual principles of human consciousness. By understanding these and removing obstacles to them, Kundalini energy is freed. When your consciousness is freed you can move towards the divine essence of your being. Otherwise you are trapped in the illusions of your karma which cause worldly entanglements, expectations and other illusions which lead to pain, sorrow and disappointment as well as reincarnation. Thus, the Serpent Power is inexorably linked to karma and fate. However, the practice of Serpent Power Yoga mitigates all negative karma because it destroys illusion and ignorance about the truth of your Higher Self. It is ignorance about the Higher Self which leads a human being to experience the endless trials and tribulations, pains and sorrows of life, like a person who is caught in the middle of a storm without any shelter.

Mental and emotional complexes and sentiments constitute the main obstacles and blocks to Kundalini, one's own spiritual consciousness. Through physical exercises, physical cleansing through diet and lifestyle changes, and meditation on the psycho-spiritual implications of each center, Kundalini Yoga is effected.

Purity of the Body

There are two important aspects to the cleansing process which must occur in order to have success in awakening the Serpent Power. The first is cleansing the physical body and the second is cleansing the heart. The Temple of Aset provides the teachings for promoting purity of the body through diet, proper eating habits and the proper was to practice the spiritual disciplines. The teachings of Maat provide the guidelines for promoting purity of mind in thought, word and deed in life. So it is important to realize here that awakening the Serpent Power cannot be accomplished just by practicing meditation or by praying to the Serpent goddess. It is an integral process which must be practiced in an integrated, balanced manner. You will not have success if your body and nervous system are weak. The Serpent Power requires a sturdy and pure nervous system in order to manifest the higher forms of spiritual consciousness. If you attempt to rush your spiritual development without first purifying yourself you may develop negative tendencies which will draw you away from true spiritual realization or even worse, the premature eruption of the Serpent Power energy will short circuit and damage the spiritual centers, sometimes permanently. Thus insanity or mental instability can occur.

Serpent Power Yoga will not work if you have a healthy body but are plagued with mental agitations and worldly desires. If you cannot control your mind the energy that you could conserve and use towards the development of the Serpent Power will be wasted and you will not have success. Therefore, you must practice the teachings, study the teachings and practice meditation while you work on simplifying your life and promote harmony in your mind. The following is a summary of the teachings of the Temple of Aset in reference to the process of studying the teachings and the diet of the Initiates (spiritual aspirants).

While the general population of Ancient Egypt was considered to be one of the most healthy groups of the ancient world, the spiritual initiates were required to keep an even more strict dietary practice. The special diets of the Ancient Egyptian initiates were a highly guarded secret as were the inner meanings of the myths which were acted out in the mystery rituals (***SHETAUT NETER***). For this reason, many of the special yogic practices which included a special diet and meditation were not committed to writing in an explicit fashion. Rather, they were committed to hieroglyphic form and carried on through the initiatic process. It was not until Greek historians and initiates into the Egyptian mystery schools began to write about their experiences that the more detailed aspects of the initiatic diets were available to a wider audience. The sect of Jews called the Essenes practiced an initiation period of two to three years and instituted purification diets and hygienic practices similar to those spoken about by Herodotus (484?-425 BCE) and Plutarch (46?-120 ACE). The Essenic health practices were presented in the Essene Gospel of Peace.

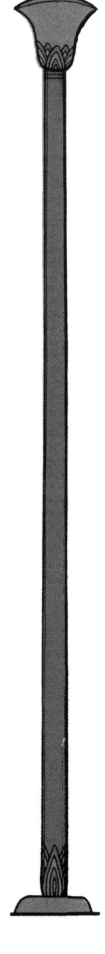

The Teachings of the Temple of Aset (Isis)

Above: The Pylons of the Temple of Aset at Agilkia island (Aswan) in Egypt, Africa.

Plutarch, a student of the mysteries of Isis, reported that the initiates followed a strict diet made up of vegetables and fruits and *abstained from particular kinds of foods* (swine, sheep, fish, etc.) *as well as indulgence of the carnal appetite.* In the following excerpts Plutarch describes the purpose and procedure of the diet observed by the Initiates of Aset and the goal to be attained through the rigorous spiritual program. This next excerpt should be studied carefully.

To desire, therefore, and covet after truth, those truths more especially which concern the divine nature, is to aspire to be partakers of that nature itself (1), and to profess that all our studies (2) and inquiries (2) are devoted to the acquisition of holiness. This occupation is surely more truly religious than any external (3) purifications or mere service of the temple can be.(4) But more especially must such a disposition of mind be highly acceptable to that goddess to whose service you are dedicated, for her special characteristics are wisdom and foresight, and her very name seems to express the peculiar relation which she bears to knowledge. For "Isis" is a Greek word, and means "knowledge or wisdom,"(5) and "Typhon," [Set] the name of her professed adversary, is also a Greek word, and means " pride and insolence."(6) This latter name is well adapted to one who, full of ignorance and error, tears in pieces (7) and conceals that holy doctrine (about Asar) which the goddess collects, compiles, and delivers to those who aspire after the most perfect participation in the divine nature. This doctrine inculcates a steady perseverance in one uniform and temperate course of life (8), and an abstinence from particular kinds of foods (9), as well as from all indulgence of the carnal appetite (10), and it restrains the intemperate and voluptuous part within due bounds, and at the same time habituates her votaries to undergo those austere and rigid ceremonies which their religion obliges them to observe. The end and aim of all these toils and labors is the attainment of the knowledge of the First and Chief Being (11), who alone is the object of the understanding of the mind; and this knowledge the goddess invites us to seek after, as being near and dwelling continually (12) with her. And this also is what the very name of her temple promiseth to us, that is to say, the knowledge and understanding of the eternal and self-existent Being - now it is called "Iseion," which suggests that if we approach the temple of the goddess rightly, we shall obtain the knowledge of that eternal and self existent Being.

Mystical Implications of the Teachings*

*Note: The numbers at the beginning of each paragraph below correspond to the reference numbers in the text above.

1- It is to be understood that spiritual aspiration implies seeking the union with or becoming one with the thing being sought because this is the only way to truly "know" something. You can have opinions about what it is like to be a whale but you would never exactly know until you become one with it. God enfolding all that exists is the one being worthy of veneration and identification. This "knowing" of Neter (God) is the goal of all spiritual practices. This is the supreme goal which must be kept in mind by a spiritual aspirant.

2- In order to discover the hidden nature of God, emphasis is placed on study and inquiry into the nature of things. Who am I? What is the universe composed of? Who is God? How am I related to God? These are the questions which when pursued, lead to the discovery of the Self (God). Those who do not engage in this form of inquiry will generate a reality for themselves according to their beliefs. Some people believe they have the answers, that the universe is atoms and electrons or energy. Others believe that the body is the soul and that there is nothing else. Still others believe that the mind is the Soul or that there is no soul and no God. The first qualification for serious aspiration is that you have a serious conviction that you are greater than just a finite individual mortal body, that you are an immortal being who is somehow mixed up with a temporal form (body). If this conviction is present, then you are stepping on the road to enlightenment. The teachings will be useful to you. Those who hold other beliefs are being led by ignorance and lack of spiritual sensitivity as a result of their beliefs. Thus, their beliefs will create a reality for them based on those beliefs. They will need to travel the road of nature which will guide them in time toward the path of spiritual aspiration.

3-4 The plan prescribed by the teachings of yoga is the only true means to effective spiritual development because it reveals the inner meanings of the teachings and it is experiential, i.e. it is based on your own personal experience and not conjecture. Otherwise, worship and religious practices remain at the level of ritualism only and do not lead to enlightenment.

5-7 The name "ISIS" represents "wisdom" itself which bestows the knowledge of the true Self of the initiate. In the Asarian Mysteries, when Set killed Asar by tearing him into pieces, he was symbolically tearing up the soul. However, Aset restores the pieces of the soul (Asar). Therefore, Pride and Insolence (Set-egoism) destroy the soul and Knowledge of the Self (Isis) restores it to its true nature. The Greek name for Aset is supported by the Ancient Egyptian scriptures. One of the names of Aset is: *Rekhit*  meaning "knowledge personified" and "Isis-Sothis." Rekhit is also a name of the God in the "Duat" or Netherworld who

possesses knowledge which can lead the soul to the abode of the Divine, thus avoiding the fiends and demoniac personalities of the Duat which lead the soul to experience hellish conditions after death. The variation, *Rekh-t* , means Sage or learned person.

8- True spirituality cannot be pursued rashly or in a fanatical way by going to extremes. Yoga spirituality is a science of balance. It has been developed over a period of thousands of years with well established principles, which when followed, produce the desired effect of leading the initiate from darkness to light, ignorance to knowledge, an un-enlightened state to enlightenment.

9-10 The foods referred to are flesh foods (swine, sheep, fish, etc.), pulse, and salt. Indulgence in sexual activity has two relevant aspects. First, it intensifies the physical experience of embodiment and distracts the mind by creating impressions in the subconscious which will produce future cravings and desires. This state of mind renders the individual incapable of concentration on significant worldly or high spiritual achievements. Secondly, control of the sexual urge leads to control of the sexual Life Force energy, which can then be directed toward higher mental and spiritual achievement.

11- See #1.

12- There are two very important points in this line. Once again we are being reminded that good association or keeping the company of sages or other enlightened personalities is a powerful means to gain knowledge of the state of enlightenment. To this end, strive to keep good company in your family relations as well as non-family relations. Read uplifting books by the sages and the teachings of the masters. When you discover a more evolved personality, seek to maintain contact by reading their teachings and through correspondence. Do not debate with those who lack spiritual sensitivity. This form of interaction will weaken your mind. As Jesus said: *Cast not your pearls before swine, for they will trample them as they turn against you.* Trust in the Omniscient Divine Self, who knows past, present and future, who manifests as Nature to lead others on the path. Spread the teachings of yoga to those who are interested only or those with whom you practice. This kind of interaction will help you both to increase your understanding and generate a positive frame of mind.

The second important point here refers to continuous reflection and meditation on the Divine which is also expressed in the opening prayer: *"Give thyself to GOD, keep thou thyself daily for God; and let tomorrow be as today."* It implies that one's mind should be constantly remembering the Divine and glorifying the Divine in all things. It means not allowing the mind to develop attachments to the fleeting events of human life be they positive experiences or negative ones. It means not allowing the negative thoughts and feelings to lead you into a pursuit of illusory pleasures of the senses which will draw you away from divine awareness and realization. It means centering the mind on self discovery and introspection at all times regardless of what your activities may be, and those activities should be based solely on the principles of virtue, justice and order. This form of spiritual practice is known as "mindfulness" in Buddhism and Vedanta Philosophies.

Plutarch further reports that the Egyptian initiates:

> *...strive to prevent fatness in Apis† as well as themselves*(1), *for they are anxious that their bodies should sit as light and easy about their souls as possible, and that their mortal part* (body) *should not oppress and weigh down their divine and immortal part...during their more solemn purifications they abstain from wine*(2) *wholly, and they give themselves up entirely to study*(4) *and meditation*(5) *and to the hearing* (3) *and teaching of these divine truths which treat of the divine nature.* † Bull which was kept as a symbol of Asar and Ptah.

The following dietary guidelines for spiritual and physical health are derived from the above statement.

1- Preventing "fatness"- obesity. This issue is very important even for those without spiritual aspirations. Some people who are overweight claim that they are happy and content as they are. Some scientists claim to have discovered a gene in the human system which causes a propensity to become overweight. Once again, all of your body's characteristics are due to your past karmic history of experiences and desires, not only in this lifetime but in previous ones as well. Physical weight is like a physical object which is possessed. The more you have, the more you try to hold onto, and the more stress you have trying to enjoy and hold onto "things." Desires of the body such as eating have a grounding effect on the soul because they engender the desire to experience the physical pleasure of consuming food. Desires of the body as well as strong emotions such as hate, greed, etc., have the effect of rendering the mind insensitive to spirituality. Excess weight on the body causes innumerable health problems to arise.

You can change the future condition of your body by first mentally resolving to change it and then employing the self-effort in that direction while at the same time invoking the help of the Neters (cosmic forces - divine energies of God) to assist your quest for self-improvement. This will not be easy since the temptation of food is very great. It is related to the first energy center of the subtle spiritual body (Uraeus-Kundalini Serpent Power)* and it is a force which needs to be controlled in order to proceed on the spiritual path. As part of your spiritual program, begin controlling your intake of food gradually, on a daily basis. Even if you cut back a tablespoonful per day until you reach a level of intake which will support the normal weight for your body structure. Be especially watchful of yourself in respect to your habits. Do you eat out of habit, for pleasure or out of necessity? If it is out of habit or for pleasure, you must break the cycle by engaging in other activities when the desire arises. Do exercise, deep breathing, study, chant, call a fellow practitioner for support. The Serpent power will be discussed in detail in two future sections. *see audio tape lecture KUNDALINI - URAEUS YOGA: Workshop and Cleansing Meditation-I.

2- Natural wines and other naturally brewed drinks are acceptable in small quantities, however, you will notice that as you purify yourself, you will not be able to tolerate even a small amount of intoxicants. Distilled liquor is not a natural substance. It is processed into a potent form which is injurious to the body and is therefore, not suitable at all for use by those advancing on the spiritual path. The same applies to narcotics and all other "recreational" drugs. All of these distort the

spiritual perception while damaging the physical body. No drug can produce a high which can be compared to spiritual bliss. Therefore, resolve to leave all drugs behind and become intoxicated with spiritual feelings and aspiration.

3,4,5- Once again, the main format for spiritual education is:

> 3- Listening to the teachings.‡
> 4- Constant study and reflection on the teachings.‡
> 5- Meditation on the meaning of the teachings.‡

‡Note: It is important to note here that the same teaching which was practiced in Ancient Egypt of **Listening** to, **Reflecting** upon, and **Meditating** upon the teachings is the same process used in Vedanta-Jnana Yoga of today.

Chapter 30B of the *Book of Coming Forth By Day* states:

> *This utterance (hekau) shall be recited by a person purified and washed; one who has not eaten animal flesh or fish.*

Chapter 137A of the *Book of Coming Forth By Day* states:

> *And behold, these things shall be performed by one who is clean, and is ceremonially pure, a man who hath eaten neither meat nor fish, and who hath not had intercourse with women* (applies to female initiates not having intercourse with men as well).

In the Mysteries of Asar and Isis, Set represents the lower human nature and Heru the Higher. Set kills Asar and usurps the throne which rightfully should belong to Heru, Asar' son. In various renderings of the characteristics of Set, it is stated that Set is promiscuous. Most interestingly, both Heru and Set are vegetarians. Their favorite food is *lettuce*. Therefore, we are to understand that vegetarianism increases the potential for spiritual advancement and for the vital sexual force. With this understanding, it is clear that control of the sexual urge to conserve potential spiritual energy and purification of the diet are necessary practices on the spiritual path which enable the aspirant to achieve increased spiritual sensitivity. When practiced correctly, the conserved energy can be transformed into spiritual energy by directing it through the various energy centers in the body until it finally reaches the center of intuitional vision (Eye of Heru-Udjat).

A most important point to remember when beginning practices for the purification of the body is that they should be implemented gradually, preferably under the supervision of an experienced person. If these changes result in an inability to perform your daily duties, then they are too extreme. The key to advancement in any area is steady, balanced practice. There must always be a balance between the practical life and the spiritual. In this way, spiritual advancement occurs in an integral fashion, intensifying every area of one's life rather than one a particular area exclusively. All areas must be mastered, secular as well as non-secular, in order to transcend the world process (illusion of time and space and the ego-self).

Since the physical body and all worldly attainments are changeable, fleeting and ultimately perishable, it would be wise to pursue a way of life which directs the mind toward understanding the Self and not to pursue health as an end in itself, but as a means to your own growth and spiritual evolution, which will continue even after the death of the your physical body if you have not attained enlightenment up to the time of physical death. The holistic development of an individual must be directed to achieving a state of consciousness which is not dependent on the physical body for peace and comfort. The body is an instrument which you have created through your thoughts to allow you to pursue the goal of enlightenment and thereby experience the fullness of life.

How to Attain Purity of Heart

Reflection on the Virtues that are to be cultivated in Spiritual Energy Centers

The goal of Serpent Power Yoga is to unlock the hidden potential of the human being which is being blocked by various psycho-spiritual forms of ignorance and negative feelings. The following diagram shows the main psycho-spiritual elements (obstacles to the full expression of consciousness) which are to be overcome at each center of psycho-spiritual consciousness.

TRANSCENDENCE - ENLIGHTENMENT

7

Obstacle: Ego self - You think you are a mortal
human being instead of an Immortal Divinity.

6

Lack of concentration. Lack of intellectual ability required to think properly and discover the true meaning of life. The intellect is clouded over by egoistic feelings, desires and illusions about what reality is.

5

Lack of self control, Getting carried away with the whims of the mind and senses.

4

Attachment, Egoistic Love

3

Desire for worldly attainments, and control of others, Greed, Hatred,

2

Gross Sexual Desire.

1

Fear of death. Survival concerns. Where will next meal come from?

The following diagram shows the virtuous qualities of each center which are to be cultivated and developed in order to transcend that center on the upward movement toward transcendence. Note that the centers 1-3 are separated by a horizontal line and that next to these the word Maat is written. This signifies that those people who are at the psycho-spiritual consciousness level between one and three are those people who have not reached the maturity for self-determination. They require rules and regulations imposed by society to guide them on the right path which promotes self-development, sex-sublimation and self-control. Therefore, they must be taught the injunctions of Maat and they must be shown the wisdom of following its principles.

Those who have gained control over the first three psycho-spiritual consciousness centers will be able to discover a new, deeper essence of their own existence as they move beyond "animal" consciousness. Otherwise, they will remain in a horizontal movement through life which will lead to pain, sorrow and disappointments as well as the development of a karmic basis for reincarnation.

Where Does True Happiness Come From?

In reality, happiness does not and cannot come from objects that can be acquired or from activities that are performed. It can only come from within. Even actions that seem to be pleasurable in life cannot be considered as a source of happiness from a philosophical point of view because all activities are relative. This means that one activity is pleasurable for one person and painful for another. This leads to the realization that it is not the activity itself that holds the happiness but the individual doer who is performing the action and assigning a value to it which she or he has learned from society to assign. Therefore, if it was learned that going out to a party is supposed to be fun then that activity will be pursued as a source of happiness. Here action is performed in pursuit of the fruit of the action in the form happiness; a result is desired from the action. However, there are several negative psychological factors which arise that will not allow true happiness to manifest. The first is that the relentless pursuit of the action renders the mind restless and agitated. The second is that if the activity is not possible there will be depression in the mind. If the activity is thwarted by some outside force, meaning that something or someone prevented you from achieving the object or activity you saw as the "source of happiness" you develop anger towards it. If by chance you succeed in achieving the object or activity you become elated and this will cause greed in the mind; you will want more and more of it. When you are not able to get more at any particular time you will become depressed and disappointed. Under these conditions a constant dependence on outside activities and worldly objects develops in the mind which will not allow for peace and contentment. Even though it is illogical to pursue activities which cause pain in life people are constantly acting against their own interests as they engage in actions in an effort to gain happiness while in reality they are enhancing the probability of encountering pain later on. People often act and shortly regret what they have done. Sometimes people know even at the time of their actions that they are wrong, yet they are unable to stop themselves. This is because when the mind is controlled by desires and expectations, the intellect, the light of reason, is *clouded* and *dull*. However, when the mind is controlled by the intellect, then it is not possible to be led astray due to the *fantasies* and *illusions* of the mind. When the individual is guided by their intellect, then only right actions can be performed no matter what negative ideas arise in the mind. Such a person cannot be deluded into negative actions. When negative actions (actions which lead to future pain and disappointments) are not performed, then unhappiness cannot exist. Thus, a person who lives according to the teachings of non-doership (without desire or expectations for the future results of their actions) lives a life of perpetual peace and happiness in the present.

Thus, true peace and inner fulfillment will never come through the pursuit of actions when there is an expectation or desire for the fruits of those actions. The belief in objects or worldly activities as sources of happiness is therefore seen as a

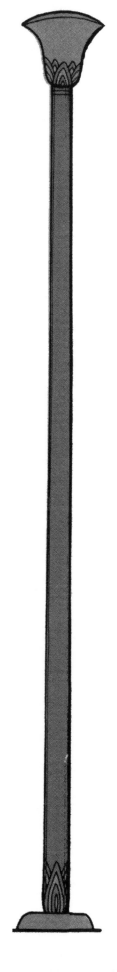

state known as *ignorance* wherein the individual is caught up in the *illusions*, *fantasies* and *fanciful notions* of the mind. However, happiness and peace can arise spontaneously when there is an attitude of detachment and dispassion towards objects and situations in life. If actions are performed with the idea of discovering peace within, based on the understanding of the philosophy outlined above, and for the sake of the betterment of society, then these actions will have the effect of purifying the heart of the individual. The desires and expectations will dwindle while the inner fulfillment and awareness of the present moment will increase. There will be greater and greater discovery of peace within, a discovery of what is truly stable and changeless within as opposed to the mind and outer world which are constantly changing and unpredictable.

Keeping The Balance

"Neither let prosperity put out the eyes of circumspection, nor abundance cut off the hands of frugality; they that too much indulge in the superfluities of life, shall live to lament the want of its necessaries."

"See that prosperity elate not thine heart above measure; neither adversity depress thine mind unto the depths, because fortune beareth hard against you. Their smiles are not stable, therefore build not thy confidence upon them; their frowns endure not forever, therefore let hope teach you patience."

-Ancient Egyptian Proverbs

As the proverbs above suggest, equanimity is one of the most important qualities that a spiritual aspirant must develop in order to practice virtuous living. Virtuous living requires strength of will because life is constantly tempting the mind and body towards the pleasures of the senses and egoistic desires. When the mind is constantly agitated, swinging back and forth, becoming elated and exuberant in prosperous conditions and angry and agitated during adversity, the mental energy is drained and dispersed. It becomes hard to concentrate, to act with clarity, to distinguish between right and wrong and to fulfill the duties of life. This is why in the *Ancient Egyptian Book of Coming Forth By Day* the initiate is constantly saying that he or she *"Kept the Balance"* and is worthy to enter into the divine realms.

Undue mental agitation is the source of angry thoughts wherein people say and do things they otherwise would not say or do and get caught in a pattern wherein they are easily provoked by others who can "push the right buttons" which can evoke anger in them. When the mind is in control and always aware of the thoughts within as well as the world outside it is impossible for it to fall prey to the provocation of others, despair or fear. This is the ideal of equanimity that is to be reached by living a virtuous life through the study and practice of the teachings of mystical spirituality.

"No one reaches the beneficent West unless their heart is righteous by doing MAAT. There is no distinction made between the inferior and the superior person; it only matters that one is found faultless when the balances and the two weights stand before the Lord of Eternity. No one is free from the reckoning. Thoth, a baboon, holds the balances to count each one according to what they have done upon earth."

Ancient Egyptian Proverb

Seek Purity of Heart Through Living a Life of Simplicity

"When opulence and extravagance are a necessity instead of righteousness and truth, society will be governed by greed and injustice."

Ancient Egyptian Proverb

The key to reducing worldly entanglements, mental agitation and negative karmic impressions which will lead to future pain and reincarnation is to reduce the desires in the mind. One important way to accomplish this is to simplify one's life. This implies reducing one's karmic entanglements and worries which constantly agitate the mind. We are indoctrinated into believing that material wealth brings happiness, so much so that having achieved a measure of success, according to societal standards, we convince ourselves that we are happy, sometimes even if it means an early grave due to overwork and increased stress attempting to support luxuries which are not needed or pursuing ideals which are wrong for us. Many who may not have the material wealth are, as if hypnotized by the idea, that they "must" pursue it and once achieved, it will yield the long sought after happiness. Despite the disappointments and frustrations, we continue to pursue the dream, not realizing that material wealth does not automatically produce happiness. Further, if those who have achieved the riches are happy, it is not because of the riches but due to a much deeper psychological integration that has occurred. Also, just as the presence of material wealth does not necessarily constitute prosperity, mental peace and happiness, in the same way, the lack of material wealth does not necessarily constitute adversity, mental agitation or unhappiness.

A life of simplicity does not mean giving up all wealth and moving somewhere in the country to live off the land. It means living according to the necessities of life and not hoarding possessions as sources of happiness or due to some family obligation. It means not indulging in the egoism of jealousy by comparing oneself to others and trying to emulate their success or trying to look good in their eyes. The divine plan has prescribed a specific path for every individual. Therefore, you should live life according to the understanding that you have been given all of the necessary tools to accomplish the goals of your life. Therefore, while continuing to strive for better conditions in life, the underlying understanding should be that if riches are to come, it will be a result of Divine will. Likewise, if adversities come it is for the same reason. Both adversities and prosperities come to a person according to their karmic history as fruits of past actions. Therefore, in order to

promote positive situations in the future, all you need to do is concentrate on correct actions in the present which are guided by the correct attitude and understanding.

Simplicity means living within one's means and watching over the mind's desires for pleasures and luxuries that are not necessary, accepting whatever comes as part of the divine plan, even while striving to better oneself. In this way, feelings of detachment, contentment and peace can be developed even while you are engaged in actions which are necessary in life.

Mysticism of the Color Green

"Hotep di si Neter iri Mettu wadj"
Peace Offering given (to) cause (the) Divine (to) make (the) vascular systems green (healthy)

In Kamitan spirituality, the divinity Asar is often represented with a green hue. The picture above, which comes from the Temple of Aset (Isis) in Egypt, shows us the reason why. Wheat, representing all vegetation in Creation, is seen growing out of the dead body of Asar. In the Asarian Resurrection Myth, Asar was killed by his brother and resurrected by his sister and wife, Aset. While his spirit resurrected and became the lord of the "Beautiful West," his body became the sustaining essence which causes vegetation to grow. He, i.e. the spirit, is the ↑ ♀ ↑ , *Uas-Ankh-Uas,* or "flow of life force essence" which causes vegetation to grow and sustains human existence. Asar (Osiris) is green because he is the essence of life in the vegetables we eat. If we learn to eat the right "green" diets for our bodies, minds and souls, we are eating Asar himself, and thereby become divine beings ourselves. Isn't the saying "you are what you eat" well known now? This is the original teaching of divine food, which was later represented in Christianity as the eucharist. But you must know that everything you eat can be a eucharist leading you to health, vitality and spiritual enlightenment.

swadj – "May you become green" – "may you flourish and thrive"

In a mystical sense, Asar is the very sustenance of life. All food that is eaten is therefore Asar also. This idea is also expressed in the benediction of the Ancient Egyptian doctors, who, upon administering medicaments, would speak the special words of power *"may your mettu flourish."* The Kamitan term for flourish is "greening." So in order to become healthy, one is to become "green" like Asar. Thus, Asar is the sustenance of the *Duat* (Astral) as well as the *Ta* (earth) realms.

This theme is present in every aspect of Ancient Egyptian culture and others. In modern times, most people do not want to think about death, especially when they are "having a good time." This would have been considered a turning away from truth, a breach of one of the fundamental injunctions of Maat philosophy (Precept #24: *I have not stopped my ears listening to the words of right and wrong*). Thus, when the subject of death is broached, one should not turn away and act as if it does not exist or try to have a "good time and not think about it" attitude. Drugs, worldly entanglements, and other distractions may soften the blow of death in the short term, but some day the issue will have to be dealt with through the death of close family members and of one's very self. If you are not ready, the experience will be harrowing and painful. If you are ready, it can be "as smooth as silk." This is the prospect that initiates of the mystical sciences look forward to and discover.

Facing death and uncovering its mystery is the most important task for every spiritual aspirant. This is because the fear of death and the sorrow caused by disease, old age and death typify the pain, misery and frustrations of life. Therefore, conquering death means conquering life.

The goal of health practices is to allow the soul to have a useful body throughout its lifetime, a body that is not obstructed by disease and suffering. The body should be healthy even up to the time of death, for death is not determined by either health or illness of the body, but by the karmic necessity of the individual. It is one's own soul who makes the determination of when and how one will die. This is why death, sometimes seem senseless.

When all healing attempts have been made and despite those efforts, health deteriorates beyond any further action, it is time to help the dying person understand and accept what is happening, and even look forward to it. This process is made easier for those who have led a righteous life because their conscience can be clear, devoid of regrets, fears, discontent, and anger. While hope should be kept alive, the truth should be openly discussed and in this way, the higher purpose of health is also served, for death means that a new body will be acquired and the opportunity to apply the lessons of this life will once again be available to that person. When a society becomes so out of touch with the spiritual reality it fears death and dreads its coming, then it searches for ways to extend life, even after the soul has left the body. This misguided idea forces many to suffer unnecessarily, hanging on by machines which sustain the pain-racked body which is little more than a useless husk. This is very degrading to the soul, but yet it is in line with the karmic basis of those who perpetuate it and those who must suffer through it as patients.

Since in the view of the Kamitan sages, the one and only purpose of life is to attain Enlightenment, then it makes sense that every aspect of one's life should be tied into this purpose, even one's diet for the physical body. This was expressed throughout the Kamitan wisdom teachings, iconography and mythology. It is

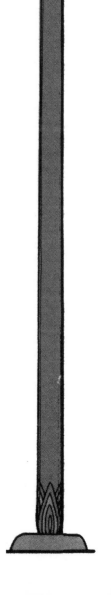

expressed in the iconography depicted on the back cover of this book with the physical body of Asar, an incarnation of the Divine, laying in a coffin and wheat growing out of his body. Since the purpose of life was to become Divine, becoming one with the Divine Self in the form of Asar was seen as the goal of life in the Asarian tradition of Kamit. Asar was often depicted as green, so the spiritual meditation related to diet and eating vegetarian foods is that as one eats "green," one becomes Asar-like, a Divine being. Becoming Asar-like, that is, becoming a spiritually Enlightened personality, was seen as the state of ultimate health. This concept of a green diet and its relationship to health and attaining unity with the divine is further expressed in the following verse that was chanted in Kamit in ancient times by healers:

"Si i(e) mettu wadj" or " mettu swaj" for short

This injunction for healing calls for a "greening" of all the vital channels (vascular system, lymphatic system, circulatory system, etc.) of the physical body to restore health. It was understood that this process of bringing "green" into these conduits and channels would restore physical health, but even more importantly, mental health and spiritual health, because automatically the use of the word "swaj" meaning "greening" would render the effect of turning the mind to Asar, the Divine, the essence of all greenery in nature and the source of all healing. As a result of this, both the doctor and the patient would have an immediate experience of divine grace in the way of an experience of Divine Presence and communion with the Divine. Thus, in the process of being healed and healing with regards to the physical body, both the patient and doctor, respectively, move closer to the attainment of Enlightenment...perpetual union with the Divine, Sema (or Sma, Smai) Tawi.

There is another aspect of healing via green foods and green juices from plants. The chlorophyll molecule of the plants and the hemoglobin molecule of the animal and human red blood cells have almost the identical chemical structure. The main difference, which is primarily one of function, is that the chlorophyll molecule in plants contains the element magnesium, which allows it to trap the sun light (solar energy) for the plant in the process know as photosynthesis, while the hemoglobin molecule contains the element iron, which allows it to carry oxygen in the physical body. In the Asarian tradition, the sun is a symbol of the Divinity Ra, who is the father of Asar, and also is representative of the Divine Self. Thus, the plant stores this divine (Ra-light) energy, which is then transferred to the human body when they are consumed, leading to a union of the person eating the plant food with the Divine. Interestingly enough, when Kirlian photography, which measures the electromagnetic radiation surrounding objects (more commonly known as the "aura") is taken of plants, there is a vibrant glow. However, when this same Kirlian photography is taken of a hamburger, the only thing that glows is the lettuce. One scientist[31] found that when he measured the frequency of meat and that of cancer, they vibrated at the same (low)

---

[31] Robert O. Young, Ph.D., D.Sc., head of the Innerlight Biological Research Center and author of "Sick and Tired?"

frequency, unlike the vibrant high energy frequency of green plant based foods, especially when in their raw unprocessed state. He literally demonstrated that you become that which you eat, so from this perspective, cancer can be described as the accumulation of "dead" meat and processed "dead" foods in the body.

Greening the Energy Channels

Figure 28: Left-An Ancient Egyptian conception of the energy centers with the caduceus of Djehuti – based on the Greenfield Papyrus.

Figure 29: Center- The Kamitan Caduceus with the central Shaft (Asar), and the intertwining serpents (Uadjit and Nekhebit, also known as Aset and Nebethet)

Figure 30: Right- The Kamitan Energy Consciousness Centers (Spheres-Chakras)

The Kamitan system of the energy spheres, and of the caduceus with its central shaft symbolizing the subtle spine, and the two intertwining serpents symbolizing the dual energies into which the central shaft differentiates, concurs in every detail with the later developments in East Indian Mysticism encompassed by the discipline known as Kundalini Yoga with its system of Chakras and the three main energy channels, Sushumna (central) and Ida and Pingala (intertwining conduits).

Uadjit
(The Green One)

Goddess Uadjit represents the totality of the Serpent Power conception in Ancient Egyptian mysticism. One of her important aspects if the greening power. She is the power behind all vegetation and the life force sustaining human beings.

This green aspect has two manifestations. The first operates in the subtle (astral) plane and then second operates in the physical plane.

In the Astral Plane she courses through the subtle *"mettu"* conduits (channels) of the astral body, sustaining the mind and senses. The grosser aspect of this same energy comes into the physical plane through the nervous system. If the nervous system is not clear (green) there will be obstructions and disease in the mental and or physical bodies will ensue. Therefore, proper diet for body, mind and soul are essential in maintaining the level of health that is necessary to sustain the proper level of life force in the astral and physical bodies in order to properly discover and cultivate the Serpent Power. [32]

The Mysticism of the number 72 and its Multiples

In the Ancient Egyptian myth of the Asarian Resurrection, the death and resurrection of the god Asar, it is told that Asar was killed as a result of a plot that was hatched against him by his brother Set and Set's 72 Sebau (demoniac companions). They killed him by placing him in a coffin that was made to especially fit the body of Asar. They placed him in it and threw it into the Nile river. Asar died and his body floated downriver. Aset, his wife and sister, found the body and revived it through special words of power which she controlled due to her attainment of spiritual enlightenment (See the book *The Mysteries of Aset* by Muata Ashby) and also due to her "blowing air on him with her wings," i.e. reinfusing his body with the life force that had been cut off from it and that led to Asar's death. In the Ancient Egyptian Hymns to Aton we are informed that the "life breath" is a form of energy that is in the air but is not air itself.[33]

The significance of this teaching is that Set represents the egoistic aspect of the human personality[34] and when the ego gets the better of the soul (represented by Asar), the seventy-two energy channels of a living human being are closed off. The coffin symbolizes the closing off of Asar's capacity to draw "life breath." Similarly in India, it is taught that there are 72,000 energy channels or *naris (nadis)* in which the life force courses and sustain life. Therefore, a practitioner of the Serpent Power should take care to maintain control of the personality and promote humility and non-violence. This can be done by following the precepts of Maat philosophy enjoined by goddess Maat.[35]

The cleansing of the energy channels, which are in the astral body, can take place when the gross impurities of the body and mind are cleansed. The gross impurities of the body are cleansed by adopting a vegetarian diet.[36] The gross impurities of the mind are cleansed by adopting study of the teachings of wisdom and keeping company with sages, and their books on wisdom teachings. Further

---

[32] See the book Kamitan Diet by Muata Ashby
[33] (See the book *The Hymn to Aton* by Muata Ashby)
[34] See the book Resurrecting Asar by Muata Ashby
[35] See the book *42 Principles of Maat, The Book of the Dead* by Muata Ashby
[36] See the book Kamitic Diet by Muata Ashby

cleansing occurs when the life force is cultivated and directed by the mind to "unclog" the channels that are blocked. Short of death, blocked channels cause diseases of all kinds along with aches and pains of the physical body. They also cause anxiety, worry, fear and psychological suffering in the astral (mental) body. Therefore, this is a critical area of the practice and cannot be overlooked. Proceeding without cleansing the channels can have detrimental consequences for the physical and astral bodies including physical disease in the physical body and mental disease in the mental body.

The Forces of Chaos

Set and Apep

In Kamitan spirituality there is no conception of a "devil" such as is described in the orthodox western religions. However, there is the notion of Apep and the Sebau. Apep or Apepi is known as a fiend who daily tries to stop the progress of the boat of Ra, the same one that emerged from the primeval waters and which Ra commands along with his company of gods and goddesses. This principle is referring to the ever relentless natural forces of entropy which degenerate all things organic and inorganic. It is the movement of the elements in nature attempting to restore themselves to their natural condition before being brought into some form and order by the forces of Creation which organized them at the beginning of time. The image below is of Apep in the form of the serpent and Set is battling it in service to Ra, thereby proving that Set, though a divinity symbolizing egoism and sensual desire, is actually not a demoniac character in Kamitan religion.

Set protecting the boat of Ra

Chapter 4: The Philosophy of the Life Force and the Process fo Spiritual Evolution

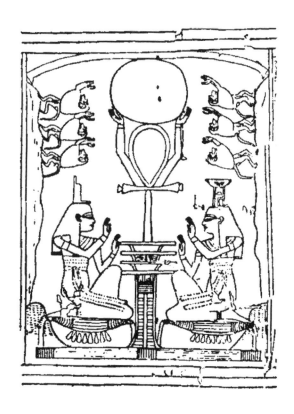

Understanding The Process of Human Evolution

The process of human evolution as reflected in seven states of consciousness was recognized by the Ancient Egyptian Sages long ago. This teaching became an integral part of the philosophy of Maat because it is indeed this aspect of a human being which is being judged in the Hall of Maat. The level of consciousness is equal to the level of purity of heart. Therefore, the heart (subconscious and unconscious mind) may be classified into one of the seven states of evolution and this classification will determine its fate. It is important to note here that all souls are responsible for their own state of consciousness and that each soul will judge itself and thereby determine its own fate.

"Though all human beings suffer fated things, those led by reason (guided by the intellect), do not endure suffering with the rest; but since they've freed themselves from viciousness, not being bad, they do not suffer bad. Though having thought fornication or murder but not having committed these, the Mind-led man will suffer just as though he had committed fornication, and though he be no murderer, as though he had committed murder because there was will to commit these things."

-Ancient Egyptian Proverb

Through your own actions and beliefs you are fashioning the content of your own mind, and this creation of yours will lead you to varied experiences during life and after death.

The following is a more detailed description of each Energy-consciousness center of the subtle spiritual body along with its function and the state of psychology which it represents. Also included are specific meditations which will act as cleansers of the centers. These are to be practiced after you have gained an understanding of the energy center and its function.

The development of the Life Force energy within every human being was practiced in ancient times by the Egyptians and then the Chinese and Indians. The Ancient Egyptian Papyruses of Kenna and Greenfield are examples of the Serpent Power in Ancient Egypt. The Ancient Egyptian deity *Arat*, who was known as the Uraeus goddess by the Greeks, presides over the Life Force energy known as Ra or Sekhem. This same Arat is an aspect of Hathor who is the scorching, fiery eye of Ra, and is also the right eye of Heru. Within this brief explanation you can see the interrelated nature of all deities as they refer to the various facets of spiritual development of a human being.

The picture from the Papyrus of Kenna shows Ammit, the monster who devours the unrighteous. Notice that he is biting the scales of MAAT between the third and fourth circles. These circles indicate levels of spiritual evolution or psycho-spiritual energy centers. The Greenfield Papyrus shows the centers as a chain with seven links. These centers refer to the judgment of the heart of the

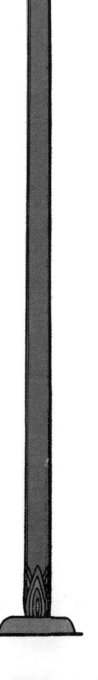

initiate. Centers 1-3 indicate immature human beings who live to seek sensual pleasures and centers 4-7 indicate individuals who are progressing on the spiritual path. The symbol of the serpent (and/or vulture) (Fig. A-1) at the level of the brow (Fig. C, D, E-1) indicates the energy consciousness at the level of the sixth energy center and the serpent on the top of the head (Fig. A-2, B) refers to the seventh energy center at the crown of the head. Figure E-2 shows both the serpent and the vulture protruding from the brow of the goddess Isis.

Above: the Sage-King Akhnaton of Ancient Egypt,
collecting Life Force from the Sun

The sun is the most visible example of the dynamic power of the Life Force energy. This is why the power of the sun has been linked with the notion of the *Uadjit*, 𝕃, the fire spitting serpent and the *Udjat*, ℱ, or the right eye of Ra (the Supreme Being). Both of these symbols imply the light and fire of intuitional spiritual realization. The scorching eye destroys ignorance and bestows the supreme bliss of self-knowledge. Further, the entire universe is pervaded by the Serpent Power energy, however, the sun and the stars are the most dynamic sources of that energy. They are like cosmic transformers which convert the cosmic energy of the Self into a physical manifestation which sustains all life in the universe. Therefore, nothing can survive without this precious energy and the energy itself is the divine touch of God Him/Herself. Thus, sunbathing in the nude (if possible) for 5 to 10 minutes a day is a vitalizing practice. Also, with the power of mental concentration and visualization, the Life Force energy of the sun and of the universe can be harnessed and accumulated in the spiritual (astral) body of a human being and may be used for healing or carrying out important work on the physical plane of existence. This is why there are so many Ancient Egyptian pictures of the initiates, and pharaohs with upraised arms propitiating the Supreme Being in the form of the sun god, Ra, and receiving the Life Force energy. Uadjit is also the right eye (fiery eye) of Ra.

RAISING ASAR

Aset Receives the Pillar of Asar – From the Temple of Abdu

In Ancient Egyptian Mythology the resurrection of the God Asar assumed primary importance. Asar is a symbol of the human soul and his resurrection is commensurate with that of the spiritual aspirant who follows the teachings of Shetaut Asar (Mystery teachings of Asar). In the myth of Asar he is killed by his brother, Set, who dumps his body in the Nile. It floats away and becomes a tree on the banks of Syria. The king of Syria liked the aroma so much that he cut the tree down and carved it into the form of a pillar. This is the pillar or Djed of Asar. Its retrieval by Aset and her subsequent prayers, propitiations and devotional rituals over the pillar, with the assistance of her sister Nephthys and the serpent goddess, signify the process of resurrecting the Higher Self.

Above Left: The Pillar of Osiris

Above right: Life is emerging out of the
Djed Pillar and it is supporting the Sundisk, the light of consciousness.

The Djed is actually the vertebrate spine or spinal column of Asar. The four tiers of the Djed or spine of Asar symbolize the planes of existence as well as the four higher psycho-spiritual centers of consciousness within every human being. When the Djed is laying on its side it signifies death and when it is upright it symbolizes life. The following is an exert from the rituals of resurrection which were practiced in the Ancient Egyptian Temples.

RAISING THE PILLAR

As stated earlier, the raising of the pillar or the subtle psycho-spiritual energy centers of the vertebrae signifies the raising of consciousness and as consciousness is raised one is leading oneself to discover the Higher Self and immortality. This "raising" is accomplished by Aset and Nephthys in their serpentine aspects. Aset and Nephthys are identified as the "the two exceedingly great uraei" (serpents of higher consciousness). Also, in the myth of the Ausarian Resurrection it is said that Set tore to pieces the body of Asar and that Isis, Anpu, and Nephthys, with the help of the Serpent god Nehebka, re-membered the pieces, all except the phallus which was eaten by the fish. In this way, assisted by the words of power of Isis, Asar was reconstituted. Following this, he (Asar) became the ruler in the realm of the dead, the beautiful West, the Amenta or Duat (Astral world).

The deeper mystical implications of the myth of Asar, Isis, Heru, Set and Nephthys involve the journey of the soul. Asar, as the symbol of the soul, experiences the passion of life and death as well as rebirth and resurrection and this is the ultimate fate of every human being when the "two ladies" as well as the psycho-spiritual qualities as represented by the other characters in the myth (Heru, Set, Anpu, Selket, Nehebka, Sebek, Hathor, Min, etc.) are harmonized and realized within one's own consciousness. In this sense, Serpent Power Yoga is a mythic experience wherein one can develop mystical insights through the understanding of the ancient myth, the practice of the rituals related to it as well as a psycho-physical discipline of meditation on the energy centers.[37]

According to the ancient scriptures there are three states of mind. These are Lucidity, Agitation and Dullness.[38] In order for you to discover the higher realms of consciousness you need to engender lucidity and harmony in your life. This will allow you to conserve energy and preserve mental calmness. These will allow you to control the mind and direct it towards the inner Self within. Lucidity and harmony can be promoted in various ways. According to the ancient scriptures your diet should consist of the following.

Many people do not realize that what they consume has a strong effect on their psyche. This implies not only foods but all manner of consumption. Just as there are three major states of relative consciousness, there are three basic kinds of foods. The first group is composed of those foods which engender restlessness and distraction.

> Ex. sugars, salty foods, dry foods, hot spices, coffee, fish, poultry, eggs, etc.

These foods promote passion, stimulate the emotions and excite the body. Also eating in a hurry promotes restlessness and distraction. The second group is composed of foods which promote dullness. This group includes:

> meats, tobacco, alcohol, fermented foods, processed foods, stale or overripe foods.

These foods promote dullness of intellect, anger, hatred, greed, volatility, negative thoughts, disease and clouded reasoning ability. These foods are filled with negativity due to the way in which they are handled in the food processing system. The addition of unnatural chemicals to food in and of itself is reason enough to classify them as tainted with poison. The killing of animals effectively poisons the food with negative hormones as well as fear vibrations from the animals. Also the human digestive tract is not designed to handle meat so the food

---

[37] For the entire myth of the Ausarian Resurrection see the book ***Resurrecting Asar***
[38] See the books ***Meditation: The Ancient Egyptian Path to Enlightenment*** and ***The Kamitic Diet***.

rots as it passes through the intestinal system, causing diseases such as cancer. Is there any wonder why medical doctors admonish those who contract cancer or experience heart trouble to stop eating meat and to stop smoking? Shouldn't they begin promoting a meat free diet for everyone (including themselves) at an early age? If smoking is known to produce cancer shouldn't it be outlawed as are other addictive drugs? Poisons are sold out of greed and ignorance. Also, such poisons are consumed due to ignorance and addictive desire.

Dull foods are not good for the body or for the mind, but much like the stimulating foods, they create an addictive form of dependency wherein even when the person has a full understanding of the deleterious effects of the foods, he or she continues to consume them anyway using the excuse "well I want to enjoy my life even if I shorten it." The weakened will disables a person's reasoning capacity as well as their willpower to resist the urge for the foods.

Lucid foods are those which promote harmony, inner mental peace, bright intellect, willpower, etc. They foster purity of the mind as well as the body. They are nutritious and enhance the body's ability to fight off disease. Lucid foods include:

whole foods, cereals, fresh vegetables and fruits, legumes, seeds, nuts, sprouted seeds, herb teas, honey.

A serious spiritual aspirant must learn about the nature of food as he or she climbs the ladder of mystical spirituality. In so doing, a healthy constitution can be created which will allow for a positive and fruitful spiritual movement towards self-discovery. Since every human being is not exactly the same as another, the exact diet which is optimal for each individual will be slightly different. Therefore each individual should experiment with their diet within the broad guidelines given above in order to discover the right combination within the Lucid Diet category which is best suited for him or her.

The most important factor in the practice of Serpent Power Yoga is not the psycho-spiritual exercises but developing a harmonized and meditative lifestyle. If you were to become knowledgeable about the myths and the mystical teachings in reference to the psycho-spiritual consciousness centers but failed to control anger and desire you will find that the energy (Serpent Power) you needed to assist you in discovering the higher realms of consciousness has been squandered uselessly in the pursuit of objects and desires which are in the end perishable as well as agitating to the mind. Thus, you must strive to control your emotions and expectations by bringing them under the control of reason.

You must strive to promote equanimity, dispassion and detachment in your life. These will lead you to reduce the illusions which you have about the world as well as the entanglements which those illusions lead to. So you must strive to not only develop the psycho-spiritual energy centers but you should strive to promote advancement in every area of your personality (reasoning, emotions, action, and will). As you practice the disciplines of studying the teachings you are promoting reason. As you practice devotion to the divine by following the myths related to the teachings you are developing stability and positivity in your emotional self. As you practice righteous living you are promoting harmony and peace in your external life which will in turn promote peace in your mind. As you practice formal meditation you will be promoting strength of will and concentration of the psycho-spiritual forces which will allow you to direct the mind to pierce through the energy blockages and other forms of ignorance and negativity which prevent you from seeing the higher reality. This manner of practice is referred to as Integral Yoga because it makes use of all yogic disciplines to develop the four major aspects of human personality, emotions, reason, action and will.

As introduced earlier, the teachings the Ancient Egyptian Temple of Aset enjoined spiritual aspirants (initiates into the mystical philosophy) to maintain leanness of the body. This implies not only refraining from overeating but to maintain a physical constitution that subsists on the basic necessities and nothing more. This practice allows the nervous system to be free from being overburdened by too much activity in the digestive tract and also the energy which would have been used for digesting unnecessary food material can be conserved and sublimated into spiritual force. These were the objectives of the Ancient Egyptian Mystical philosophy which is evinced in the spiritual scriptures as well as the Ancient Egyptian Temple architecture itself.

The Meaning of the Tiers of the Djed Pillar

The deeper implications of Serpent Power Yoga involve the control of thoughts and actions, understanding, and sublimation of desires and urges and the cleansing out of negative impressions in the energy centers which are blocking psycho-spiritual energy, the serpent power, which will allow you to discover the higher realms of existence. Thus the four tiers of the vertebrae of Asar have a mystical reference to the higher planes of existence as well as the higher psycho-spiritual energy-consciousness centers of the spiritual anatomy of a human being.

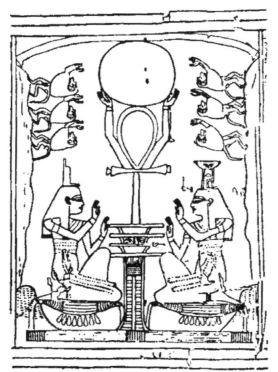

The Pillar of Asar, flanked by the two serpent goddesses Aset and Nebthet

Below right: The Ancient Egyptian God Asar with the Djed Pillar showing the four tiers of the vertebrae.

Below left: The Ancient Egyptian God Ptah with the Djed Pillar showing the four tiers of the vertebrae.

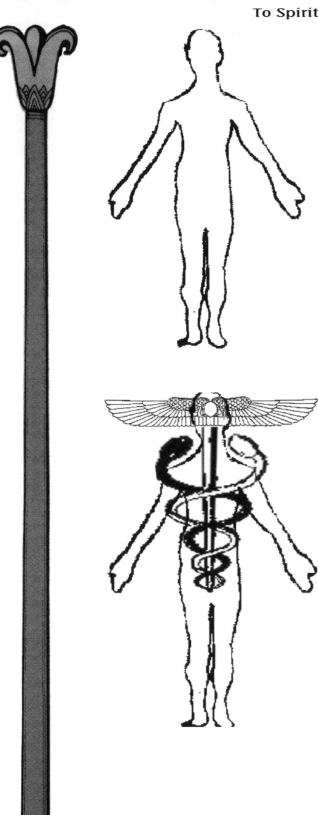

The Serpent sustains the life of human being at all times. However, if it is operating only at the lower energy-consciousness centers, the individual (male or female) will not have access to cosmic consciousness, peace or bliss in ordinary human life.

When the Serpent Power is in full operation it moves from the base of the spine up, uniting all opposites, all contradictions, into one at the head where it engenders cosmic consciousness, bliss, peace, and an awareness of all-encompassingness, all-pervasiveness and union with the Divine.

Chapter 5: Cultivation of the Serpent Power

INTRODUCTION

The Psycho-spiritual Energy Centers and the Process of Awakening them

The process of discovering the psycho-spiritual energy centers and the higher levels of consciousness first involves the understanding of their nature. Secondly, it will involve the sustained practice of intense meditation upon them and finally it will involve experiencing their nature first hand. Therefore, the following section should be studied well before you begin to actually practice the meditations. Also you should at the same time begin to practice the teachings of the mythology behind the theory of serpent power as well as controlling your actions, emotions, thoughts and speech in your day to day activities as mentioned earlier. This form of practice will allow you to realize the teachings in a balanced manner and not to overload one aspect of your being with negativity while improving in another. What benefit will you derive if you are developing the serpent power energy if you cannot control your emotions or if you are so weak willed that you cannot resist temptations such as food or sexuality?

The movement of the Serpent Power involves two modes, creation and dissolution. In the process of creation the energy moves to progressively grosser forms until it reaches a solid state. In the dissolution phase it dissolves by becoming more and more subtle until it reaches its natural state, the subtlest, and this is the nature of the Divine. Therefore, the objects which seem so solid in Creation, including the human body, are in reality condenses subtle spiritual matter. Thus, the process of Serpent Power Yoga involves the dissolution of grossness and the discovery of the subtle nature of the inner Self.

In reality everything is subtle and not solid. Even modern science accepts this now. The problem is that the human mind and senses have come to hold the objects which the senses perceive as solid and gross. However, through the process of the Serpent Power Yoga, this misunderstanding can be corrected. When this occurs the discovery of the transcendental reality, that all is the subtle Self (God), it is the discovery of ones own sublet, immortal and infinite nature as well.

The Three Bodies

Above: The diagram of a household light bulb. It works by creating a "resistance" to the flow of electricity, which is generated

by the power station. The power station sends energy in a circuit. One line is positively charged and the other is negatively charged. This flow of electricity in the lines is called the current. Therefore, a particular balance of resistance must be maintained in order to effect the proper functioning of the appliance.

Ancient Mystical Philosophy maintains that there are many parts or aspects of human existence. Most people feel that their psycho-physical constitution is all that their is. However, those who practice yoga and other forms of mystical spirituality quickly discover that the psycho-physical aspect is only the tip of the iceberg as it were. In reality you are much more than what you know and the objective of yoga is to assist you in discovering that exalted and transcendental reality. Essentially there are three basic bodies. These are the physical, astral and causal. They correspond to the three planes of existence (Physical, Astral and Causal Planes) and they also have connections to other dimensions and subplanes. For our practice it is necessary to understand that they are all intertwined as it were by the thread of thought. Also, each body is subtler than the previous one. The Astral Body is more subtle than the Physical and the Causal Body is more subtle than the Astral and Physical Bodies. The Self transcends all bodies and is the subtlest. Thus, it permeates all existence.

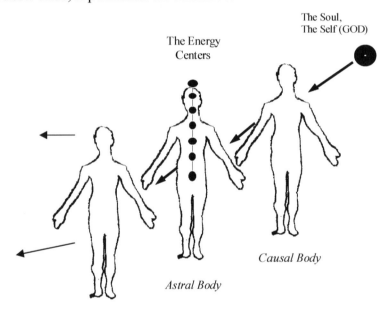

The Soul,
The Self (GOD)

The Energy
Centers

Causal Body

Astral Body

Physical Body

Essentially there are three basic bodies. These are the physical, astral and causal. They correspond to the three planes of existence (Physical, Astral and Causal Planes) and they also have connections to other dimensions and subplanes.

The psycho-spiritual energy centers of the Serpent Power are located in the astral Body.

The Physical body consists of the waking consciousness, physical constitution, nervous system and sense organs. The Astral Body consists of the subconscious mind, dream consciousness and intellect, subtle senses and the subtle astral channels. The Causal Body consists of deep mental impressions gathered over many lifetimes. These impressions "cause" the desires, thoughts, feelings and circumstances of the Astral and Physical realities. They determine the fate of an individual.

The energy centers are located in the Astral body (see above) though they have corresponding centers or glands in the Physical body as well. The spiritual work that is performed at the level of the Causal and Astral bodies will have its effect in the Physical Body and waking consciousness. The process of Serpent Power Yoga has the effect of allowing consciousness to be propelled, as it were, into the Astral and Causal planes and finally to transcend these and to discover the Higher Self instead of it being directed downward towards the physical body and the physical world. When the higher aspects of one's own existence are discovered, the ignorance as to one's true identity and negativity caused by that ignorance (anger, hatred, greed, etc.) which are lodged in the Causal Body become dissolved or cleansed as it were. This cleansing process gives rise to "purity of heart." Purity of heart allows the positive qualities of the soul to emerge as the sun emerges after a storm passes. This new vision is known as Enlightenment, resurrection, liberation, the Kingdom of Heaven, etc.

The human body is much like an appliance in that it receives spiritual energy from the soul through the mind and transforms it into physical energy to perform physical work. Feelings of peace, contentment, harmony, equanimity, dispassion and understanding allow the proper flow of spiritual energy.

Feelings of anger, hate, fear and passionate desire cause blockages in the flow of spiritual energy through the parts of the spirit, mind and body, thereby causing illness. Also, depletion of energy occurs when the energy dissipates or flows out (open circuit) of the body due to mental attention on worldly objects (attachment), desire, worry, passion, sexual ejaculation, etc. These activities hasten the death of the individual because the energy is "used up" sooner. Therefore, one aim of concentration and meditation is to prevent the foolish loss of energy (closed circuit).

Reincarnation occurs when the soul decides to "switch off" its identification with a particular bulb (death), and then to send its light (Life Force) power to another bulb (body).

Far left (above): Ordinary flow of energy through the body is outward through the mental attention on the senses and mental desires (A) and sexual ejaculation (B). This mode of energy flow serves the purposes of gratification of the senses and procreation of the species, and therefore does not lead to higher spiritual attainments.

The Body-Mind-Soul Relationship

Figure 31: The Body-Mind-Soul-Spirit Connection

It is very important to understand that the soul is not a development of the body or mind and that the soul is not dependent upon the body for its existence. In fact, the body and the mind are developments of the soul, which it creates through the karmic desires of the unconscious and sustains through the Life Force. So the Spirit which is transcendental and unlimited, becomes conditioned, confined as it were, as a soul or individual focus of consciousness. This soul creates the Astral Body, and the Astral Body creates the Physical Body. A human being gains experiences through the ego (false aspect of the personality that develops as a result of the soul's identification with the mind and body as being who it is, rather than the transcendental Spirit), and its interactions with the world. When the teachings and disciplines of yogic mysticism are practiced, a human being is able to discover that there is more than the physical body and mind, that there is a larger world beyond the physical and mental planes. The more expansive a human being becomes in consciousness, the closer they are moving to the discovery of the Higher Self, the unlimited Spirit, God, and this is the glorious essential reality of every human being. In the diagram above, notice that there is no circle encompassing the Spirit. It encompasses all. Therefore, the Spirit (Universal or

Cosmic Soul) is not in the body. Rather, the body is within the mind, the min within the individual soul, and the individual soul is within the Spirit (Soul). It should be noted here that the mind (conscious, subconscious and unconscious) and the brain are not synonymous. The mind is in the Astral Body. Mental energy flows into the physical body through the nervous system (brain and spinal column) where it operates through the gross senses of the Physical Body. The Spirit is all-pervasive and transcendental, beyond time and space. The Soul, Mind and Body all exist within the realm of time and space and are therefore, limited and finite. Discovering this supreme teaching in life is referred to as Spiritual Enlightenment. It is the greatest human achievement.

Working With The Psycho-spiritual Energy Centers

Begin your practice by concentrating on each energy center for as long as you like until you are comfortable that you are in control of the elements and psycho-spiritual issues of that center. Pay special attention to the proper breathing instructions as you practice the meditations. Only then will you be able to productively move on to the next center. We will use both Ancient Egyptian and Indian symbols in this section as complementary teachings in order to gain a deeper insight into the nature of the energy centers. In Ancient Egyptian Mystical iconography the energy centers are depicted as either rings in a chain or as circular discs on the balance scales of goddess Maat. In Indian iconography they are depicted as circular discs, spinning discs or as lotuses. The word *chakra* in Indian mysticism signifies "discus." The Ancient Egyptian and Indian symbols for each center will be included preceding the definition of each center. When you feel comfortable with the process of visualization you may begin to practice the Integral Serpent Power Meditation presented at the end of this volume.

ᵖ **vement of the Serpent Power According to the Ancient Egyptian**
e

movement of the Serpent Power is described in a special scripture from
Ancinet Egypt. The hieroglyphic text is presented below with an original
translation by Muata Ashby.

ORIGINAL SERPENT POWER TEXT RANSLATION

Wadjit comes to you in the form of the Serpent Goddess to anoint
you on your head. She is the mistress

of
fire.

She is also the double goddess Wadjit and Nekhebit.
The rise up to your head through the left side and through

the west right side also and shine there on the top of your head.
Not with words (in silence, stillness) they rise to the top of your
head encompassing all time, as they do for their

father Ra. They speak to you from within and illumine those
becoming venerable Blessed Spirits.

It is they who give souls perfection, as they work their way, up to
the brow, to their dwelling place on the brow, which is their
throne.

They firmly establish themselves on your brow as they do on Ra's
brow. Not

leaving, taking away the enlightenment, they stay there for you
forever.

The preceding scripture from the Ancient Egyptian embalming ceremonies is echoed in the *Book of Coming Forth By Day*. The state of enlightenment is further described in Chapters 83 and 85 where the initiate realizes that the seven Uraeus deities or bodies (immortal parts of the spirit) have been reconstituted:

> ***"The seven Uraeuses are my body... my image is now eternal."***

These seven Uraeuses, *Iarut,* are also described as the *"seven souls of Ra"* and *"the seven arms of the balance (Maat)"* (referring to the Energy Centers). Thus, we are to understand that the seven primordial powers (Uraeuses) are our true essence. Further, the same seven are GOD. Thus, GOD'S soul and our souls are identical. It is this same soul which will judge us in the balance. Therefore, we came into existence of our own free will, and we are the supreme masters (judges) of our own destiny. We may put together our divine form by attaining a purified heart or live in ignorance, ruled by passion and mortality. In Chapter 30, the initiate affirms that his / her vertebrae, back, and neck bones are firm.

Note: Arat originates as a power of the Sun God, Ra. She is often described as being the embodiment of Ra himself. As such she is the fire spitting serpent who "scorches evil." Thus, she represents the light of reason and the dynamic force of nature. In Hindu mysticism *Arati* means "light."

In the *Book of the Dead* (Chap. xvii. 30), the initiate identifies with Amsu-Min and says:

> *"I am the god Amsu (or, Min) in his coming forth; may his two plumes be set upon my head for me."* In answer to the question, *"Who then is this?"* the text goes on to say, *"Amsu is Heru, **the avenger of his father**, and his coming, forth is his birth. The plumes upon his head are Aset and Nephthys when they go forth to set themselves there, even as his protectors, and they provide that which his head lacketh, or (as others say), they are **the two exceedingly great uraei** which are upon the head of their father Tem, or (as others say), his two eyes are the two plumes which are upon his head."*

The passage above provides an exact idea about the true nature of Aset and Nephthys. Nephthys is associated with the life which comes forth from her death in Isis. They are complementary goddess principles which operate to manifest life-death-life or the cycle of birth-death-rebirth known as reincarnation. Another important teaching presented here is that Aset and Nephthys are identified as the "the two exceedingly great uraei." They are the two forces of the Serpent Power. The Serpent Power refers to the Life Force energy which manifests in the physical human body in the form of two opposites. In Ancient Egyptian mythology and yoga these two opposites are known as "Uadjit (Uatchit, Udjat, Uatchet) and Nekhebet" or "Aset and Nephthys" or "The Two Ladies." Uadjit is the solar serpent while Nekhebet symbolizes the lunar serpent. In India they are known as "Ida and Pingala." The opposites refer to the solar pole and the lunar pole or the active and passive nature of the energies. In reality the energy is the same. It originates from the same source but it manifests as opposite due to the polarization it assumes. Thus, it may be seen as male and female. The Serpent Power energy resides at the base of the spine and when aroused through spiritual evolution (practice of yoga) it courses through the energy centers of the subtle body, finally reaching the crown of the head and re-unites into its original oneness; the poles dissolve, leaving oneness of consciousness or enlightenment.

In the *Book of Coming Forth by Day,* Uatchet is the destroyer of the evil forces which try to defeat the initiate. In the Asarian resurrection story she assists Aset when she is fleeing from Set. Arat was also known as "Apuat" or "Opener of Lands." The Serpents Uatchet and Nekhebet are equal to the *Ida and Pingala* respectively of Indian Kundalini Yoga. The central staff of Djehuti (caduceus) represents the Sushumna, the central astral channel. Ida is associated with lunar energy and it is cooling, coalescing, passive. Uatchet (Pingala) is associated with solar energy and it is dynamic and heating. They are both related to the left (lunar) and right (solar) nostrils. If you take notice of your breathing habits you will see that you are usually breathing out of either the left or the right nostril and rarely out of them both at the same time. This is because at particular times one form of Life Force energy may be dominant. The interaction of these two forces (solar and lunar) cause movements in the Life Force energy that is available to each living being and support their practical existence in the physical realm. This interaction is what causes the appearance of matter in the various forms of nature. However, all forms are in reality one essential essence. This is the secret of the Serpent Power. If the opposing forces were to be harmonized there would be no separation or differences between the objects of nature. In other worlds the underlying unity would emerge. This is the task of Serpent Power Yoga, to discover the underlying unity behind the multiplicity of Creation.

Thought is also intimately related to the movements in the Life Force energy, therefore, in an unenlightened personality, if there is much movement (agitation) in the mind, there will be much mental distraction and unrest. This will in turn agitate the Life Force Energy and obstruct its flow, resulting in inability to see the subtle realities beyond physical existence and also this process will engender both mental and physical tension, anxiety and disease. The object of Serpent Power Yoga is to harmonize the two opposites. When this is accomplished, there is free flow of the Serpent Power Life Force energy which may then be directed towards the *brow* and *the crown of the head* where the serpents rise up and there anoint the practitioner bestowing enlightenment, contentment, peace and bliss. This process is known as, Christhood (Christ means *anointed one*) in Christianity and the anointing of *Amrita,* the mystic nectar, in Indian Kundalini Yoga and by other names in other systems.

The two opposing forces in the Serpent Power Life Force energy of a human being are balanced by practicing the various disciplines of yoga in an integral fashion. Increasing wisdom, reflection, practice of virtues, purification of the diet, exercise and specific serpent power breathing exercises all serve to balance and harmonize the Life Force energy, enabling it to dissolve the

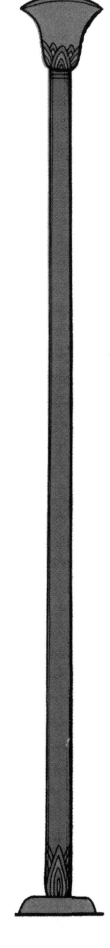

opposites and then they rise through the central subtle channel up the spine and into the head where they eventually become established, providing a continuous shower of bliss to the practitioner.

The Ancient Egyptian Temple Architecture and the Serpent Power

.

The Ancient Egyptian temple consisted of three main sections. The teaching of the Serpent Power was integral to the architecture of the facility as it was very much related to the process of spiritual evolution. The three main sections were preceded by the entranceway pylons (A). Several rooms that were used for various purposes were attached to the main sections. These sections were (B) the Court, (C) the Hypostyle Hall and (D) the Chapel (Holy of Holies). This format follows the system of the Trinity, which among other things, implies the teachings related to the three levels of religion, the three steps of spiritual study prescribed by the ancient Temple of Aset and the three Ancient Egyptian initiatic education levels of aspirants.

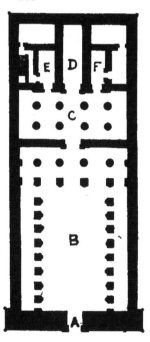

Above: a diagram of the Temple of Amun-Ra at Karnak, Egypt, showing the Pylons (A), the Court (B), the Hypostyle Hall (C), the Chapel of Amun (Holy of Holies - D), the Chapel of Mut (E), the Chapel of Chons (F).

The typical Ancient Egyptian temple incorporated the Serpent Power mysticism within its architecture. The temple sections relate to the parts of the human anatomy as follows and the serpentine movement is a precursor for the Hermetic Caduceus (Late Period Kamitan Philosophy).

Figure 32: Below: a diagram of the Temple of Amun-Ra at Karnak, Egypt, showing the Pylons (A), the Court (B), the Hypostyle Hall (C), the Chapel of Amun (Holy of Holies - D), the Chapel of Mut (E), the Chapel of Chons (F).

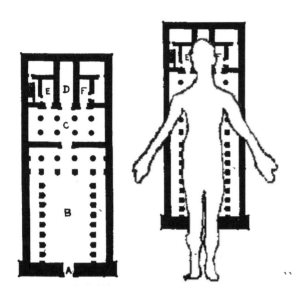

An artistic rendition of the human body and the Ancient Egyptian Temple. Notice that the lower part of the body, which supports the activities of the higher, is at the level of the outer court. Notice that the vital part of the body, which includes the heart and lungs, is at the level of the middle court. Notice that the head, and higher centers of spirituality are located at the level of the inner sanctuary (Holy of Holies) and at either side are located the chambers of Uatchet and Nekhebet, just as the Ancient Egyptian Scripture describes.

Just as it is described in the Ancient Egyptian Serpent Power scripture, (above) the two serpents meet each other at the area of the temple which correlates to the head of the individual human being. These sections of the temple are known as the "great house" (left side) and the "house of fire" (right side).

Below: Ancient Egyptian artistic representation of the yogi seated in the lotus posture displaying the three main channels of the *Arat Shekhem* (Serpent Power) and the 7 *Sefech Ba Ra* (Life Force energy centers) 5th dynasty (4th millennium B.C.E.)

Table 2: The Life Force:

Ancient Egypt	India	China
Sekhem	Prana (Kundalini)	Chi

The energy centers (chakras) wherein the Life Force energy is transformed from subtle to gross energy for use by the body are seven in number and are depicted as follows.

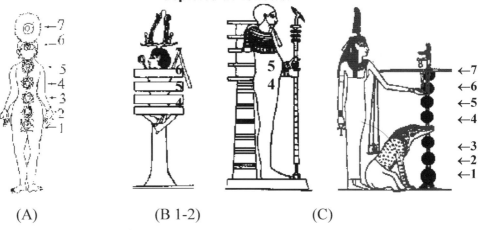

(A)   (B 1-2)   (C)

Figure 33: Left (A), the East Indian rendition of the Life Force energy centers (chakras) in the subtle spine of the individual.

Figure 34: Center (B 1-2), Ptah-Asar-Ancient Egyptian rendition of the Life Force energy centers in the subtle spine of the individual. The god Asar displays the four upper centers as centers of higher consciousness.

Figure 35: The figure at right (C) shows the scale of Maat displaying the seven spheres or energy centers called the "seven souls of Ra" and "the seven arms of the balance (Maat)."

Figure (C), above, includes the Ammit demon, (composite beast combining one third hippopotamus, one third lion and one third crocodile), symbolic devourer of unrighteous souls, biting between the 3rd & 4th sphere (energy center-chakra). This means that those who have not attained a consciousness level higher than the 3rd center will continue to suffer and reincarnate. The spheres represent levels of spiritual consciousness from the most ignorant (1) to the most enlightened (7). The lower three spheres are related to worldly consciousness and the upper four are related to spiritual consciousness and enlightenment, therefore, the lower must be sublimated into the higher levels. This is the project of spiritual evolution. Those who have attained higher (3rd through the 7th) will move on and attain enlightenment. This Kamitan system of energy spheres and the caduceus with its central shaft symbolizing the subtle spine, and the two intertwining serpents, symbolizing the dual energies into which the central shaft differentiates, concurs in every detail with the later developments in East Indian Mysticism encompassed by the discipline known as Kundalini Yoga with its system of Chakras and the three main energy channels, Sushumna (central) and Ida and Pingala (intertwining conduits).

Figure 36: Left-An East Indian depiction of the Chakras with the Sushumna (central) and Ida and Pingala (intertwining conduits).

Figure 37: Center- the Hermetic[39] Caduceus with the central Shaft (Asar), and the intertwining serpents (Uadjit and Nekhebit, also known as Aset and Nebethet); Ancient caduceus motif: Asar with the serpent goddesses.

Figure 38: Right- The Kamitan Energy Consciousness Centers (depicted as Spheres-Chakras or serpentine chains)

---

[39] Late Ancient Egyptian motif.

More Examples of the Kamitan Caduceus:

The Kamitan Caduceus is not just a symbol of Djehuiti (Hermes) but rather, it is one of the fundamental symbols denoting the concept of the Serpent Power which can be found throughout Kamitan Religion.

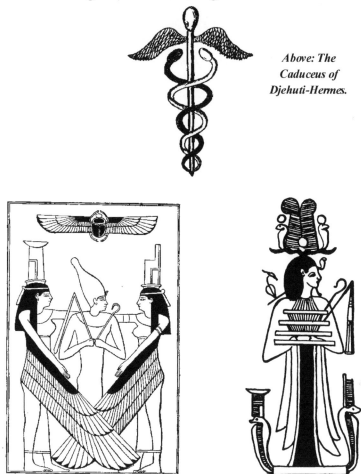

Above: The Caduceus of Djehuti-Hermes.

Figure 39: Above: The Iconography of the Caduceus is present in the most ancient images of the Divine Trinity of Asar (Osiris), Aset (Isis) and Nebthet (Nephthys.

The goddesses are depicted as women or as serpents and Asar's back (Pillar of Asar) is actually the central shaft of the caduceus that the two (Serpent) goddesses intertwine and raise up, symbolizing the raising of cosmic consciousness.

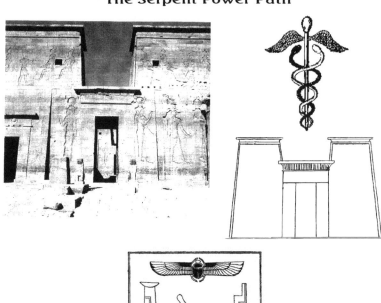

Above: Temple of Aset (Isis), Egypt-Africa, facade entrance showing two Pylons and the single opening. In an inscription at Edfu the pylons are referred to as Aset and Nephthys, the two goddesses of Asar who raise him up to attain resurrection and immortality (picture below, left). The single opening symbolizes non-duality and singularity of consciousness. Thus, on entering into the Temple, there is a symbolic ritual-meditation leading toward a spiritual movement out of the world (duality - ASET AND NEPHTHYS) and into the shrine wherein the underlying oneness of the universe is to be explored and discovered. Thus, the temple is a place wherein the duality and multiplicity of human existence can be transcended. Therefore, the architecture of the temple, in and of itself, is a meditation on spiritual enlightenment and nonduality.

The Caduceus of Goddess Sekhmit- Goddess of the Sekhem Life Force

The goddess Sekhmit transfers the leonine (Sekhem) energy through air and breath. Therefore, the process of breathing can be uses to harness the life force energy and cultivate the serpent power.

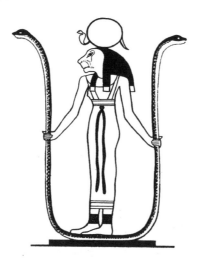

Understanding the Principles of the Energy Centers

(General Outline of the Spheres)

ARAT SHEKHEM or Serpent Power system.

The system of Psychology incorporates Psychological and cosmic energy-consciousness states within the human being and in creation.

Each center represents a psycho-spiritual state of mind wherein the divine essence creates or manifests itself from the transcendent realm which is without name, form, time or space at level 7, to the realm of time, space, and material forms from centers 1-6. Each of these represents specific emotional and energy states of mind which interact with eachother throughout the spiritual evolution of the individual regardless of sex, religion or cultural beliefs. These changes occur over several life times leading to a reunion of the individual soul with its transcendental self.

7 — Fearlessness-Absolute freedom
No element - all forms transcended

6 — Spiritual - impersonal love, divine vision
Element: mind-intellect-ego

5 — Self control
Element: Ether

1

4 — Human love - personal
Element: Air

3 — Will, power over things/people, desire emotions. Element: Fire

2 — Sexual desire, passion - sexual frustration
Element: Water

1 — Fear, Fight or flight, survival, food worry, reactionary Element: Earth

In order to understand the Serpent Power and how it affects human consciousness we will trace its movement through the psycho-spiritual energy centers of the subtle body in the next several pages.

"Wa-Ba-Ra"
soul of Ra #1

Psycho-spiritual Energy Center #1

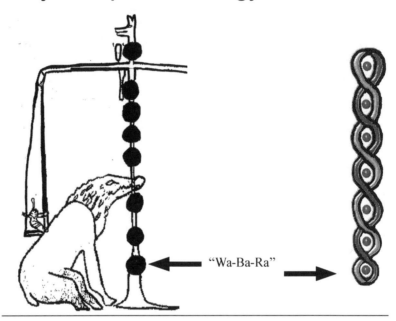

"Wa-Ba-Ra"

The First Psycho-spiritual Energy Center is Located: in the root-base energy center which is found at the base of the spine.

The symbols of this center consists of: A square (earth element) inside of which is the *lingam-yoni* or male and female organs, symbolizing that the pairs of opposites are contained in the field of matter, time and space.

The element of this center is: Earth. The attributes of this element are: collecting, greed, stability, saving.

The Barrier of this sphere is Iron. This is the boundary that must be pierced in order to attain this level of consciousness.

The psychological principle here is: *Behaviorism.* Here the consciousness of the individual is reactive rather than active. The type of character who lives at this level has been described as a "creep." The energy here is concerned with survival issues and in the unbalanced state, manifests as fear, selfishness, possessiveness, concern with finding food, etc.

<u>Desires include:</u> Physical comforts, physical security, shelter, biological needs for survival.

<u>The animal symbol of this center is:</u> The elephant. The elephant is a slow, massive creature which possesses immense strength. Such is the energy at this level which acts to slow down the action of spiritual energy. It becomes grounded in the earth element. If the subject is given to flights of fancy or unfounded fears (paranoia), this could be a signal that there is a disturbance at this center.

<u>The way to awaken the energy at this center is:</u> Concentrate on it while mentally or vocally chanting the sound of this center. The sound is *"Am"* with the "a" pronounced as the "o" in the word *"what."*

<u>The beginners meditation for this center is:</u> After chanting the sound of the center for several minutes: "Om," "Om," "Om," "Om," etc., sit quietly observing the proper breathing techniques as you relax the mind and body. Gently search for those feelings within one's actions, thoughts, feelings in the past or present where fear, excessive concern over providing for one's needs, anger, hate, greed, etc., arose. Then one must clear these thoughts which block the flow of energy by asserting the facts of wisdom, that you are essentially one with the Transcendental Deity (God) and that just as all creatures in nature are perfectly provided for, our needs will also be provided for. We are an inseparable part of nature and if we perform our daily duties in harmony with Maat, nature will provide for all of our needs. Therefore, we need not worry, cheat, scheme, or resent others. We know that the insult or wrong that has been done to us was due to the ignorance of the fact that we are all one. If there is ignorance in the mind then there is a karmic basis to experience all that that ignorance will lead to (pain, disappointment, unrest, discontent, etc.). If there is wisdom, strength, peace and contentment in the mind, then there is a positive karmic basis which will lead to greater and greater experience of the Divine and this divine experience is transcendent of all worldly pleasures and positive developments. The positive karmic basis can be promoted through righteous action and spiritual practice. So we can forgive them and not hold unto any animosity since we know that they will have to answer to nature for any wrongs they have done since nobody can escape their karmic depts. Forgiving oneself and others is the key to mental peace and the flow of emotional energies. As the conflicts and discordant feelings at this level are resolving themselves, visualize them as the earth element dissolving into the next energy center which is water.

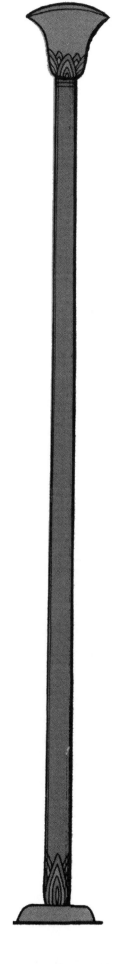

"Sn-wy-Ba-Ra"
soul of Ra #2

2- THE SECOND ENERGY-CONSCIOUSNESS CENTER

Location: It is in the area of the organs of procreation.

The Indian symbols of this center consists of: the moon, referring to the tides of life, the cycles of the reproductive system, sexual desire and of activity and rest which are inherent in all of nature.

The element of this center is: Water. The attributes of this element are: coolness, attachment, flowing outward.

The Barrier of this sphere is Copper. This is the boundary that must be pierced in order to attain this level of consciousness.

The predominant psychic activity here is: Reproduction and Sexuality. Propensity to disregard other worldly activities in order to pursue sexual satisfaction. Craving for the fulfillment which comes from temporary sexual fulfillment and sensual pleasures. This center would translate to the Freudian idea as the main motivator of the human mind. The primary need of this state is creativity. Every human being needs to create. This is the very essence of existence and it is why every atom in the universe is constantly moving and changing into something else. Thus, if there is a vision of higher creativity a human being can produce wondrous works of literature and other art forms or they can create great institutions for humanity. If there is only a limited understanding of creativity nature will force a human being to become entangled in domestic situations wherein they will feel the need to create offspring or somehow they will create negative situations for themselves in other ways. The wisdom teachings point the way towards higher creativity. The mass culture of television and materialism emphasizes sensual pleasures and wealth. The struggle to acquire these leads a human being to multitudinous situations of adversity and stress of human existence, never to find true happiness and inner peace. *For more on the spiritual path of Sex Sublimation [40]

---

[40] see the book *Egyptian Tantra Yoga: The Art of Sex Sublimation and Universal Consciousness* by Dr. **Muata Ashby**

Desires include: procreation, infatuation, fantasies, family relationships and sensuality.

The possible psychic dysfunctions are: Frustration and disillusionment at the discovery that sexual feelings cannot always be pursued, and also that when pursued, they are never totally quenched. If these feelings are properly coped with the individual will accept the realities of sexual life and pursue other activities an a balanced manner along with the search for sexual fulfillment. This process is known as sublimation. If the individual is stuck here, then there will be constant preoccupation with sexual matters along with feelings of guilt due to repudiation from society.

The Indian animal symbol of this center is: a *Makara* creature, the mythical crocodile type animal representing the Ganges river and all of its energy, the power of sexual energy.

The way to awaken the energy at this center is: Concentrate on it while mentally or vocally chanting the sound of this center. The sound is *"Om"* with the "a" pronounced as the a in the word *"what."*

Psycho-spiritual Energy Center #2

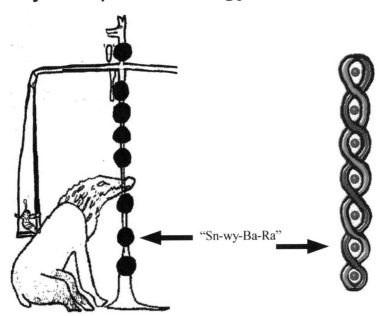

"Sn-wy-Ba-Ra"

"Souls, Heru, son, are of the self-same nature, since they came from the same place where the Creator modeled them; nor male nor female are they. Sex is a thing of bodies not of Souls."

Ancient Egyptian Proverb from *The teachings of Aset to Heru*

Sexual feelings and sexual arousal come about through the ignorance of the higher reality. The soul has no sex but when it is identified with matter, time and space (physical nature) it succumbs to feelings of individuality and ego-identification. These feelings delude the soul into believing that it is a physical, mortal being instead of a subtle, immortal and transcendental being. In reality, the sexual energy is trying to push the mind towards higher experiences of transcendental consciousness. However, due to ignorance of the higher purpose and the lack of proper guidance, human beings fall prey to the philosophy of modern culture which pushes people to become more sexual, more greedy, etc. and these movements lead a human being away from inner discovery. When people live in ignorance they settle for the ideals of mass culture and they do not realize that they have greater potential that they can possibly understand. In this state they willingly become involved in sexual relationships mistaking these for love and they think they are doing well if they can acquire possessions like their friends. The prospect of life centers around gaining material wealth and engaging in situations which will bring sensual pleasures. However, when the ramifications of these in the form of pain and sorrow due to misunderstandings and disappointments from loved ones or other relations comes they feel the pain of life and again fall prey to the delusion of mass culture, "that life." The Sages and Saints from time immemorial have admonished those who have been wise enough to listen that sensual pleasures are like chains that bind a person to the limited existence as a human being. However, they also show, by their own experience, that when sublimated it can be the most powerful means to spiritual realization. This is why they enjoined practices of celibacy and sex sublimation to assist the process of spiritual evolution.

> And behold, these things shall be performed by one who is clean, and is ceremonially pure, a man who hath eaten neither meat nor fish, and who hath not had intercourse with women (applies to female initiates not having intercourse with men as well).

Chapter 137A of the
Book of Coming Forth By Day

Sexual energy can be used as a vehicle which can carry the mind to transcendental levels of consciousness like a rocket carries astronauts into outer space. Otherwise the mind remains on the lower levels, interested in hanging onto the meager and fleeting pleasures and the even more frequent adversities of ordinary life. You will use the energy as your vehicle to transport yourself back to the original primordial state of consciousness which is vast and all-encompassing.

<u>The beginners meditation for this center is:</u> After chanting the sound of the center for several minutes: "Om," "Om," "Om," "Om," etc. Sit quietly observing the proper breathing techniques and then begin to relax the mind and body. Gently search for those feelings within one's actions, thoughts, feelings in the past or present where sexual feelings emerge. Do not be concerned if they seem to be wrong feelings, the important idea here is to allow them to surface so that they may be understood. Try not to allow them to make you feel erotic. Try to be detached, looking at them as if at a set of clothes you have worn or are contemplating to wear. Examine these feelings and try to understand why you have them. Realize that you have these feelings because you are in search of fulfillment, but there has never been complete fulfillment in the world of objects or people of the world. Now see if there is a place within you where you can take those feelings. A quiet place which is free from judgment, a place where there is unconditional acceptance. Offer these feelings to that place as an offering on an altar. Give them to your Higher Self while asking for communion. Now in complete silence feel the warmth which comes over your entire being, the gentle flow of peace and contentment. As the conflicts and discordant feelings at this level are resolving themselves, visualize them as the earth element dissolving into the next energy center which is fire.

Second visualization: Become conscious of your sexual energies and desires at this center. See them as a flowing river. Visualize them as the Nile river, flowing on. Become one with this energy, do not fight it. Flow on with the river as it travels, like all rivers do, toward the ocean. All rivers flow to the ocean and merge with it. See yourself as water, traveling up the river of your spine toward the endless ocean of primordial energy which is at the crown of your head. This primordial ocean is the same primordial ocean of creation. It is the same energy that surges when there is sexual arousal.

"Chmt-Ba-Ra"
soul of Ra #3

3- THE THIRD ENERGY-CONSCIOUSNESS CENTER

Location: Its location is in the solar plexus.

The symbols of this center consists of: The downward pointing triangle, the Yoni or downward pointing triangle, the womb of creation symbolizing energy that is moving downward towards the earth and towards earthly behavior patterns, emotions and animal passions and desires.

The element of this center is: Fire. The attributes of this element are: hot-headed, anger, achievement, ambition.

The Barrier of this sphere is Wood. This is the boundary that must be pierced in order to attain this level of consciousness.

The predominant psychic activity here is: The vital fire which sustains the physical body is located here. This energy center gives one a sense of power and will. Also, this is the center of emotion energy.

Desires include: longevity, fame, name, power, wealth, authority, immortality as an individual personality.

The possible psychic dysfunctions are: Inability to control emotions. Desire to control environment in an attempt to provide for one's own security. Lack of consideration of others while attempting to fulfill goals and desires. Imbalance or obstruction in this energy center manifests as feelings of inadequacy and powerlessness; one feels incapable of expressing their willpower.

The animal symbol of this center is: Ram.

The way to awaken the energy at this center is: Concentrate on it while mentally or vocally chanting the sound of this center. The sound is *"Om"* with the "o" pronounced as the a in the word *"what."*

The beginners meditation for this center: Meditation on this spot sends SEKHEM or vital energy (Prana, Chi) to this center which promotes health by increased digestion and equal distribution of energy throughout the body; the effect is physical and emotional balance. This is a prerequisite for higher spiritual advancement.

After chanting the sound of the center for several minutes: "Om," "Om," "Om," "Om," etc., sit quietly observing the proper breathing techniques and then begin to relax the mind and body. Gently search for those feelings within one's actions, thoughts, feelings in the past or present where one has tried to assert oneself over others. See yourself as equal to others and equal to nature. Serving others as you would serve yourself, feeling peaceful in the wisdom of yoga, that all needs are taken care of in a most mysterious but unfailing way. Visualize these conflicts and issues resolving and being burned up by the fire that they themselves produced. Visualize them becoming thinner and thinner until they become diffused in the next element, air.

In Egyptian Symbolism the Ammit monster who is the "devourer of souls" bites the string of energy centers which symbolizes the subtle spine of the initiate between the third and fourth Energy Center. In doing this Ammit is showing the separation of those who are worldly minded, and over whom he has power, that is those who have not progressed beyond the first three centers, and those who have raised their consciousness beyond the first three centers. When the aspirant goes beyond these first three centers he or she begins to experience expansion beyond the physical being and beyond the ego self. So the first three centers are under the domain of Set, the deity of worldliness, impulsive behavior and basic instincts and those above are presided over by Heru, the deity of divine realization or the Higher Self.

Psycho-spiritual Energy Center #3

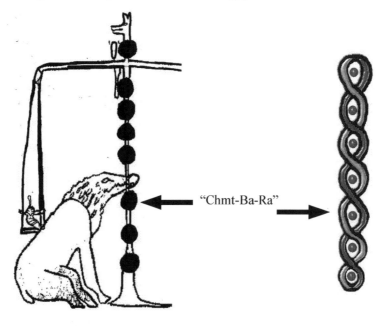

"Chmt-Ba-Ra"

"Fdw-Ba-Ra"
soul of Ra #4

4- THE FOURTH ENERGY-CONSCIOUSNESS CENTER

Location: Its location is at the heart. This center opens up the possibility of the *"virgin birth"* which signifies the birth of spiritual consciousness, as opposed to the lower animal consciousness. At this level, your spiritual essence becomes revealed in the caring (expressing love) for others.

The Kheper or Anahata chakra is related to a gland in the body known as the thymus. Being very large in babies, the thymus shrinks as we mature. The thymus is intricately related to the immune system, producing antibodies to ward off infections.

The symbols of this center consists of: The six pointed star composed of the upward and downward triangles. This is the center where the upward flowing energy of spiritual realization and the downward flowing energy of creation can be balanced according to the will of the individual.

The element of this center is: Air. The attributes of this element are: restless, sex, activity, movement, task oriented.

The Barrier of this sphere is Ivory. This is the boundary that must be pierced in order to attain this level of consciousness.

The predominant psychic activity and desires include: love, sharing, selfless service, devotion, compassion.

Psychic dysfunctions are:

Inability to love selflessly, absence of sharing, selfishness, absence of devotion and compassion. Heart troubles. Love sickness.

The fourth to the seventh energy-consciousness centers (chakras) represent the evolution of spiritual life, the divine nature which is latent in every one. The lower energy centers (3 - 1) represent the lower nature, the animal nature which seeks survival and supremacy over others and gratification of the senses. The

movement of the Serpent Power from the lower to the higher consciousness centers represents the second birth, the birth of the spirit.

It is not surprising then, that when you are stressed, your immune system weakens and we become ill. If you evaluate yourself when you become ill, you will find that you usually are involved with self-defeating and self-destructive attitudes and behaviors---overworking, frustration, drugs, alcohol, bad relationships---and are not in a situation to freely give love to your very self, much less to all humanity. If you are not cautious, you become trapped in this negative way of existence which becomes a vicious cycle. How do you break this cycle? By performing self-less service to others, a very difficult task when you feel as though you are the one who needs to be served. However, you must remember the divine rule (Cosmic Law): To give is to receive.

Psycho-spiritual Energy Center #4

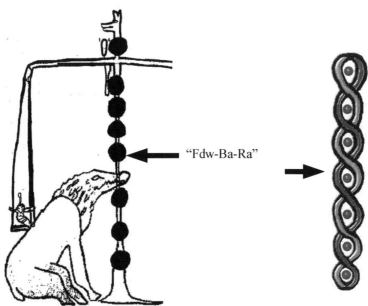

"Fdw-Ba-Ra"

The Heart Center holds special importance in Ancient Egyptian, Hindu, Christian, and Buddhist symbolism and mythology. The heart is seen as the seat of the mind and of emotions of love and compassion as well as the seat of the soul, it it viewed as a powerful center for spiritual development when it is awakened and developed. The pictures of Jesus on the cross are powerfully evocative images which evoke feelings of compassion followed by love of the divine personality (Jesus). In later iconography up to modern times pictures which depict Jesus in a heavenly locale pointing to his "flaming heart" have emerged. These are equal to the pictures of Buddha which show his heart overflowing with life force energy to the world. In Buddhism, the Diamond Heart is purity and indestructibility of one's consciousness since one has experiences one's true nature. It is the man whom can not be "cut" or disturbed by anything.

The animal symbol of this center is: Antelope or Gazelle.

<u>The way to awaken the energy at this center is:</u> to concentrate on it while mentally or vocally chanting the sound of this center. The sound is *"Om"* with the "a" pronounced as the "o" in the word *"what."*

<u>The beginners meditation for this center is:</u> After chanting the sound of the center for several minutes: "Om," "Om," "Om," "Om," etc., sit quietly observing the proper breathing techniques and then begin to relax the mind and body. Gently search for those feelings within your actions, thoughts, feelings in the past or present where you were hurt or did not act in a loving and giving way. See these as expressions of your past ignorance and know that the Divine Self has already forgiven you. Visualize situations in which you were loving and received love from others and visualize yourself being loving and giving. Visualize all conflicts as being resolved in the wisdom of oneness with all things and all dissolving into the air element.

"Dwa-Ba-Ra"
soul of Ra #5

5- THE FIFTH ENERGY-CONSCIOUSNESS CENTER

<u>Location:</u> Throat area.

<u>The symbols of this center consists of:</u> A circle within the same Yoni or downward pointing triangle representing the womb of creation from the third energy center number three and the flying elephant with seven trunks. The deity of this center is the five headed Shiva, symbolizing the five senses brought to one pointed attention.

<u>The element of this center is:</u> Ether. The attributes of this element are: ego, space, solitude.

<u>The Barrier of this sphere is Ebony.</u> This is the boundary that must be pierced in order to attain this level of consciousness.

<u>Desires include:</u> knowledge, self-control, re-definition of self.

<u>The predominant psychic activity here is:</u> Thoughts and ideas, divine speech and action. This center is involved with your ability to receive love from others--- your self-value, but most importantly, it is the center where the energies of the other centers, especially the third, are sublimated and used for self-development. This idea is known as the turning around of the Shakti (energy). No longer you we directing energy outward towards controlling others, but inwards to controlling yourself and developing your spiritual life.

<u>The possible psychic dysfunctions are:</u> Imbalance in this energy center may be expressed as the inability to communicate your needs to people around your and the world at large. Thus, it is linked to illnesses such as hoarseness and sore throats, which usually occur as a result of communication difficulties such as shouting and screaming in an attempt to be heard.

<u>The animal symbol of this center is:</u> The elephant is now a celestial symbol. It is no longer bound to the earth and is the sustainer of the other realities.

<u>The way to awaken the energy at this center is:</u> Concentrate on it while mentally or vocally chanting the sound of this center. The sound is *"Om"* with the "a" pronounced as the "o" in the word *"what."*

<u>The beginners meditation for this center is:</u> After chanting the sound of the center for several minutes: "Om," "Om," "Om," "Om," etc., sit quietly observing the proper breathing techniques and then begin to relax the mind and body. Visualize that you are an accomplished disciple who is on the path to Heruhood (Enlightenment), intent on using all available energies to realize the truth of your own existence. Visualize yourself exercising self-control and wisdom in all situations. Visualize yourself as the ether element, beyond all of the gross elements and their qualities.

Psycho-spiritual Energy Center #5

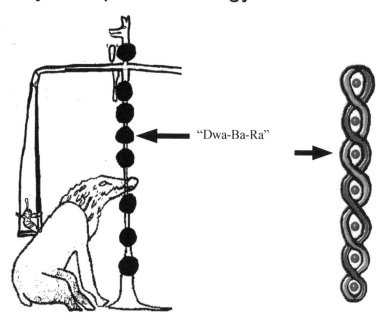

"Dwa-Ba-Ra"

"Shu-Ba-Ra"
soul of Ra #6

6- THE SIXTH ENERGY-CONSCIOUSNESS CENTER IS:

Egyptian - *Mer,* Indian - Sanskrit - *"Ajna Chakra"* meaning: "Command wheel" or commanding center. See illustration #6

Location: Middle of the head at the level of the eyebrows.

The symbols of this center consists of: The Ancient Egyptian system used a single eye here, either the eye of Asar or the eye of Heru, 👁, to symbolize the single vision which has dawned at this level of consciousness. Also, the serpent, 𓆙, at the forehead signifies the same idea of consciousness having reached this level. In Indian iconography a two petalled lotus is used. It symbolizes two entities, God and the individual who is beholding God. There is also the *linga* or phallus of Shiva, the creative male principle, within the *Yoni* or womb of the female creative power.

The element of this center is: Mind (Cosmic mind). The attributes of this element are: intellectuality and intuitive reasoning.

The Barrier of this sphere is Silver. This is the boundary that must be pierced in order to attain this level of consciousness.

Desires include: enlightenment, self-realization, Christhood, Heruhood, Buddha consciousness, the Tao, etc.

The predominant psychic activity here is: It is the third eye, the level of intuitive wisdom that does not require "thinking or the mind processes." This is the Eye of Heru, the light of intuitive vision. It is the level of "knowing" something instead of "thinking" we know something. Herein lies the ability to perceive the spirit as well as matter, and to live in both equally.

The possible psychic dysfunctions are: disintegrated psychic experiences leading to psychotic behavior or aberrant social behaviors.

<u>The animal symbol of this center:</u> No animal symbol. No longer do you see a multiplicity of objects in the world. Now you see with the "inner eye" that there is one underlying essence to all things.

There are many references to this energy center in the Ancient Egyptian Pyramid Texts wherein the initiate is continually reminded of his/her true self and is directed to accept the "Eye" of intuitional vision. This same teaching was given over a period of over 5,000 years through the early Christian period.

In the *Ancient Egyptian Book of Coming Forth By Day* the "Eye" represents the spiritual vision which every human being has the capacity to attain. This vision is blocked by the *excrement* which Set throws into it (C. 17:66), as well as the *hair* (ignorance) which obstructs the spiritual vision faculty of the Eye which is on the *forehead* or *brow* (C. 17:72, 144). The process of clearing up the *Eye* is accomplished overcoming Set in battle (acting with righteousness and resisting temptations and egoism and through intuitional realization of the wisdom teachings of Djehuti.

Psycho-spiritual Energy Center #6

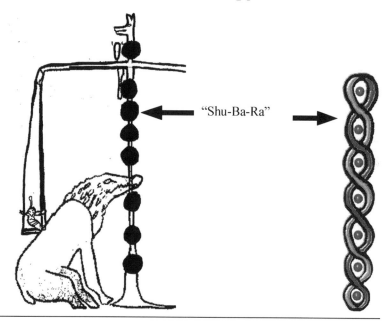

"Shu-Ba-Ra"

<u>The way to awaken the energy at this center:</u> Concentrate on it while mentally or vocally chanting the sound of this center. The sound is *"Om," "Aum,"* Amun.

<u>The meditation for this center:</u> After chanting the sound of this center for several minutes: "Om," "Om," "Om," "Om," etc., sit quietly, observing the proper breathing techniques, and then begin to relax the mind and body. This center commands all of the other lower centers. Visualize yourself as a mental being only. You are now beyond even the ether element. See how all things, the earth, the planets, stars, people, your body, are all manifestations of the transcendental reality.

In the beginning of your practice you may not notice significant changes in the first few days. However, you must proceed with perseverance and faith. As you cleanse your mind and body with these exercises and the other disciplines presented here, you will begin to feel the emergence of a new feeling of hope, inner beauty and strength of will. Later you may have different types of psychic experiences, however, you must not waver on your journey. See yourself as a shepherd who is guiding the Serpent Fire on the path of the central conduit from the base of the spine to the sixth energy center at the forehead using the meditation and illustrations presented here. Visualize the energy flowing up and down each center. See it in your mind's eye, moving down to the base center with each inhalation, hold for a few moments and then see it moving up through your subtle spine. Bring it up to center #6 and continue holding for as long as is comfortable. Now with your exhalation see it returning back to the base of the spine at #1.*

*The *Kundalini-Uraeus* audio cassette meditation tape #1 will be beneficial when used along with this Chapter.

The main Ancient Egyptian symbols of the sixth energy center are the Udjat Eye (A), also referred to as the "third eye" of spiritual vision, the cat goddess Bast, (B), the Arat Serpent, (C), who are all aspects of the goddess Hathor-Aset (D).

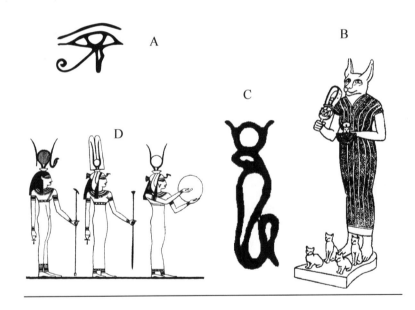

"Sefech-Ba-Ra"
soul of Ra #7

7- THE SEVENTH ENERGY-CONSCIOUSNESS CENTER

<u>Location:</u> At the crown of the head, extending upward beyond the physical body.

<u>The symbols of this center consists of:</u> In Ancient Egyptian iconography the Uraeus serpent encircling the sundisk, 🜚, at the crown of the head is used. Also, in the papyrus of Ani an unguent cone at the crown of the head is used to symbolize the anointing of transcendental consciousness which occurs when the lower self is transcended. In Indian iconography a thousand-petalled lotus at the top of the head with the "Lotus Feet of God" in the center, symbolizing the fact that you must transcend even the experience of oneness with God in order to experience the transcendental being-ness without attributes, or associations of any kind.

Psycho-spiritual Energy Center #7

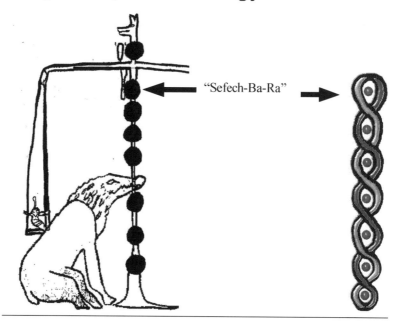

"Sefech-Ba-Ra"

<u>The element of this center is:</u> This center is beyond the concepts of symbols, desires, indifference, being and non-being,

<u>The Barrier of this sphere is Gold.</u> This is the boundary that must be pierced in order to attain this level of consciousness.

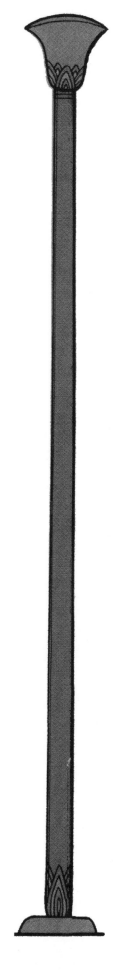

The predominant psychic activity: This is the energy-consciousness level where the dualistic mind symbolized by Apopis and the *"life giving fire"* (primal energies) become united into one whole. This is where Apopis (lower Self) is transformed into the Uraeus (Higher Self), the highest achievement of all spiritual movement. This consciousness level represents the level of transcendence where the Christ anointing occurs. It is here where the merging of the individual soul with the Absolute reality (The Universal Soul) occurs. The same symbolism is expressed in the idea of the Sphinx wherein the lion body (lower self) of the Sphinx merges with the human head (Higher Self, GOD). In Indian terms, goddess Kundalini, the energy force of the body, unites with the god Shiva, the creative force of the universe, thus, going beyond male and female.

The way to achieve this energy center: Cleanse the subtle and gross energy channels to dissolve all traces of mental and physical blockage. This psychic state is achieved when the elements of the body are all dissolved into infinity (a thousand petals). Earth (1st energy center) dissolves into water (2nd energy center) , water dissolves into fire (3rd energy center), fire dissolves into air (4th energy center), air dissolves into ether (5th energy center), ether dissolves into the cosmic mind (6th energy center). When all traces of ego consciousness (ego-identification) with the elements is dissolved, all elements dissolve into infinity, the transcendental Absolute (7th energy center). Behold the transcendental reality of which you are a reflection and dissolve yourself in it. Constantly bring the mind back to this realization. You are the ocean of existence. You are the source from which all things arise. All of the different levels of consciousness are expressions of the one consciousness. Pull them all in to yourself and experience the bliss that comes from wholeness.

The Movement of the Serpent Power

Above: The goddess Sekhmet. Sekhmet is the counterpart of the god Ptah. The name Ptah signifies supporter of heaven and earth. He sustains Creation through his goddess.

The term Sekhmet comes from Sekhem. Sekhem is the divine Life Force energy which emanates from the Divine (God) and which causes Creation to exist and which engenders all life. Thus, Ptah is the cause while Sekhmet is the dynamic aspect of the Divine.

Thus, Sekhmet is holding the two forces (positive and negative) which together manifest as the opposites of creation. So in this aspect Sekhmet is likened to the caduceus of Djehuti. Sekhmet is the central channel while the two serpents symbolize the solar and lunar. Note that the two serpents are in reality one serpent with two heads. This signifies that the energy, while appearing as opposites in the form of two serpents (positive and negative), is in reality two aspects of the same energy. When the opposite forces in the mind and body are harmonized there is a dawning of the vision of universality and union which underlies all.

The Serpent Power

A

B

The latent spiritual energy lies dormant, coiled up as it were, at the base of the spine and when awakened spirals upward awakening the spiritual energy centers in the subtle spiritual body.

In Indian iconography (B) the three main *nadis* or astral channels through which the Serpent Power travels are depicted as one straight channel or central shaft which runs vertically, and two intertwining channels representing the two opposite poles of the same Serpent Power energy.

This is the same depiction used in Ancient Egyptian iconography (A) with the staff of the god Djehuti which later became known as the Caduceus of Hermes Trismegistus.

A Yogi in the Lotus Pose
Meditating on the
Psycho-spiritual Energy Centers

Energy Centers and the Movement of the Serpent Power

...am of the Psycho-Spiritual Energy Centers of Human consciousness
...s the Serpent Power for concentration and meditation exercises.

MEDITATIVE PRINCIPLE

7-I am The Self.

6-Spirit and matter have the same

5-I have the power to control my

4-I love and care for others and not just myself.

3-I will understand my potential to serve others.

2-I will control and harness my Sexuality and Create positive thoughts, feelings and impressions.

1-I am sustained and provided for by the Self.

Instruction:

Practice concentrating on one meditative principle each month. As you reflect on each meditative principle chant the words of power of your choice and direct your heart and mind toward one-pointedness on that principle. Then remain in silence and allow the Divine feeling to rise within you, lifting you above all weakness and difficulty (ignorance, obstruction) in each particular center. Allow yourself to be cleansed and the Serpent Power will rise within you

Arat: The Serpent Power Goddess of Ancient Egypt.

164

The mystical symbolism of the three and a half turns of the Serpent Power.

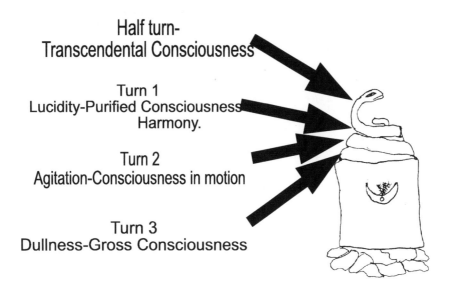

Half turn-
Transcendental Consciousness

Turn 1
Lucidity-Purified Consciousness
Harmony.

Turn 2
Agitation-Consciousness in motion

Turn 3
Dullness-Gross Consciousness

Above: The Serpent Basket of Isis

Below: Goddess Kundalini from India.

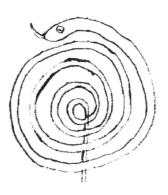

There are two forms of movement in the Serpent Power. The first movement is from the cosmos to the physical plane. In this movement the energy of the Serpent Power comes "down" from the heavens to sustain life on earth. This is called the "Creation" movement. The energy enters the personality and "lays" dormant at the base of the spine. The second form of movement is an upwards. This is called the "dissolution" movement. When a spiritual practitioner causes the energy to move upward it eventually rises through all of the energy centers and "reunites" with its cosmic source. In the process it takes with it the conscience of the individual and the individual thereby also joins the cosmic Self and attains "enlightenment."

The Serpent Power has two forms of movement. The first is a creative expression and the second is a movement towards dissolution, the opposite of creation. When a practitioner engages in the disciplines of the Serpent Power a movement is engendered in which the Serpent Power reverses its flow and ceases to sustain the reality of the world. It moves up above the surface of the world into the higher planes of existence. This is what allows a human being to experience the higher planes of existence.

Figure 40: The Serpent Power in the process of Creation.

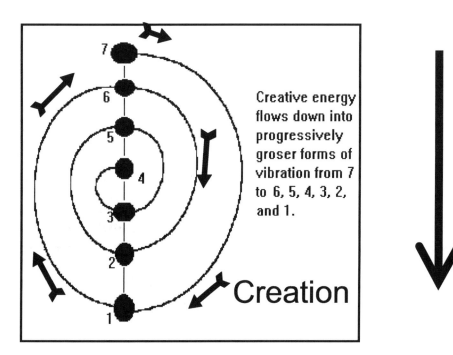

Creative energy flows down into progressively groser forms of vibration from 7 to 6, 5, 4, 3, 2, and 1.

Creation

Figure 41:The Serpent Power in the process of Dissolution.

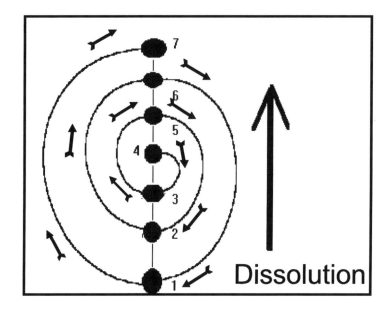

Dissolution

When a human being raises the serpent power by sublimating the first three lower energy centers. The advanced process of spiritual enlightenment begins when the fourth centers is awakened and cultivated.

Figure 42: Movement from center 4 to center 3.

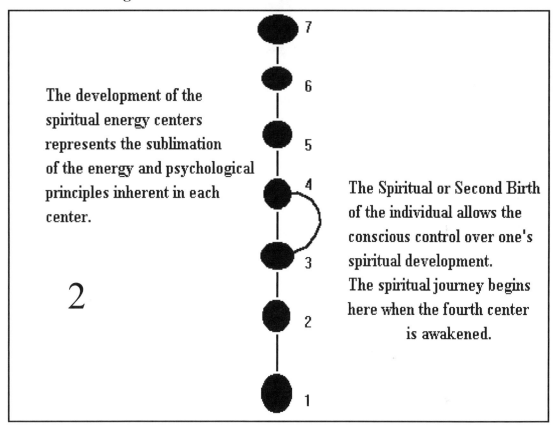

The development of the spiritual energy centers represents the sublimation of the energy and psychological principles inherent in each center.

The Spiritual or Second Birth of the individual allows the conscious control over one's spiritual development. The spiritual journey begins here when the fourth center is awakened.

The upwardly spiraling movement of the Serpent Power begins at sphere #4 and then begins "collecting" the sublimated energies from each of the lower centers and carries it to their corresponding upper centers.

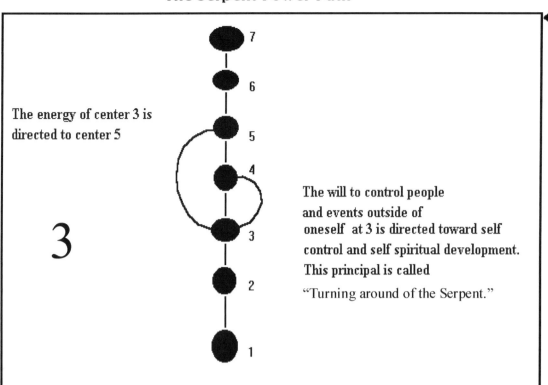

The energy of center 3 is directed to center 5

3

The will to control people and events outside of oneself at 3 is directed toward self control and self spiritual development. This principal is called

"Turning around of the Serpent."

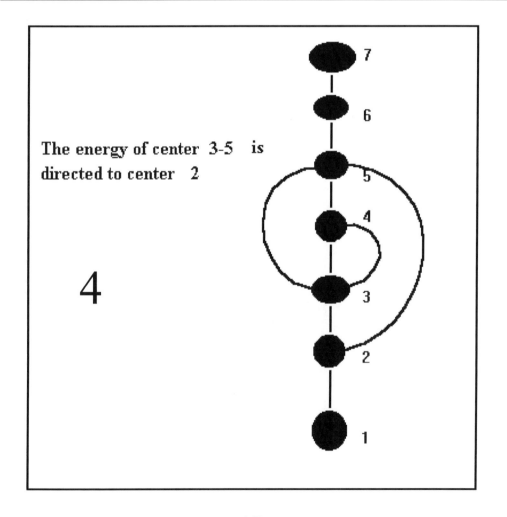

The energy of center 3-5   is directed to center   2

4

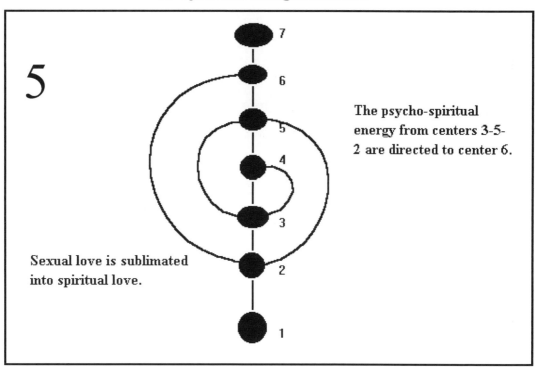

5

The psycho-spiritual energy from centers 3-5-2 are directed to center 6.

Sexual love is sublimated into spiritual love.

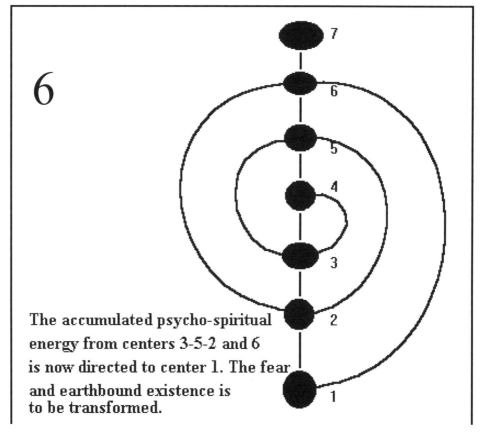

6

The accumulated psycho-spiritual energy from centers 3-5-2 and 6 is now directed to center 1. The fear and earthbound existence is to be transformed.

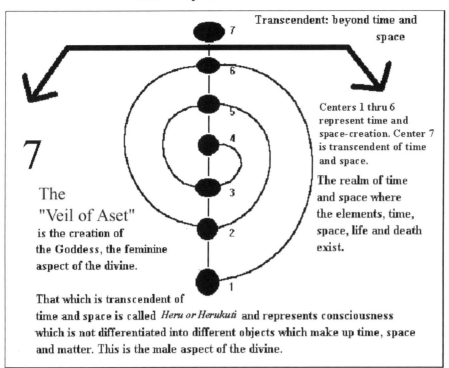

Transcendent: beyond time and space

7

Centers 1 thru 6 represent time and space-creation. Center 7 is transcendent of time and space.

The realm of time and space where the elements, time, space, life and death exist.

The "Veil of Aset" is the creation of the Goddess, the feminine aspect of the divine.

That which is transcendent of time and space is called *Heru or Herukuti* and represents consciousness which is not differentiated into different objects which make up time, space and matter. This is the male aspect of the divine.

For more on the "Veil of Aset" see the book The Mysteries of Isis.

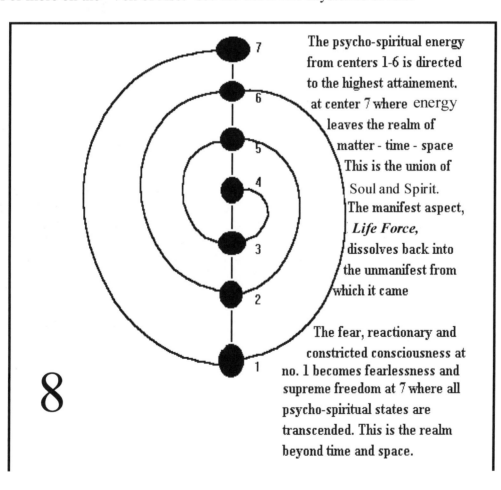

The psycho-spiritual energy from centers 1-6 is directed to the highest attainement. at center 7 where energy leaves the realm of matter - time - space This is the union of Soul and Spirit. The manifest aspect, *Life Force*, dissolves back into the unmanifest from which it came

The fear, reactionary and constricted consciousness at no. 1 becomes fearlessness and supreme freedom at 7 where all psycho-spiritual states are transcended. This is the realm beyond time and space.

8

How to Make the Serpent Power Move

The Importance of virtuous living for cleansing the energy centers and conduits.

The importance of practicing Maat to purify the personality cannot be understated in the practice of the Serpent Power Yoga discipline. This is the frst step in making the Serpent Power effective along with cleansing the body and mind.

The following diagram shows the virtuous qualities of each center which are to be cultivated and developed in order to transcend that center on the upward movement toward transcendence. Note that the centers 1-3 are separated by a horizontal line and that next to these the word Maat is written. This signifies that those people who are at the psycho-spiritual consciousness level between one and three are those people who have not reached the maturity for self-determination. They require rules and regulations imposed by society to guide them on the right path which promotes self-development, sex-sublimation and self-control. Therefore, they must be taught the injunctions of Maat and they must be shown the wisdom of following its principles.

**Transcendental
Union with the Absolute**

↑

Vision of Oneness with Creation and the Absolute

↑

Self Control

↑

Divine Love

\- -

Power-   ↑
Control of Others   ↑
Emotions →→→→→→→←←←   MAAT

↑
↑
↑

Sexuality-Creativity →→→→→→→←←←   MAAT

↑
↑
↑

Survival/Reactionary →→→→→→→←←←   MAAT
Food Concerns

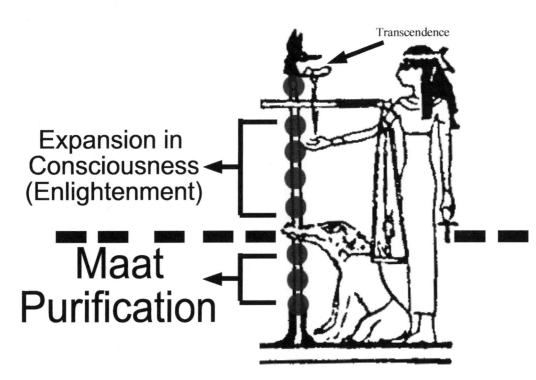

Transcendence

**Expansion in
Consciousness
(Enlightenment)** ←

**Maat
Purification** ←

This diagram illustrates the meaning of the Qenna Papyrus judgment scene in succinct terms. Those who live out of the lower three spheres of psycho-spiritual consciousness need to be purified through living life in accordance with the precepts of Maat. Then

they will be ready to experience the higher spheres of consciousness (4th thru 7th).

The flow of the Life Force energy is from most subtle and powerful at the top to the least subtle (at the bottom):

Universal Spirit
⬇
Life Force Energy
⬇
Individual soul
⬇
The Energy Centers of the Astral Body of each human being-mind.
⬇
The Nervous System
⬇
The Endocrine System
⬇
The organs and muscles, etc.

If there is a disturbance in the mind (Astral Body), the distribution of Life Force energy to the associated energy center will be disrupted and imbalances may occur that could lead to diseases in the areas wherein the Life Force is deficient or overabundant. This is the basis of the mind-body connection spoken about so much in current new age and alternative healing discussions. For example, anger (mental disturbance) effecting the 3rd energy center will result in the liver withholding or secreting too much bile, and the stomach secreting too much acid or not enough, resulting in physical illness. In order for the Life Force to be in harmony and function properly, the mind needs to be in harmony, peace and ease instead of dis-ease. Also evident from the above flow chart is that even higher than affecting disease at the mental level (Astral Body) is affecting it at the soul level. This is most effectively done through the practice of meditation. Thus, true freedom from stress can only come when there is a proper lifestyle, which provides for the needs of the body, mind and soul. Therefore, the practices of cleansing the mind from negative thought, meditation, and right actions are extremely important in promoting health, which is dependent to a great extent on the subtle aspects of the personality (mind and soul).

Thus, we will work with the gross energy and gradually move to the subtler forms. The Serpent Power is one energy but it is classified in accordance with its form of manifestation in the following ways.

Neberdjer
⇕
Ra-Khepri (Heru)
⇕
Tefnut
⇕
Sekhmit
⇕
Sekhemti
⇕

Uadjit and Nekhebit, Aset and Nebethet, The Maati Goddesses, The Uadjti etc.

According to the teachings of Anunian theology (See book Anunian Theology by Muata Ashby) The subtlest cosmic principle, Neberdjer, gives rise to Ra-khepri, within the Nun (primeval waters, i.e. undifferentiated matter-consciousness). This principle (Ra-khepri) gives rise to a grosser form of energy called Tefnut which is the leonine goddess of water. Tefnut, gives rise to Sekhmit (life Force energy in air which sustains life) and Sekhmit gives rise to Sekhemti, the dual forms of the serpent (Uadjit and Nekhebit, Aset and Nebethet, The Maati Goddesses, etc.). The Uadjti form (dual serpent goddesses) are the ones who move up the subtle spine and meet at the point between the eyebrows, causing spiritual enlightenment to occur but this will only happen when the movement towards duality is reversed and the serpents are made to harmonize and coalesce at the top of the Djed or Pillar of Asar. So there is a movement of duality (Creation) and a movement towards non-duality (dissolution) which is actually a return to the primordial state which was in the beginning. Therefore, the dual state of matter is but an illusory manifestation of the true state, allowed by the duality of the Serpent Power.

Those who have gained control over the first three psycho-spiritual consciousness centers will be able to discover a new, deeper essence of their own existence as they move beyond "animal" consciousness. Otherwise, they will remain in a horizontal movement through life which will lead to pain, sorrow and disappointments as well as the development of a karmic basis for reincarnation.

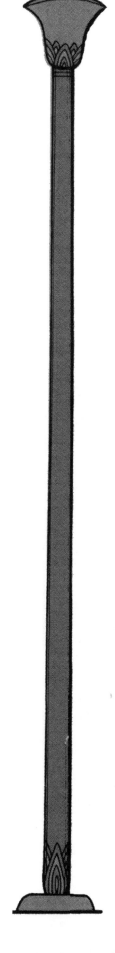

Vibration, Hekau, Life Force and the Serpent Power

Principle of Vibration – From The Ancient Egyptian Kybalion Text

"Nothing rests, everything moves; everything vibrates.

"To change your mood or mental state, change your vibration."

"To destroy an undesirable rate of mental vibration, concentrate on the opposite vibration to the one to be suppressed."

The Ancient Egyptian Concept of Vibration

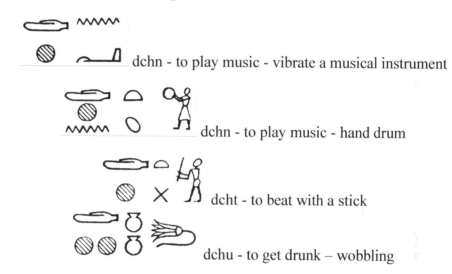

dchn - to play music - vibrate a musical instrument

dchn - to play music - hand drum

dcht - to beat with a stick

dchu - to get drunk – wobbling

As Djehuti is the God of intellect (mind), he also presides over mental vibrations and thus is the master of mind. Thus, vibration is an important concept in mental transmutation as well as the management of the Serpent Power energy. *Dech* or *vibration* is one of the seven principles of metaphysics presented by Hermes-Djehuti in the Kybalion text. And, as the evidence above shows, the teachings related to Vibration, go back to the hieroglyphic text that Djehuti himself brought into being. All the derivative terms from the original term "dch" convey an aspect of vibration related to the shaking or oscillating effect that occurs in nature.

Vibration is the means by which the individual mind (human beings and astral beings) creates thoughts and also the means by which the cosmic mind (God) brings into being and sustains Creation. The faster the vibration, the subtler the manifestation of matter will appear. Conversely, the slower the vibration, the more gross the material manifestation will appear.

In the practice of the Sema Arat Shekhem (Ancient Egyptian Serpent Power Yoga), the practitioner directs attention to the base of the spine and causes the energy of the Life Force to concentrate and accumulate there. Then it is cultivated and raised. The Life Force is controlled by the mental meditation on the point that causes it to focus and become dynamic, as opposed to being unfocused and diffused (weak).

A

m

n

(The Ancient Egyptian Hieroglyphic symbols of the term Amun)

The sound Am is used to harness the Life Force energy. Special attention is given to the "m" in Am, which is the universal sound of the original vibration enjoined by the Spirit to bring Creation into being. In this sense the "m" becomes an emphatic "M" that carries the grosser vibration at the beginning of the syllable to a greater level of subtlety as the "M…" is carried into infinity "…" and silence which eventually gives rise to the next chant of "AM…."

(The Ancient Egyptian Hieroglyphic symbols of the letter "m")

The letter "m" in Kamitan grammar signifies "transformation" from one form to another. Specifically in the religious texts it relates to developing from a person with ordinary consciousness to a person possessing enlightened consciousness, hence the term "Pert m Heru." This program of transformation is accomplished by the transmutation engendered through the cultivated Life Force. A metamorphosis of consciousness occurs in which the earlier personality "becomes enlightened" by coming into the light of the Supreme Spirit, Heru.

Pert   -   m   -   Heru
book (of) - transforming into - the light."

Am is a universal word of power which was used in ancient Kamit (Egypt) and is used extensively in India by yogis. Om or AUM is related to the word Amun from Kamit and Amun is related to the Amen of Christianity. More importantly, it has the same meaning as Amun and is therefore completely compatible with the energy pattern of the entire group. According to the Ancient Egyptian Leyden papyrus, the name of the "Hidden God", referring to Amun, may be pronounced as *Om,* or *Am.* Therefore, Om is generally useful for spiritual practice. Om* is also not related to a particular deity but is common to all. It is also the hekau-mantra of the 6th energy center at the point between the eyebrows known as the ancient Egyptian *Arat* or Uraeus serpent. You will use hekau for chanting during your worship periods, and at idle times during the day. You will use it from now on to dig deeply into the unconscious regions of your mind as a miner uses a pick to cut into a mountain in search of gold. Concentration opens the door to transcendental awareness and spiritual realization. Various estimates are given as to when you may expect to feel results; these vary from 500,000 repetitions to 1,200,000 or more. The

number should not be your focus. Sustained practice, understanding the teachings about the Self and practicing the virtues and self-control in an integral, balanced fashion are the most important factors determining your eventual success.

The movement, "dchn" of objects in Creation causes the illusion in the mind due to the illusory senses, that solid objects exist and that one is a solid personality. When the vibrations (fluctuations) of the mind are controlled and caused to become subtler, the illusoriness of the physical world becomes evident. Therefore, the chant of Am (Aum, Om) along with the visualization exercises is to be practiced along with purity of body through righteous diet and job occupation as well as actions in the world based on righteous Maatian principles. Also, the mind is to be purified by studying the righteous principles. Then, with the assistance of the Serpent Power, the mind will open to the higher levels of consciousness. So during the practices of focusing and accumulating the Life Force the Am chant or chants that incorporate the Am (Aum, Om) will be used.

Included below are two types of words of power: short, containing one or two syllables, medium length, containing two to three and average, containing six to eight. They are presented as guidelines for the practice of hekau-mantra repetition.

	Number per minute			Number per hour		
	Low	Med	High	Low	Med	High
1. OM	140	250	400	8400	15000	24000
2. Om Amun Ra Ptah	80	120	140	4800	7200	9000
3. Om Asar Aset Heru	80	120	140	4800	7200	9000
4. Om Maati Maakheru	80	120	140	4800	7200	9000

If using the ancient Kamitan music during meditation practice the practitioner will take care to use only those songs that use the appropriate chants and vibrational rate (steady and processional as opposed to variable and festive).

Great pains are being taken here to outline the concept of vibration because this is the means by which the Serpent Power is affected and cultivated. Gross sound, thought and will, are forms of vibration that affect the movement of the Serpent Power and these are affected by one's understanding of who one is, i.e. knowledge of Self. Therefore, the philosophy behind vibrations is central to the discussion about the Serpent Power.

Poles of Vibration

Everything in the universe vibrates and their manifestations are dependent on the particular rate of vibration. Modern Physics has already shown that matter is actually not solid, but only appears so to our limited "physical" senses. If we were able to raise our vibrational level we would be able to elevate our consciousness and thereby perceive other levels of existence beyond the physical which are vibrating at a higher rate. The universe is set up with two poles. The source is the Self (God) which vibrates at the highest rate. Its farthest vibrational emanation is the physical world which has the lowest rate of vibration. The higher rate of vibration is faster and more compact. The lower rate of vibration is slower and expanded. This also means that the energy that sustains creation permeates Creation and thus comes from "within" and not from outside. The Life Force that sustains a human being comes from the Self and sustains the soul. The soul sustains the astral body and the astral body sustains the physical reality. The universe has astral bodies and souls just as living (sentient) beings do.

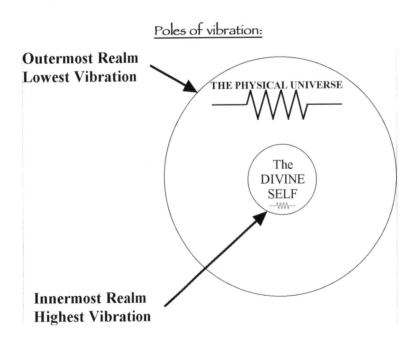

Poles of vibration:

Outermost Realm Lowest Vibration

THE PHYSICAL UNIVERSE

The DIVINE SELF

Innermost Realm Highest Vibration

Self – The All	Physical universe
High energy	Low energy
Fast rate of vibration	Slow rate of vibration
Psychological tendency:	Psychological tendency:
Virtue	*vice*

The objective of the Serpent Power disciplines is to raise the frequency of the vibration of the personality: this means making the personality subtle. This occurs when the gross personality is purified by living in accordance with the teachings of Maat. Then the cleansing of the subtle body must take place. Then the manipulation of subtle energies which cleanse the unconscious mind (soul) takes place. Then, consciousness, unobstructed, can perceive the transcendental and unfathomable vibration of the Supreme Being. The poles should therefore be understood as extreme tendencies that are manifesting different aspects of the same energy-thought consciousness.

Music and Color

Music is a form of vibration which impresses our auditory senses. All music emanates from one vibration, and this is called OM (Aum, Am, Amun). From this single sound (Om) seven recurring vibrations (notes) emerge. These repeat every octave step away from the initial sound in either direction (up or down). The higher the octave range, the higher the vibration. The lower the octave range the lower the vibration. Therefore, if one wants to elevate the vibration of the personality (gross physical body, astral body {mind and senses}, then one should play "elevating music," that is, music in the upper ranges or music that is based in the elevating ranges. Elevating music is music that lifts the feeling and makes one feel calm, virtuous, spiritually devoted, optimistic and altruistic, i.e. lucid. Music that is agitating to the mind and which insights anger, hatred, desire for sense pleasures, etc., has a lower vibration and should be avoided by aspirants. Also, people have vibrations and this is why the company of people with "negative vibes" should be avoided. Sages and enlightened souls have a higher rate of vibration and their company should be sought.

Music can aid in the process of transforming the personality at the subatomic level by acting on the emotional level of vibration in the personality which is the center of the most powerful feeling, love. Therefore, music extolling divine love for the Divinity is the highest form of musical practice. This is why priests and priestesses in Kamit were also students of music and there were professional musicians at the temples who served in the capacity of musicians at the varied ritual programs.[41] Pythagoras and Plato, who were documented students at the Ancient Egyptian temples, wrote about music theory and its effect on the personality. Special music has been prepared for this practice by Sebai Muata,

---

[41] See the book *Egyptian Yoga Chant and Songbook by Muata Ashby.*

which is designed to work on each energy center, to cleanse it and elevate its vibrational potential.[42]

Color and Spiritual Evolution

Just as music has its audible range of sound and there are lower and higher sounds beyond the human range of hearing, there is a visible range of colors and below it and above it there are colors that cannot be perceived by the gross human sense organs (eyes). However, as the vibration of the personality is raised and as one is liberated from the constrictions of perception through the gross physical senses, one can become aware of the higher range of light (Gamma Rays X- Rays, etc.).

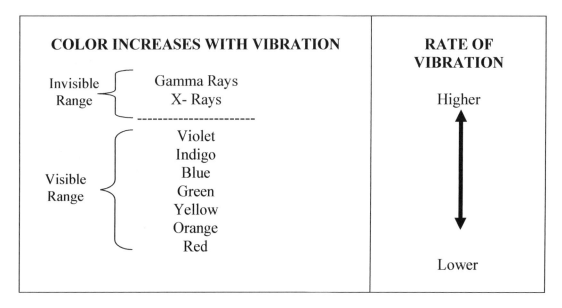

COLOR INCREASES WITH VIBRATION	RATE OF VIBRATION
Invisible Range { Gamma Rays X- Rays -------------------------	Higher ↕ Lower
Visible Range { Violet Indigo Blue Green Yellow Orange Red	

As with music, color has been shown to affect moods. For example, the color red incites action, and agitation. Blue is soothing and calming. Indigo promotes subtlety of mind and the opening of the Third Eye. Violet promotes complete transcendence. Therefore, the color of the particular psycho-spiritual energy center being worked upon should be presented to the eyes when that center is being cultivated, using a poster, sheet or mental visualization.

- When matter is caused to vibrate, a process of disintegration (dissolution) is enjoined:

  o At a certain point the object, which is composed of molecules, disintegrates into atoms.
  o Further vibration disintegrates it into ethereal substance.
  o Further vibration disintegrates it into mind substance.
  o Further vibration disintegrates it into the ALL – Absolute.

---

[42] Contact the Sema Institute for details – see catalog at the back of this book

Higher vibration has more power so – a higher vibrating mind controls a lower vibrating mind. This was illustrated in the story of the Asarian Resurrection in the episode where goddess Aset (who represents wisdom) tricked Set into admitting his guilt in the murder of Asar.

- If the art of concentrating on a particular vibration is learned and mastered, vibrations can be reproduced at will like music. This has the following implications.

  - a person can control their mental states and moods at will and not be a slave to them since all moods and mental states are rates of vibration of the mind which people have learned based on reactions to nervous stimuli and human interactions.

  - a person can control lower minds and objects – this act is not to be practiced by aspirants, but only by masters who have gained higher insight into the nature of Self in order to perceive what is proper, i.e. they have become one with the cosmic forces of the Supreme Being, which direct the cosmic plan. Use of this power by unenlightened persons makes them particularly susceptible to more powerful forces than ordinary worldly "Ari" (Karmic entanglement) in the law of cause and effect (Maat).

- Thus when the mind is vibrating on a higher level it is liberated from the world, which is vibrating at a lower level. This highlights the importance of practicing virtuous action and controlling the lower human urges.

Precautions

The teaching presented in this book does not provide the full method to awaken the Serpent Power through the secret meditations, breathing exercises and chants because the misuse of these before the personality has been prepared could lead to injury of the practitioner. Those interested in the Serpent Power path should follow the instructions below.

1. work with a qualified preceptor someone with experience in awakening the serpent power and can guide you should any problems develop if it is awakened prematurely or in the wrong manner.
2. become a vegetarian and cleanse the physical body for at least 3 years before beginning the more advanced disciplines of the Serpent Power. Do not overeat and do not starve yourself. Find the balance. See the book Kemetic Diet.
3. study the Serpent Power philosophy during the cleansing period. Thereby purify your mind.
4. control the sex urge during the purification period. Prepare to practice abstinence during the advanced phase of the Serpent Power discipline.
5. make sure you do not have high blood pressure or other medical conditions before beginning the advanced phase of the Serpent Power discipline. The advanced disciplines are stressing to the body in the beginning and good health is necessary for success.
6. stabilize your home life. Practice Maat at home and at play.
7. stabilize your job or occupation. Practice Maat at work.

When the practice is successful, energies of higher vibration that are locked within matter which is vibrating at a lower rate are liberated. The energy of the liberated mind is more powerful than a liberated atomic explosion. The energy of the liberated mind can manifest in the form of heat, light, sound, etc., of great intensity, even more powerful than physical forms of energy (including nuclear bombs). Before this happens the personality must be prepared to handle those forces. Otherwise this can have a detrimental effect on the personality even leading to disease or insanity (psychotic breaks). Therefore, the practitioner should follow the instruction of his/her preceptor. There can be pain involved with the development of the Serpent Power as its awakening restructures the nervous system. Any remaining impurities in the nervous system, caused either by physical impurities or psychological ones, will be met with immense force. If the personality is not ready to handle this, physical and or emotional breakdown can occur. Therefore, follow the instructions laid out here for gradual development and do not skip to the advanced practice without guidance..

If this teaching is mastered it is said that the practitioner will control the Caduceus of Djehuti, i.e. the power of the Life Force energy centers and the two serpents that lead to the knowledge of "Above and Below." This is why it is said that:

"The one who has grasped the principle of vibration, has grasped the scepter of power."

Chapter 6: Meditations and Exercises For Serpent Power Cultivation and Spiritual Transcendence

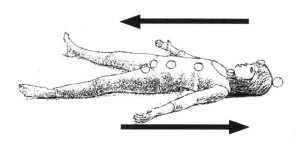

INTEGRATED SERPENT POWER MEDITATION

There are four main components of meditation: posture, breath-life force control, sound and visualization.

Before you begin, practice some light physical exercises (yoga, tai chi, etc.) for several minutes. This will serve to free up any energy blockages and wake up the mind by stimulating the circulation of the vital forces within the body.

Next practice some chanting or prayers. These will serve to set the general mood for your meditation session and to set up positive vibrations in your physical and astral bodies.

Now choose a comfortable posture. If you consistently practice meditation, you will gradually be able to stay in one position for longer periods of time. If you practice regularly, you will discover that your body will develop a daily rhythm which will be conducive to your meditation time.

Next practice alternate nostril breathing so as to balance the positive and negative charges within the body and open up the central channel of vital energy as we discussed in the last section. Choose a particular visualization exercise or hekau. This will serve the purpose of helping to occupy the attention of the mind and prevent it from straying. It will also help you to develop sensitivity and control over the vital energy so that eventually you will be able to direct it according to your will.

A meditation on the energy centers will be used here or you may use the format presented in the audio tape (Ushet I: Morning Worship and Meditation).

See the diagram provided for the location of the energy centers. Visualize yourself gaining cosmic energy. See it accumulating in the body. Place your concentration on the first energy center at the base of the spine as you inhale. See the energy tapping that spot, then see it rising through the other energy centers going up to the sixth center where the pineal gland is situated (The Uraeus). Hold the breath for a few seconds. Exhale and see the energy go back down to the first center. Inhale and repeat the exercise. Feel the increasing levels of PEACE *(htp)* develop. Also, you will notice that you are gaining a subtle form of vitality. This is *Sekhem* or spiritual Life Force energy, also known as *Chi* or *Prana* in China and India, respectively.

Inhale and visualize the energy flowing up from the first energy center, through the second, and then through the third, fourth, fifth and sixth up to the seventh, the highest energy center and hold the breath a few seconds. Then as you exhale, visualize the energy flowing back through the centers from the highest to the first center at the base of the spine.* As you visualize the energy flowing from center to center you are controlling the Life Force energy and the direction of the mind at the same time.

Now we will add sound to the meditation. You may choose a hekau of your choice, one you feel especially drawn to and one that you understand the deeper meaning of, to some degree, or the one suggested by your spiritual preceptor. Repeat it with meaning and feeling as you breath. Visualize and remain steady in your pose. You can link your breath and hekau repetition by reciting the first part of your hekau upon inhalation as the energy is moving up and the second part upon exhalation as the energy is moving back down.

In the beginning it may seem as though not much is happening, but within a short time, you will begin to notice changes within yourself. Your level of relaxation will improve immediately and your awareness of yourself will increase gradually. Eventually, you will begin to perceive various new sensations and psychic expansion. You will hear your heart beat. A feeling of peacefulness will develop. When you succeed in transcending your body consciousness you will be going beyond the exercises. You will not feel your arms or legs. This is an initial stage of transcendence. Your inner vision will open and you will perceive reality beyond the mind and body. At this point, do not worry about the components of the meditation. Simply relax and remain a witness to all you perceive. Do not try to run away from or to anything you notice. Gradually allow yourself to go deeper and deeper until you become one with the source of all thoughts. This is the real you. Continue practicing this "communion" exercise with the Divine until you are fully established in this level of being at all times. This is the state of Enlightenment. *(For more specific instructions and meditation music listen to the Serpent Power audio tapes.)

Instruction

"The Meditation on the energy centers. From the base of the spine to the "Uraeus", third eye, pineal gland, 6th center between the eye brows.

As the Serpent Power is cultivated it moves through the conscious, subconscious and unconscious levels of the mind and the Physical and Astral bodies. It effects a dissolution of these, revealing the consciousness of the innermost Self as the true reality which was there all the time.

Sound is an important factor of meditation because it imbues the mind with positive vibrations that allow it to gain concentration and calmness and thus to transcend ordinary consciousness. In the Serpent Power Meditation we will use sound in a special way. First sit or lay in a comfortable posture. Using the Hekau-mantram *"Om Asar Aset Heru"* we will visualize that we are drawing energy from the universe and that we will bring it to the body, store it and use it to cleanse the body. Also you will use it to carry your mind to discover the higher realms of existence. The hekau signifies The Supreme Power (OM) manifesting as Asar (Asar), Aset (Aset) and Heru (Heru), the Trinity of consciousness and the three planes of existence. Begin by visualizing cosmic energy as light. See that light coming into your body from all directions and landing on the base of the spine while at the same time uttering "Om". Then moving it (with your thought) to the second energy center with "As". Then to the third with "Ar" and so on until the crown center is reached with "Ru." When you reach the crown allow a few moments of silence. Allowing the sound to fade into infinity and remain motionless. This symbolizes the absolute and transcendental Self. Allow yourself to abide in this silent place in between one cycle of chanting and the next. Repeat this cycle as many times as you like and you will gradually feel that the Sekhem energy and the Hekau are gaining power over stray and negative thoughts. Eventually you will be able to utter these words and immediately feel calm and transcendental, no matter where you are. This is the power of the Serpent within you. After some time you will lead yourself to discover the higher energy centers, *"Iarut"* (the seven energy centers), as you gradually release their potential. You may utter the hekau vocally or mentally according to your level of concentration. The more distracted the mind the greater volume should be used.

The Serpent Power Path

Phase 1: Draw in cosmic energy (Sekhem)

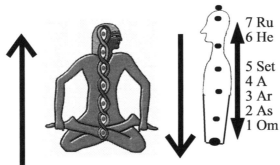

7 Ru
6 He
5 Set
4 A
3 Ar
2 As
1 Om

Phase 2: Visualize the energy going to the base of the spine and then rising up as a rearing cobra to the crown of the head. Pause. Then see it return to the base again. Start over.

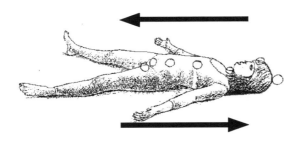

As you breath in (a) see the energy moving down to the base of the spine. As you chant (b) see it rising up toward the crown of the head as it passes through the energy centers. Suck in with your abdomen and draw the energy of the lower centers up to the crown. Hold the breath for a few seconds and then release and see the energy coming to rest at the base. Begin again.

The Power Breath

The power breath is an exercise for developing concentration on the breath and for developing the Serpent Power. It is practiced by making a labored breath through the nose while inhaling and exhaling with the mouth closed.

In this exercise the partitioned breathes in naturally and slowly while making a point to "force" the breath in and out of the lungs. This practice is enjoined for 5 minutes for beginners and developing practitioners develop a longer duration but for no longer than the first hour of meditation practice. After this period the breath is allowed to go back to the normal autonomic level and it is simply observed by the aspirant who at that point begins concentrating more on the life force and the energy centers.

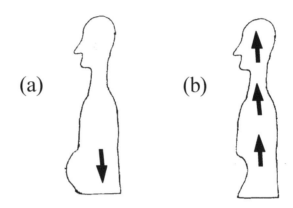

(a)   (b)

Meditation on the Spiritual Energy Centers

The goal of Serpent Power Yoga is to unlock the hidden potential of the human being which is being blocked by various psycho-spiritual forms of ignorance and negative feelings. The following diagram shows the main psycho-spiritual elements (obstacles to the full expression of consciousness) which are to be overcome at each center of psycho-spiritual consciousness.

TRANSCENDENCE - ENLIGHTENMENT

7

Obstacle: Ego self - You think you are a mortal
human being instead of an Immortal Divinity.

6

Lack of concentration. Lack of intellectual ability required to think properly and
discover the true meaning of life. The intellect is clouded over by egoistic
feelings, desires and illusions about what reality is.

5

Lack of self control, Getting carried away with the whims of the mind and senses.

4

Attachment, Egoistic Love

3

Desire for worldly attainments, and control of others, Greed, Hatred,

2

Gross Sexual Desire.

1

Fear of death. Survival concerns. Where will next meal come from?

Meditation to increase vitality: To increase vitality lie in a comfortable position (F) and relax the muscles of your body. Visualize the energy centers and envision that the energy from the sun (G-1) is entering your being at the point of the energy center you have chosen (H). You may also visualize that you are receiving life itself in the form of sunrays (I). Work with the breath by inhaling the energy in and holding the breath while concentrating on the particular energy center. If there are any psychic difficulties or health issues related with that center they will be alleviated. Practice this exercise for as long as you like each day and feel revitalized and renewed.

G-1

H

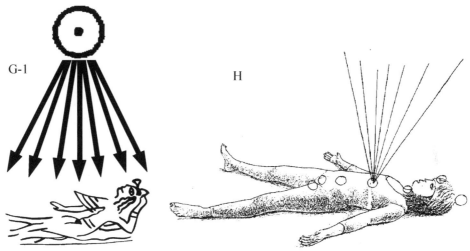

I

The Heart Pyramid

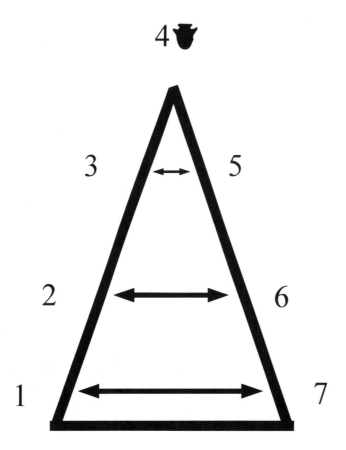

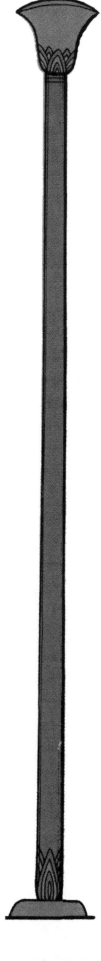

The heart pyramid symbolizes the relationship between the energy centers. Each one has an opposite correspondent except the heart center. The heart psycho-spiritual center, #4, is at the center of the entire scheme of the Serpent Power. Thus, once all of the centers are realized and opened it is necessary to balance them so as to continue living in the world of ordinary human experience. Otherwise there would be continuous transcendence and it would be impossible to sustain the ordinary day to day realities of life. This balancing and harmonizing can be accomplished by meditating on the heart center. This practice is also useful when there is stress or anxiety in the mind.

Psychic Powers and Spiritual Experiences

As you gain success in Serpent Power Yoga you will experience many new thrills of discovering the inner Self. However, at the beginning you may feel fear since this is new territory. As you move forward you will discover unimaginable heights of enjoyments such as none that you can find in ordinary human life. Never forget however that these are all transient thrills and that the ultimate thrill, discovering the Self, awaits you at the end of the journey. So be a detached witness to the experiences even as you experience them. Psychic powers such as the ability to perceive at a distance, clairvoyance, telepathy, etc can be yours as the hidden potential of the energy centers unfold, if you desire them but remember that these can be a distraction like worldly hobbies and gifts can be as well. The most important psychic power you should look for are inner peace and contentment because these allow you to be free from all worldly miseries while engendering a sensation not unlike the fulfillment of sexual desire but multiplied manifold. For this reason Serpent Power Yoga is known as the style of Yoga which bestows fulfillment in all planes (Physical, Astral and Causal - body, mind and soul). It is also why all forms of yoga depend on the Serpent Power for spiritual advancement. A practitioner of Wisdom Yoga elevates the Serpent Power by cleansing the mind and body through reason. A practitioner of Devotional Yoga elevates the Serpent Power by cleansing the mind and body through pure emotion directed towards the Divine. A practitioner of Action Yoga elevates the Serpent Power by cleansing the mind and body through righteous living and actions directed towards the Divine through selfless service to humanity. A practitioner of Meditation Yoga elevates the Serpent Power by cleansing the mind and body through pure will and concentration directed towards the Divine. Therefore, all forms of yoga practices need to have insight into the Serpent Power.

As the Serpent Power is awakened in a natural way there is increasing peace and greater understanding of the teachings. Greater understanding comes from expansion in consciousness that is brought about by the work of the Serpent Power as it increases conscious awareness and the capacity of the nervous system to accommodate the expanded perceptions. The senses become expansive. The sense of smell, touch, hearing, seeing become subtle and begin to perceive beyond the physical plane. This leads to a perennial awareness of life, an all-encompassing appreciation of existence and this is Nehast or spiritual enlightenment, the great awakening.

May Djehuti and Arat lead you to the highest attainment of
Higher Consciousness!

Assignment: Using the Serpent Power workshop-meditation audio cassettes begin incorporating the beginners meditation in Tape 1 to your daily spiritual program. Record your impressions. Feel free to experiment without the tape when you feel comfortable with the process of meditation. Also you may use the music only side along with your chosen word or words of power. Don't forget to follow the previous instructions given. Find a quiet place in which to practice. Use your favorite incense and prayers and perform light exercise prior to commencing your meditation practice.

Questions for Reflection and Study.

The following questions and exercises are designed for those taking the Egyptian Yoga course and are based on this volume and on Egyptian Yoga: The Philosophy of Enlightenment. However, anyone who works through them will gain a deeper insight into the themes expressed in this book.

1- What are the names of the Serpent Power in Ancient Egypt? What is the name of the Serpent Power in India?

_____

_____

_____

_____

2- Which nation of Africa is also known to practice the Serpent Power Yoga besides the Ancient Egyptians?

_____

_____

_____

_____

3- List the Ancient Egyptian names of the energy centers and the area of the astral body where they are located?

_____

_____

_____

_____

4- List the Indian names of the energy centers?

_____

_____

_____

_____

5- Name two Ancient Egyptian Papyruses where the Serpent Power is referred to?

6- How is the Serpent Power related to the God Shu who represents air and breath?

_____

_____

_____

_____

7- How is the Serpent Power related to the God Djehuti?

_____
_____
_____
_____

8- What are references to the Serpent Power which are in the Bible?

_____
_____
_____

9- If you reflect and rationalize about the Divine what kind of Yoga are you practicing?

_____
_____
_____
_____

10- How is the Life Force or Serpent Power form of Yoga related to all others?

_____
_____
_____
_____

11- How is the Serpent Power likened to a tree?

_____
_____
_____
_____

12- How and where does the Serpent Power energy flow?

_____
_____
_____

13- Which are the three important subtle channels through which the Serpent Power energy flows?

_____
_____
_____
_____

14- What is the name of the Serpent Power Cobra Goddess who presides over magical spells?

_____
_____
_____
_____

15- How is the Ancient Egyptian Serpent Power Goddess related to Anpu (Apuat)?

_____
_____
_____
_____

16- What are the two stages of practice in the Yoga of Life Force development?

_____
_____
_____
_____

17- What are the obstacles to the flow of the Serpent Power and how may these obstructions be overcome?

_____
_____
_____
_____

18- What are the elements associated with each energy center?

_____
_____
_____

19- What are the animals associated with each energy center?

_____
_____
_____

20- What is the process of Creation and how is the Serpent Power related to it?

_____

_____

_____

_____

21- What is the process of Dissolution and how is the Serpent Power related to it?

_____

_____

_____

_____

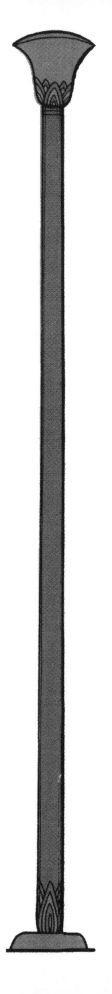

Index

Abdu, 11, 35, 120
Absolute, 32, 42, 70, 162, 172, 207
Absolute reality, 162
Absolute XE "Absolute" Reality, 42
Africa, 4, 8, 9, 10, 13, 15, 16, 28, 46, 48, 53, 57, 59, 64, 101, 142, 193
Air, 153
Ajna Chakra, 158
Akhenaton, 202
Akhnaton, 11, 74, 119
Alexandria, 82, 83
Amen, 176
Amenta, 122, 213
Amma, 224, 227
Ammit, 118, 140, 152
Amun, 11, 18, 137, 138, 159, 176, 177, 207, 224, 227
Amun-Ra-Ptah, 11, 207, 227
Ancient Egypt, 3, 4, 8, 10, 11, 12, 13, 15, 16, 17, 18, 20, 22, 24, 25, 26, 27, 29, 31, 32, 35, 36, 37, 38, 44, 46, 47, 49, 50, 51, 52, 53, 54, 55, 56, 57, 58, 61, 63, 64, 66, 67, 69, 72, 73, 76, 77, 78, 80, 82, 83, 94, 100, 102, 105, 109, 110, 111, 112, 114, 115, 118, 119, 120, 121, 122, 124, 126, 133, 134, 135, 137, 138, 139, 140, 148, 154, 158, 159, 160, 161, 175, 176, 193, 195, 202, 203, 205, 207, 208, 210, 211, 212, 213, 214, 215, 218, 219, 220, 221, 222, 223, 225, 227, 228, 229, 230, 231, 232
Ancient Egyptian Book of the Dead, 202
Ancient Egyptian Pyramid Texts, 159, 202
Ancient Egyptian Wisdom Texts, 202, 225
Ani, 161, 202
Ankh, 25, 111
Anu, 11, 215
Anu (Greek Heliopolis), 11, 215
Anubis, 18
Anunian Theology, 174
Apedemak, 46

Arabs, 8, 13
Arati, 7, 135
Architecture, 82, 137
Aristotle, 14
Aryan, 205
Asar, 11, 12, 14, 15, 17, 18, 27, 28, 29, 35, 43, 44, 45, 53, 56, 61, 63, 70, 80, 83, 85, 86, 87, 101, 102, 104, 105, 111, 113, 114, 115, 120, 121, 122, 125, 126, 139, 140, 141, 142, 158, 177, 185, 212, 213, 218, 219, 224, 227, 230, 232
Asarian Resurrection, 37, 69, 82, 83, 86, 92, 111, 115, 211
Aset, 4, 11, 17, 18, 27, 29, 31, 32, 35, 43, 53, 56, 62, 63, 67, 79, 80, 84, 85, 86, 87, 92, 95, 101, 102, 111, 114, 115, 120, 121, 126, 135, 136, 140, 141, 142, 148, 160, 174, 177, 185, 212, 213, 217, 218, 219, 223, 224, 227, 230
Aset (Isis), 4, 11, 17, 18, 27, 29, 31, 32, 43, 53, 56, 62, 63, 67, 79, 80, 84, 85, 86, 87, 92, 95, 101, 102, 111, 114, 115, 120, 121, 126, 135, 136, 140, 141, 142, 148, 160, 174, 177, 185, 212, 213, 217, 218, 219, 223, 224, 227, 230
Ashoka, 46
Asia, 28, 42, 57
Asoka, 46
Aspirant, 223
Astraea (Themis), 18
Astral, 39, 65, 112, 115, 122, 130, 131, 132, 173, 185, 191, 213
Astral Plane, 39, 65, 112, 115, 122, 130, 131, 132, 173, 185, 191, 213
Aten, see also Aton, 232
Athena, 18
Aton, 11, 74, 115, 202
Attachment, 107, 188
Augustus, 12, 15
Aum (Om), 159
Awareness, 19

Ba (also see Soul), 36, 44, 55, 139, 145, 147, 151, 153, 156, 158, 161
Balance, 109
Bas, 57
Being, 22, 45, 102, 120, 153, 207, 217
Bhagavad Gita, 22
Bible, 58, 69, 194, 218, 223
Big Bang, 17
Blackness, 16
Book of Coming Forth By Day, 58, 105, 109, 135, 149, 159, 213, 223
Book of Enlightenment, 12, 36
Book of the Dead, see also Rau Nu Prt M Hru, 12, 73, 82, 115, 135, 202, 214
Brahman, 32, 70
Buddha, 44, 70, 154, 158
Buddhism, 4, 46, 103, 154
Buddhist, 45, 154
Bull, 104
Buto, 62
Caduceus, 70, 114, 137, 140, 141, 143
Caribbean, 4
Catholic, 218
Causal Plane, 65, 98, 130, 131, 191
Chakras, 52, 54, 99, 114, 140
Chakras (see energy centers of the body), 52, 54, 99, 114, 140
Chanting, 32, 224, 227
Chi, 64, 139, 151, 184
China, 24, 25, 42, 64, 69, 139, 184
Christ, 70, 136, 162, 213
Christhood, 136, 158
Christian Yoga, 225
Christianity, 8, 20, 29, 46, 111, 136, 176, 203, 218
Church, 218, 225
Civilization, 24, 25
Cobra Goddess, 195
Coffin Texts, 17
Color, 111
Concentration, 176, 223, 225
Conception, 44
Consciousness, 8, 15, 23, 28, 77, 86, 114, 140, 191, 212, 224
Coptic, 213

Cosmic consciousness, 22
Cosmic mind, 79, 158
Cosmos, 42
Cow, 82
Creation, 7, 28, 39, 42, 43,
    44, 45, 56, 67, 72, 79, 80,
    89, 95, 97, 111, 129, 136,
    163, 165, 166, 172, 174,
    175, 176, 177, 196, 207,
    211, 215, 225
Crete, 42
Culture, 205, 211, 221
Cymbals, 230, 232
Death, 224
December, 217
Demotic, 12, 16, 89
Denderah, 11, 213
Desire, 107, 151, 188
Dharmakaya, 45
Diaspora, 9
Diet, 115, 122, 123, 204
Diodorus, 12, 14, 15, 17
Discipline, 4, 31, 34, 98
Divine Consciousness, 77
Djehuti, 1, 18, 27, 29, 59,
    70, 75, 76, 77, 78, 79, 80,
    81, 82, 83, 84, 85, 86, 87,
    89, 91, 94, 95, 96, 97,
    114, 136, 159, 163, 175,
    191, 194, 202, 224
Djehuti-Hermes, 59
Drugs, 112
Drum, 229, 232
Duat, 102, 112, 122
Earth, 94, 145, 162
Edfu, 11, 33, 142, 213
Egoism, 224
Egyptian Book of Coming
    Forth By Day, 61, 69, 213
Egyptian civilization, 13, 29,
    50
Egyptian Mysteries, 20, 29,
    205
Egyptian Physics, 216
Egyptian proverbs, 27, 208
Egyptian religion, 8, 18, 28
Egyptian Yoga, 4, 8, 15, 20,
    22, 24, 25, 26, 27, 29, 38,
    45, 48, 69, 193, 203, 205,
    207, 211, 213, 214, 223,
    224, 227, 228, 229, 230,
    231
Egyptian Yoga see also
    Kamitan Yoga, 4, 8, 15,
    20, 22, 24, 25, 26, 27, 29,
    38, 45, 48, 69, 193, 203,
    205, 207, 211, 213, 214,
    223, 224, 227, 228, 229,
    230, 231
Egyptologists, 8, 15, 27, 47
Emotions, 172

Energy Centers, 94, 99, 107,
    129, 133, 135, 144, 164,
    173, 188
Enlightenment, 8, 12, 15, 20,
    21, 23, 24, 28, 29, 36, 49,
    69, 83, 112, 113, 122,
    131, 133, 157, 185, 193,
    205, 207, 209, 210, 222,
    224, 225
Essene Gospel of Peace, 100
Essenes, 100
Ethics, 33
Ethiopia, 12, 14, 15, 16, 17,
    46
Ethiopian priests, 12, 16
Eucharist, 213
Eudoxus, 221
Evil, 58
Exercise, 211, 224, 227
Eye of Heru, 105, 158
Fear, 107, 188, 225
Feelings, 131
Feuerstein, Georg, 37, 38
Geb, 18, 37, 39, 43, 44, 212
Geography, 82
Giza, 13
Gnostic, 20, 82
Gnostic Christianity, 20
Gnostics, 83
God, 9, 22, 27, 28, 29, 30, 32,
    34, 36, 42, 43, 57, 59, 70,
    78, 83, 84, 85, 86, 87, 97,
    102, 103, 104, 119, 120,
    126, 129, 132, 146, 158,
    161, 163, 175, 176, 193,
    194, 202, 208, 213, 216,
    227, 232
Goddess, 43, 54, 70, 85, 114,
    134, 143, 195, 217, 228,
    232
Goddesses, 7, 18, 39, 174,
    211
Gods, 12, 14, 15, 18, 39, 77,
    85, 86, 211, 227
Good, 95, 96, 223
Good Association, 223
Gospels, 218
Greece, 14, 17, 24, 25, 205,
    221
Greed, 107, 188
Greek philosophy, 203
Greeks, 14, 76, 78, 83, 118,
    221
Green, 111, 114
Grimaldi, 16
Guru, 79
Haari, 227, 231
Hatha Yoga, 37, 38
Hathor, 18, 58, 118, 122,
    160, 212, 213, 217, 222
Hatred, 107, 188
Hawk, 53
Health, 4, 203, 223, 225

Heart, 107, 110, 153, 154,
    220
Heart (also see Ab, mind,
    conscience), 107, 110,
    153, 154, 220
Heaven, 12, 84, 86, 94, 218
Hekau, 36, 84, 94, 175, 185,
    224, 232
Heliopolis, 11, 221
Hermes, 1, 14, 18, 76, 82,
    84, 85, 86, 141, 175, 202
Hermes (see also Djehuti,
    Thoth), 1, 14, 18, 76, 82,
    84, 85, 86, 141, 175, 202
Hermes (see also Tehuti,
    Thoth), 14, 18
Hermetic, 83, 137, 140
Herodotus, 14, 17, 100
Heru, 11, 12, 17, 18, 24, 26,
    27, 29, 33, 38, 43, 44, 57,
    72, 79, 80, 81, 82, 83, 84,
    85, 92, 95, 105, 118, 122,
    135, 148, 152, 158, 174,
    176, 177, 185, 202, 212,
    213, 214, 217, 218, 219,
    223, 224, 227, 230, 232
Heru (see Horus), 11, 12, 17,
    18, 24, 26, 27, 29, 33, 38,
    43, 44, 57, 72, 79, 80, 81,
    82, 83, 84, 85, 92, 95,
    105, 118, 122, 135, 148,
    152, 158, 174, 176, 177,
    185, 202, 212, 213, 214,
    217, 218, 219, 223, 224,
    227, 230, 232
Hetep, 25
Hetheru, 11, 18, 27, 29, 37,
    38, 67, 80, 82, 222, 229
Hetheru (Hetheru, Hathor),
    11, 18, 27, 29, 37, 38, 67,
    80, 82, 222, 229
Hidden God, 176
Hieroglyphic Writing,
    language, 176, 202, 210
Hindu, 36, 46, 135, 154
Hinduism, 46
Hindus, 77, 83
Holy of Holies, 137, 138
Horemakhet, 56
Hor-m-Akhet, 13
Horus, 18, 43, 44, 78, 230
Hymns to Aton, 115
Ibis, 76
Ice Age, 16
Ida and Pingala, 70, 114, 135,
    136, 140
Identification, 23, 87
Illusion, 224
India, 4, 9, 14, 17, 22, 24, 25,
    26, 28, 31, 32, 35, 37, 38,
    42, 44, 46, 47, 49, 51, 53,
    54, 64, 69, 70, 115, 135,

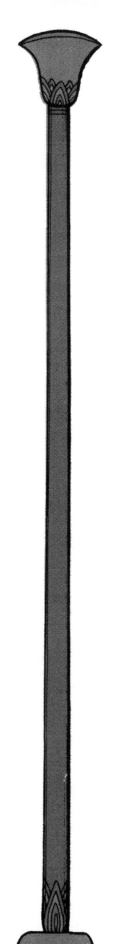

139, 176, 184, 193, 205, 209, 227, 231

Indian Yoga, 4, 22, 64, 205, 231

Indus, 24, 25, 53, 69, 205, 223, 227

Indus Valley, 24, 25, 53, 69, 205

Initiate, 204

Isis, 18, 31, 32, 43, 44, 53, 56, 62, 63, 85, 101, 102, 105, 111, 119, 121, 122, 135, 141, 142, 170, 230

Isis, See also Aset, 18, 31, 32, 43, 44, 53, 56, 62, 63, 85, 101, 102, 105, 111, 119, 121, 122, 135, 141, 142, 170

Islam, 8, 203

Jesus, 9, 103, 154, 213, 218

Jesus Christ, 213

Jews, 9, 100

Jnana Yoga, 31, 32, 105

Judaism, 8, 203

Jyotirmayananda, Swami, 36

Ka, 59

Kabbalah, 203

Kali, 44

Kali XE "Kali" position, 44

Kali Position, 44

Kamit, 8, 10, 13, 18, 48, 57, 98, 113, 176, 223, 227

Kamit (Egypt), 8, 10, 13, 18, 48, 57, 98, 113, 176, 223, 227

Kamitan, 4, 8, 9, 13, 18, 23, 34, 39, 40, 43, 44, 45, 46, 47, 53, 57, 67, 72, 82, 111, 112, 114, 115, 137, 140, 141, 176, 177, 221

Karma, 17, 23, 209, 224

Karnak, 137, 138

Kemetic, 4, 9, 18, 40, 43, 44, 45, 46, 47, 53, 111, 140, 205, 217, 228, 230, 231

Khepra, 224

Khepri, 72, 174

Ki (see also Life Force, Ra, Buto, Kundalini), 64

Kia (also see Samadhi, meditation, altered states of consciousness), 64

Kingdom, 12, 17, 29, 38, 70, 131, 218

Kingdom of Heaven, 12, 70, 131, 218

KMT (Ancient Egypt). See also Kamit, 13, 16

Know Thyself, 25

Knowledge, 102

Krishna, 70, 218

Kundalini, 4, 17, 23, 44, 49, 51, 52, 53, 54, 57, 64, 69,

70, 99, 104, 114, 136, 139, 140, 160, 162, 192

Kundalini XE "Kundalini" Yoga see also Serpent Power, 4, 49, 51, 53, 57, 69, 99, 114, 136, 140

Kush, 223, 227

Kybalion, 175, 202

Lake Victoria, 16

Latin, 82, 83

Liberation, 12

Life Force, 17, 26, 49, 54, 55, 64, 65, 66, 67, 72, 73, 80, 87, 94, 99, 103, 117, 118, 119, 131, 132, 135, 136, 139, 143, 163, 173, 175, 176, 184, 194, 195, 211

Lingam-Yoni, 46

Listening, 31, 32, 34, 105, 224

Logos, 14

Lotus, 26, 54, 161, 225

Love, 3, 19, 22, 23, 34, 107, 153, 172, 188, 209, 224

Lower Egypt, 24, 26, 46, 89

Maakheru, 177

Maat, 18, 23, 33, 76, 100, 107, 112, 115, 118, 133, 135, 140, 146, 171, 172, 209, 217, 220, 221, 223, 225, 227

MAAT, 110, 118, 172, 208, 209

Maati, 56, 174, 177

MAATI, 209

Magic, 87

Mahabharata, 22

Manetho, 17

Manetho, see also History of Manetho, 17

Mantras, 36

Mary Magdalene, 69

Matter, 216

Meditating, 31

Meditation, 2, 22, 23, 32, 33, 35, 36, 77, 104, 105, 122, 133, 151, 184, 185, 188, 189, 191, 204, 208, 210, 220, 223, 224, 225, 227, 232

Mediterranean, 42

Medu Neter, 76, 84

Memphis, 11, 89, 90, 95, 96, 221

Men-nefer, see also Het-Ka-Ptah, Memphis, 11

Mental energy, 133

Mer, 89, 90, 92, 95, 158

Merikara, 202

Mertseger (She who loves silence), 52

Metaphysics, 216

Middle East, 8, 203

Min, 122, 135, 212

Mind, 79, 118, 132, 133, 158

Moksha, 83

Mookerjee, Ajit, 42

Moon, 14, 16, 77

Morals, 221

Music, 4, 69, 175, 177, 185, 192, 230, 231, 232

Muslims, 9

Mysteries, 20, 29, 86, 102, 105, 115, 170, 205, 217

Mysticism, 4, 8, 27, 34, 111, 114, 115, 140, 205, 212, 213, 216, 222

Mythology, 8, 15, 27, 80, 120, 212

Nadis, 70

Nature, 94, 97, 103, 223, 224

Neberdjer, 57, 174, 207

Nebethet, 53, 62, 114, 140, 174, 232

Nebthet, 18, 56, 67, 126, 141

Nefer, 25, 229, 232

Nefertari, Queen, 38

Nehast, 83

Nephthys, 18, 53, 56, 62, 63, 120, 121, 122, 135, 141, 142

Net, goddess, 11, 18, 232

Neter, 8, 22, 27, 28, 29, 102, 111, 224, 227

Neterianism, 18, 46

Neters, 27, 30, 42, 104

Neteru, 38, 42, 211, 227, 230, 232

Netherworld, 39, 102

New Kingdom, 38, 50

Non-violence, 225

North East Africa . See also Egypt Ethiopia Cush, 10

North East Africa. See also Egypt Ethiopia Cush, 10

Nu, 79, 202

Nubia, 17, 57

Nubian, 57

Nubians, 14, 57

Nun, 39, 79, 174

Nun (primeval waters-unformed matter), 39, 79, 174

Nun (See also Nu), 39, 79, 174

Nut, 18, 39, 43, 44, 212

Old Testament, 9

Om, 146, 148, 150, 151, 152, 155, 157, 159, 176, 177, 185, 224, 227, 230, 231

Oneness, 172

Orion Star Constellation, 217

Orthodox, 8

Osiris, 11, 18, 43, 44, 53, 61, 79, 84, 85, 111, 121, 141, 230, 232
Pa Neter, 224, 227
Papyrus Greenfield, 54
Papyrus Qenna, 54
Patanjali, 22, 36
Paul, 52
Paut, 38
Peace (see also Hetep), 111
Persia, 14
Pert Em Heru, See also Book of the Dead, 26, 202, 213, 223
phallus, 122, 158
Phallus, 46
Pharaonic headdress, 50
Philae, 11, 35, 213
Philosophy, 2, 3, 4, 8, 15, 18, 19, 20, 24, 25, 26, 27, 29, 30, 36, 42, 49, 69, 87, 117, 130, 137, 193, 205, 207, 208, 214, 215, 220, 223, 225
Physical body, 131
Pillar of Asar, 120, 126, 141, 174
Plato, 14, 221
Plutarch, 14, 100, 101, 104, 221
Prana (also see Sekhem and Life Force), 70, 139, 151, 184
Primeval Ocean, 79
Psychic Power, 191
Psycho-spiritual consciousness, 54
Ptah, 11, 18, 96, 104, 126, 139, 163, 177, 207, 216, 224, 227
PTAH, 216
Ptahotep, 202
Puerto Rico, 4
Purity of heart (see purity of mind), 131
Pyramid, 11, 57, 202
Pyramid of Unas, 202
Pyramid Texts, 11, 57, 202
Pythagoras, 221
Qi (see also Life Force, Ra, Prana), 64
Ra, 11, 18, 35, 36, 39, 55, 58, 61, 67, 70, 72, 73, 78, 79, 80, 85, 86, 95, 96, 113, 118, 119, 134, 135, 137, 138, 139, 140, 145, 147, 151, 153, 156, 158, 161, 174, 177, 207, 211, 224, 227, 229, 232
Race, 223
Ram, 151
Ramases, 89
Ray, Sudhansu Kumar, 47
Reality, 42

Red, 46
Reflecting, 31
Reflection, 32, 107, 193
Reincarnation, 131
Religion, 4, 8, 15, 27, 29, 141, 213, 218, 219, 221, 223, 225, 230
Resurrection, 37, 79, 80, 83, 111, 121, 122, 211, 213, 217, 218, 219, 220, 223
Right action, 77
Righteousness, 33
Ritual, 23, 34
Rituals, 217
Roman, 20, 76, 82, 89
Roman Catholic, 20
Romans, 76
Rome, 221
Sages, 19, 20, 29, 69, 118, 149, 207, 212, 214, 220
Saints, 149, 214
Sais, 11, 221
Sakkara, 11, 72
Salvation, 27, 30
Salvation, See also resurrection, 27, 30
Samadhi (see also Kia, Satori), 64
Sanskrit, 12, 24, 26, 79, 158
Satori (see also Kia, Samadhi), 64
Sebai, 4, 78
Sebau, 115
Seers, 19
Sekhem, 49, 56, 67, 70, 118, 139, 143, 163, 184, 185, 186
Sekhemit, 67
Sekhmet, 56, 58, 163
Self (see Ba, soul, Spirit, Universal, Ba, Neter, Heru)., 2, 12, 23, 24, 25, 26, 27, 28, 29, 30, 31, 32, 33, 38, 43, 48, 54, 65, 66, 69, 70, 76, 77, 79, 80, 81, 87, 93, 95, 99, 102, 103, 106, 113, 119, 120, 121, 122, 129, 131, 132, 150, 152, 155, 162, 165, 172, 177, 185, 191, 206, 209, 212, 219, 224, 225
Self (seeBasoulSpiritUniversal BaNeterHorus)., 12, 23, 24, 25, 31, 32, 33, 38, 43, 76, 177, 206, 209, 212, 219, 224, 225
Sema, 3, 4, 8, 12, 24, 25, 26, 28, 38, 113, 175, 225
Sema XE "Sema" Paut, see also Egyptian Yoga, 38
Sema Tawi, 12
Semite, 16
Semitic, 16

Serpent, 1, 2, 22, 23, 35, 48, 49, 50, 51, 52, 53, 55, 56, 58, 62, 65, 66, 69, 70, 72, 82, 87, 93, 94, 97, 98, 99, 100, 104, 107, 114, 115, 118, 119, 121, 122, 123, 125, 128, 129, 130, 131, 133, 134, 135, 136, 137, 138, 139, 141, 144, 154, 160, 163, 164, 165, 166, 167, 171, 174, 175, 177, 185, 187, 188, 190, 191, 192, 193, 194, 195, 196, 225, 227
Serpent Power, 1, 2, 22, 23, 35, 48, 49, 50, 51, 52, 55, 56, 58, 65, 66, 69, 70, 72, 82, 87, 93, 94, 97, 98, 99, 100, 104, 107, 114, 115, 118, 119, 122, 123, 125, 128, 129, 130, 131, 133, 134, 135, 136, 137, 138, 139, 141, 144, 154, 163, 164, 165, 166, 167, 171, 174, 175, 177, 185, 187, 188, 190, 191, 192, 193, 194, 195, 196, 225, 227
Serpent Power (see also Kundalini and Buto), 1, 2, 22, 23, 35, 48, 49, 50, 51, 52, 55, 56, 58, 65, 66, 69, 70, 72, 82, 87, 93, 94, 97, 98, 99, 100, 104, 107, 114, 115, 118, 119, 122, 123, 125, 128, 129, 130, 131, 133, 134, 135, 136, 137, 138, 139, 141, 144, 154, 163, 164, 165, 166, 167, 171, 174, 175, 177, 185, 187, 188, 190, 191, 192, 193, 194, 195, 196, 225, 227
Serpent Power see also Kundalini Yoga, 1, 2, 22, 23, 35, 48, 49, 50, 51, 52, 55, 56, 58, 65, 66, 69, 70, 72, 82, 87, 93, 94, 97, 98, 99, 100, 104, 107, 114, 115, 118, 119, 122, 123, 125, 128, 129, 130, 131, 133, 134, 135, 136, 137, 138, 139, 141, 144, 154, 163, 164, 165, 166, 167, 171, 174, 175, 177, 185, 187, 188, 190, 191, 192, 193, 194, 195, 196, 225, 227
Set, 12, 18, 24, 26, 27, 29, 81, 82, 101, 102, 105, 115, 120, 121, 122, 136, 152, 159, 224, 225
Seti I, 33, 35, 36, 70

Seven, 69, 223
Sex, 17, 147, 148, 212
Sexual energy, 66, 149
Sexuality, 147, 172, 224
Shakti (see also Kundalini), 44, 156
Shankaracarya, 54
Shankaracarya, see also Shankara, 54
Shetaut Neter, 8, 15, 22, 27, 213
Shetaut Neter See also Egyptian Religion, 8, 15, 22, 27, 213
Shiva, 44, 45, 156, 158, 162
Shiva XE "Shiva" and Shakti, 44
Shu (air and space), 39, 158, 193
Silence, 225
Simplicity, 110, 111
Sirius, 217
Sma, 24, 26, 113
Smai, 8, 12, 22, 24, 25, 26, 27, 30, 38, 48, 113
Smai Tawi, 22, 24, 25, 26, 30, 38, 48
Solon, 221
Soul, 8, 15, 27, 30, 65, 102, 132, 133, 162, 224
Sphinx, 13, 29, 48, 49, 50, 56, 69, 162
Spinal twist, 39
Spirit, 27, 36, 54, 67, 77, 87, 132, 173, 176
Spiritual discipline, 204
Study, 28, 77, 193, 223, 225
Sublimation, 66, 147, 212
Sudan, 10
Sufi, 64
Sufi, see also Sufism, 64
Sumer, 24, 25
Sun, 84, 119, 135
Sun Gods, 135
Sundisk, 35, 39, 121
Supreme Being, 17, 22, 28, 45, 78, 119, 207, 217
Survival, 107, 172, 188
Sushumna, 70, 114, 136, 140
Swami, 36
Swami Jyotirmayananda, 36
Syria, 120
Tantra, 42, 147, 212
Tantra Yoga, 35, 42, 147, 212
Tantric Yoga, 19, 22, 23
Tanzania, 16
Tao, 70, 158
Taoism, 203
Tawi, 8, 12, 22, 25, 38, 113
Tefnut, 56, 67, 174
Tefnut (moisture), 56, 67, 174
Tem, 135

Temple, 111
Temple XE "Temple" of Aset, 111
Temple of Aset, 4, 31, 32, 35, 100, 101
Temple of Aset, 124
Temple of Aset, 137
Temple of Aset, 142
Temple of Aset, 223
Temple of Aset, 223
Thales, 221
The Absolute, 207
The God, 70, 211, 227
The Gods, 211, 227
The Hymns of Amun, 17
The Pyramid Texts, 17, 57
The Self, 54, 65, 130
The way, 146, 148, 151, 155, 157, 159, 162
Thebes, 11, 35, 207, 210
Themis, 18
Thoth, 18, 78, 110
Thoughts (see also Mind), 33, 156
Thrice Greatest Hermes, 202
Time, 223
Tobacco, 122
Tomb, 35, 36, 38, 72, 210, 232
Tomb of Seti I, 35, 36, 210, 232
Tree, 69
Tree of Life, 69
Triad, 207
Trilinga, 45
Trinity, 11, 137, 141, 185, 207, 213, 227, 232
Truth, 8, 225
Tutankhamon, 50, 59
Tutankhamun, 50
Tutankhamun, Pharaoh, 50
Unas, 202
Understanding, 118, 144, 224
union, 8
Universal Consciousness, 27, 28, 54, 147, 212
Upanishads, 214
Upper Egypt, 24, 26, 46
Uraeus, 23, 62, 70, 99, 104, 118, 119, 135, 160, 161, 162, 176, 184, 185
Vedanta, 20, 28, 29, 31, 32, 36, 103, 105
Vedic, 205
Vegetarianism, 223
Veil, 170
Veil of Aset, 170
Virtues, 107, 223
Waset, 11, 35, 52, 207
Water, 147
Western Culture, 225
Wheat, 111
Whirling Dervishes (see also ! Kung of Africa), 64

Wisdom, 22, 23, 31, 32, 35, 82, 83, 87, 191, 202, 207, 211, 223, 225
Wisdom (also see Djehuti), 23, 31, 32, 35, 202, 207, 211, 223, 225
Wisdom (also see Djehuti, Aset), 22, 23, 31, 32, 35, 82, 83, 87, 191, 202, 207, 211, 223, 225
Wisdom teachings, 31, 32
Wisdom texts, 82
Words of power, 36
Yoga, 2, 3, 4, 8, 12, 15, 19, 20, 22, 23, 24, 25, 26, 27, 28, 29, 31, 32, 35, 37, 38, 42, 45, 48, 49, 53, 65, 66, 69, 70, 80, 99, 100, 103, 107, 122, 123, 124, 125, 129, 131, 136, 140, 171, 175, 188, 191, 193, 194, 195, 203, 204, 205, 209, 211, 212, 214, 216, 220, 223, 225, 227, 228, 229, 230, 231
Yoga of Action, 23, 66
Yoga of Devotion (see Yoga of Divine Love), 19, 22, 23, 66
Yoga of Divine Love (see Yoga of Devotion), 23
Yoga of Meditation, 19, 22, 23, 66
Yoga of Selfless Action. See also Yoga of Righteous, 19, 22, 23
Yoga of Wisdom, 31
Yoga of Wisdom (see also Jnana Yoga), 19, 22, 23, 31, 66
Yoga Sutra, 22
Yogic, 22, 37
Zen Meditation (see also Samadhi, Kia), 64
Zeus, 18

1. *EGYPTIAN YOGA: THE PHILOSOPHY OF ENLIGHTENMENT* An original, fully illustrated work, including hieroglyphs, detailing the meaning of the Egyptian mysteries, tantric yoga, psycho-spiritual and physical exercises. Egyptian Yoga is a guide to the practice of the highest spiritual philosophy which leads to absolute freedom from human misery and to immortality. It is well known by scholars that Egyptian philosophy is the basis of Western and Middle Eastern religious philosophies such as *Christianity, Islam, Judaism,* the *Kabala*, and Greek philosophy, but what about Indian philosophy, Yoga and Taoism? What were the original teachings? How can they be practiced today? What is the source of pain and suffering in the world and what is the solution? Discover the deepest mysteries of the mind and universe within and outside of your self. 8.5" X 11" ISBN: 1-884564-01-1 Soft $19.95

2. *EGYPTIAN YOGA: African Religion Volume 2-* Theban Theology U.S. In this long awaited sequel to *Egyptian Yoga: The Philosophy of Enlightenment* you will take a fascinating and enlightening journey back in time and discover the teachings which constituted the epitome of Ancient Egyptian spiritual wisdom. What are the disciplines which lead to the fulfillment of all desires? Delve into the three states of consciousness (waking, dream and deep sleep) and the fourth state which transcends them all, Neberdjer, "The Absolute." These teachings of the city of Waset (Thebes) were the crowning achievement of the Sages of Ancient Egypt. They establish the standard mystical keys for understanding the profound mystical symbolism of the Triad of human consciousness. ISBN 1-884564-39-9 $23.95

3. *THE KEMETIC DIET: GUIDE TO HEALTH, DIET AND FASTING* Health issues have always been important to human beings since the beginning of time. The earliest records of history show that the art of healing was held in high esteem since the time of Ancient Egypt. In the early 20th century, medical doctors had almost attained the status of sainthood by the promotion of the idea that they alone were "scientists" while other healing modalities and traditional healers who did not follow the "scientific method' were nothing but superstitious, ignorant charlatans who at best would take the money of their clients and at worst kill them with the unscientific "snake oils" and "irrational theories". In the late 20th century, the failure of the modern medical establishment's ability to lead the general public to good health, promoted the move by many in society towards "alternative medicine". Alternative medicine disciplines are those healing modalities which do not adhere to the philosophy of allopathic medicine. Allopathic medicine is what medical doctors practice by an large. It is the theory that disease is caused by agencies outside the body such as bacteria, viruses or physical means which affect the body. These can therefore be treated by medicines and therapies The natural healing method began in the absence of extensive technologies with the idea that all the answers for health may be found in nature or rather, the deviation from nature. Therefore, the health of the body can be restored by correcting the aberration and thereby restoring balance. This is the area that will be covered in this volume. Allopathic techniques have their place in the art of healing. However, we should not forget that the body is a grand achievement of the spirit and built into it is the capacity to maintain itself and heal itself. Ashby, Muata ISBN: 1-884564-49-6 $28.95

4. INITIATION INTO EGYPTIAN YOGA Shedy: Spiritual discipline or program, to go deeply into the mysteries, to study the mystery teachings and literature profoundly, to penetrate the mysteries. You will learn about the mysteries of initiation into the teachings and practice of Yoga and how to become an Initiate of the mystical sciences. This insightful manual is the first in a series which introduces you to the goals of daily spiritual and yoga practices: Meditation, Diet, Words of Power and the ancient wisdom teachings. 8.5" X 11" ISBN 1-884564-02-X   Soft Cover $24.95 U.S.

5. *THE AFRICAN ORIGINS OF CIVILIZATION, RELIGION AND YOGA SPIRITUALITY AND ETHICS PHILOSOPHY* HARD COVER EDITION Part 1, Part 2, Part 3 in one volume 683 Pages Hard Cover First Edition Three volumes in one. Over the past several years I have been asked to put together in one volume the most important evidences showing the correlations and common teachings between Kamitan (Ancient Egyptian) culture and religion and that of India. The questions of the history of Ancient Egypt, and the latest archeological evidences showing civilization and culture in Ancient Egypt and its spread to other countries, has intrigued many scholars as well as mystics over the years. Also, the possibility that Ancient Egyptian Priests and Priestesses migrated to Greece, India and other countries to carry on the traditions of the Ancient Egyptian Mysteries, has been speculated over the years as well. In chapter 1 of the book *Egyptian Yoga The Philosophy of Enlightenment,* 1995, I first introduced the deepest comparison between Ancient Egypt and India that had been brought forth up to that time. Now, in the year 2001 this new book, *THE AFRICAN ORIGINS OF CIVILIZATION, MYSTICAL RELIGION AND YOGA PHILOSOPHY,* more fully

explores the motifs, symbols and philosophical correlations between Ancient Egyptian and Indian mysticism and clearly shows not only that Ancient Egypt and India were connected culturally but also spiritually. How does this knowledge help the spiritual aspirant? This discovery has great importance for the Yogis and mystics who follow the philosophy of Ancient Egypt and the mysticism of India. It means that India has a longer history and heritage than was previously understood. It shows that the mysteries of Ancient Egypt were essentially a yoga tradition which did not die but rather developed into the modern day systems of Yoga technology of India. It further shows that African culture developed Yoga Mysticism earlier than any other civilization in history. All of this expands our understanding of the unity of culture and the deep legacy of Yoga, which stretches into the distant past, beyond the Indus Valley civilization, the earliest known high culture in India as well as the Vedic tradition of Aryan culture. Therefore, Yoga culture and mysticism is the oldest known tradition of spiritual development and Indian mysticism is an extension of the Ancient Egyptian mysticism. By understanding the legacy which Ancient Egypt gave to India the mysticism of India is better understood and by comprehending the heritage of Indian Yoga, which is rooted in Ancient Egypt the Mysticism of Ancient Egypt is also better understood. This expanded understanding allows us to prove the underlying kinship of humanity, through the common symbols, motifs and philosophies which are not disparate and confusing teachings but in reality expressions of the same study of truth through metaphysics and mystical realization of Self. (HARD COVER) ISBN: 1-884564-50-X $45.00 U.S.   81/2" X 11"

6. *AFRICAN ORIGINS BOOK 1 PART 1* African Origins of African Civilization, Religion, Yoga Mysticism and Ethics Philosophy-Soft Cover $24.95 ISBN: 1-884564-55-0

7. *AFRICAN ORIGINS BOOK 2 PART 2* African Origins of Western Civilization, Religion and Philosophy (Soft) -Soft Cover $24.95 ISBN: 1-884564-56-9

8. *EGYPT AND INDIA* AFRICAN ORIGINS OF *Eastern Civilization, Religion, Yoga Mysticism and Philosophy*-Soft Cover $29.95 (Soft) ISBN: 1-884564-57-7

9. *THE MYSTERIES OF ISIS: **The Ancient Egyptian Philosophy of Self-Realization*** - There are several paths to discover the Divine and the mysteries of the higher Self. This volume details the mystery teachings of the goddess Aset (Isis) from Ancient Egypt- the path of wisdom. It includes the teachings of her temple and the disciplines that are enjoined for the initiates of the temple of Aset as they were given in ancient times. Also, this book includes the teachings of the main myths of Aset that lead a human being to spiritual enlightenment and immortality. Through the study of ancient myth and the illumination of initiatic understanding the idea of God is expanded from the mythological comprehension to the metaphysical. Then this metaphysical understanding is related to you, the student, so as to begin understanding your true divine nature. ISBN 1-884564-24-0 $22.99

10. *EGYPTIAN PROVERBS:* collection of —Ancient Egyptian Proverbs and Wisdom Teachings -How to live according to MAAT Philosophy. Beginning Meditation. All proverbs are indexed for easy searches. For the first time in one volume, ——Ancient Egyptian Proverbs, wisdom teachings and meditations, fully illustrated with hieroglyphic text and symbols. EGYPTIAN PROVERBS is a unique collection of knowledge and wisdom which you can put into practice today and transform your life. $14.95 U.S   ISBN: 1-884564-00-3

11. *GOD OF LOVE: THE PATH OF DIVINE LOVE The Process of Mystical Transformation and The Path of Divine Love*   This Volume focuses on the ancient wisdom teachings of "Neter Merri" – the Ancient Egyptian philosophy of Divine Love and how to use them in a scientific process for self-transformation. Love is one of the most powerful human emotions. It is also the source of Divine feeling that unifies God and the individual human being. When love is fragmented and diminished by egoism the Divine connection is lost. The Ancient tradition of Neter Merri leads human beings back to their Divine connection, allowing them to discover their innate glorious self that is actually Divine and immortal. This volume will detail the process of transformation from ordinary consciousness to cosmic consciousness through the integrated practice of the teachings and the path of Devotional Love toward the Divine. 5.5"x 8.5" ISBN 1-884564-11-9 $22.95

12. *INTRODUCTION TO MAAT PHILOSOPHY: Spiritual Enlightenment Through the Path of Virtue* Known as Karma Yoga in India, the teachings of MAAT for living virtuously and with orderly wisdom are explained and the student is to begin practicing the precepts of Maat in daily life so as to promote the process of purification of the heart in preparation for the judgment of the soul. This judgment will be understood not as an event that will occur at the time of death but as an event that occurs continuously, at every moment in the life of the individual. The student will learn how to

become allied with the forces of the Higher Self and to thereby begin cleansing the mind (heart) of impurities so as to attain a higher vision of reality. ISBN 1-884564-20-8 $22.99

13.   *MEDITATION The Ancient Egyptian Path to Enlightenment*   Many people do not know about the rich history of meditation practice in Ancient Egypt. This volume outlines the theory of meditation and presents the Ancient Egyptian Hieroglyphic text which give instruction as to the nature of the mind and its three modes of expression. It also presents the texts which give instruction on the practice of meditation for spiritual Enlightenment and unity with the Divine. This volume allows the reader to begin practicing meditation by explaining, in easy to understand terms, the simplest form of meditation and working up to the most advanced form which was practiced in ancient times and which is still practiced by yogis around the world in modern times. ISBN 1-884564-27-7 $22.99

14.   *THE GLORIOUS LIGHT MEDITATION* TECHNIQUE OF ANCIENT EGYPT New for the year 2000. This volume is based on the earliest known instruction in history given for the practice of formal meditation. Discovered by Dr. Muata Ashby, it is inscribed on the walls of the Tomb of Seti I in Thebes Egypt. This volume details the philosophy and practice of this unique system of meditation originated in Ancient Egypt and the earliest practice of meditation known in the world which occurred in the most advanced African Culture. ISBN: 1-884564-15-1 $16.95 (PB)

15.   *THE SERPENT POWER: The Ancient Egyptian Mystical Wisdom of the Inner Life Force.*   This Volume specifically deals with the latent life Force energy of the universe and in the human body, its control and sublimation. How to develop the Life Force energy of the subtle body. This Volume will introduce the esoteric wisdom of the science of how virtuous living acts in a subtle and mysterious way to cleanse the latent psychic energy conduits and vortices of the spiritual body. ISBN 1-884564-19-4 $22.95

16.   *EGYPTIAN YOGA The Postures of The Gods and Goddesses* Discover the physical postures and exercises practiced thousands of years ago in Ancient Egypt which are today known as Yoga exercises. Discover the history of the postures and how they were transferred from Ancient Egypt in Africa to India through Buddhist Tantrism. Then practice the postures as you discover the mythic teaching that originally gave birth to the postures and was practiced by the Ancient Egyptian priests and priestesses. This work is based on the pictures and teachings from the Creation story of Ra, The Asarian Resurrection Myth and the carvings and reliefs from various Temples in Ancient Egypt 8.5" X 11" ISBN 1-884564-10-0 Soft Cover $21.95   Exercise video $20

17.   *SACRED SEXUALITY: EGYPTIAN TANTRA YOGA: The Art of Sex* Sublimation and Universal Consciousness This Volume will expand on the male and female principles within the human body and in the universe and further detail the sublimation of sexual energy into spiritual energy. The student will study the deities Min and Hathor, Asar and Aset, Geb and Nut and discover the mystical implications for a practical spiritual discipline. This Volume will also focus on the Tantric aspects of Ancient Egyptian and Indian mysticism, the purpose of sex and the mystical teachings of sexual sublimation which lead to self-knowledge and Enlightenment. 5.5"x 8.5" ISBN 1-884564-03-8 $24.95

18.   *AFRICAN RELIGION Volume 4: ASARIAN THEOLOGY: RESURRECTING OSIRIS* The path of Mystical Awakening and the Keys to Immortality NEW REVISED AND EXPANDED EDITION! The Ancient Sages created stories based on human and superhuman beings whose struggles, aspirations, needs and desires ultimately lead them to discover their true Self. The myth of Aset, Asar and Heru is no exception in this area. While there is no one source where the entire story may be found, pieces of it are inscribed in various ancient Temples walls, tombs, steles and papyri. For the first time available, the complete myth of Asar, Aset and Heru has been compiled from original Ancient Egyptian, Greek and Coptic Texts. This epic myth has been richly illustrated with reliefs from the Temple of Heru at Edfu, the Temple of Aset at Philae, the Temple of Asar at Abydos, the Temple of Hathor at Denderah and various papyri, inscriptions and reliefs.   Discover the myth which inspired the teachings of the *Shetaut Neter* (Egyptian Mystery System - Egyptian Yoga) and the Egyptian Book of Coming Forth By Day. Also, discover the three levels of Ancient Egyptian Religion, how to understand the mysteries of the Duat or Astral World and how to discover the abode of the Supreme in the Amenta, *The Other World*   The ancient religion of Asar, Aset and Heru, if properly understood, contains all of the elements necessary to lead the sincere aspirant to attain immortality through inner self-discovery. This volume presents the entire myth and explores the main mystical themes and rituals associated with the myth for understating human existence, creation and the way to achieve spiritual emancipation - *Resurrection.* The Asarian myth is so powerful that it influenced and is still having an effect on the major world religions. Discover the

origins and mystical meaning of the Christian Trinity, the Eucharist ritual and the ancient origin of the birthday of Jesus Christ. Soft Cover ISBN: 1-884564-27-5 $24.95

19. *THE EGYPTIAN BOOK OF THE DEAD MYSTICISM OF THE PERT EM HERU* " I Know myself, I know myself, I am One With God!–From the Pert Em Heru "The Ru Pert em Heru" or "Ancient Egyptian Book of The Dead," or "Book of Coming Forth By Day" as it is more popularly known, has fascinated the world since the successful translation of Ancient Egyptian hieroglyphic scripture over 150 years ago. The astonishing writings in it reveal that the Ancient Egyptians believed in life after death and in an ultimate destiny to discover the Divine. The elegance and aesthetic beauty of the hieroglyphic text itself has inspired many see it as an art form in and of itself. But is there more to it than that? Did the Ancient Egyptian wisdom contain more than just aphorisms and hopes of eternal life beyond death? In this volume Dr. Muata Ashby, the author of over 25 books on Ancient Egyptian Yoga Philosophy has produced a new translation of the original texts which uncovers a mystical teaching underlying the sayings and rituals instituted by the Ancient Egyptian Sages and Saints. "Once the philosophy of Ancient Egypt is understood as a mystical tradition instead of as a religion or primitive mythology, it reveals its secrets which if practiced today will lead anyone to discover the glory of spiritual self-discovery. The Pert em Heru is in every way comparable to the Indian Upanishads or the Tibetan Book of the Dead." $28.95   ISBN# 1-884564-28-3 Size: 8½" X 11

20. *African Religion VOL. 1- ANUNIAN THEOLOGY THE MYSTERIES OF RA* The Philosophy of Anu and The Mystical Teachings of The Ancient Egyptian Creation Myth Discover the mystical teachings contained in the Creation Myth and the gods and goddesses who brought creation and human beings into existence. The Creation myth of Anu is the source of Anunian Theology but also of the other main theological systems of Ancient Egypt that also influenced other world religions including Christianity, Hinduism and Buddhism. The Creation Myth holds the key to understanding the universe and for attaining spiritual Enlightenment. ISBN: 1-884564-38-0 $19.95

21. *African Religion VOL 3: Memphite Theology: MYSTERIES OF MIND* Mystical Psychology & Mental Health for Enlightenment and Immortality based on the Ancient Egyptian Philosophy of Menefer -Mysticism of Ptah, Egyptian Physics and Yoga Metaphysics and the Hidden properties of Matter.   This volume uncovers the mystical psychology of the Ancient Egyptian wisdom teachings centering on the philosophy of the Ancient Egyptian city of Menefer (Memphite Theology). How to understand the mind and how to control the senses and lead the mind to health, clarity and mystical self-discovery. This Volume will also go deeper into the philosophy of God as creation and will explore the concepts of modern science and how they correlate with ancient teachings. This Volume will lay the ground work for the understanding of the philosophy of universal consciousness and the initiatic/yogic insight into who or what is God? ISBN 1-884564-07-0 $22.95

22. *AFRICAN RELIGION VOLUME 5: THE GODDESS AND THE EGYPTIAN MYSTERIESTHE PATH OF THE GODDESS THE GODDESS PATH* The Secret Forms of the Goddess and the Rituals of Resurrection The Supreme Being may be worshipped as father or as mother. *Ushet Rekhat* or *Mother Worship*, is the spiritual process of worshipping the Divine in the form of the Divine Goddess. It celebrates the most important forms of the Goddess including *Nathor, Maat, Aset, Arat, Amentet and Hathor* and explores their mystical meaning as well as the rising of *Sirius*, the star of Aset (Aset) and the new birth of Hor (Heru). The end of the year is a time of reckoning, reflection and engendering a new or renewed positive movement toward attaining spiritual Enlightenment. The Mother Worship devotional meditation ritual, performed on five days during the month of December and on New Year's Eve, is based on the Ushet Rekhit. During the ceremony, the cosmic forces, symbolized by Sirius - and the constellation of Orion ---, are harnessed through the understanding and devotional attitude of the participant. This propitiation draws the light of wisdom and health to all those who share in the ritual, leading to prosperity and wisdom. $14.95 ISBN 1-884564-18-6

23. *THE MYSTICAL JOURNEY FROM JESUS TO CHRIST* Discover the ancient Egyptian origins of Christianity before the Catholic Church and learn the mystical teachings given by Jesus to assist all humanity in becoming Christlike. Discover the secret meaning of the Gospels that were discovered in Egypt. Also discover how and why so many Christian churches came into being. Discover that the Bible still holds the keys to mystical realization even though its original writings were changed by the church. Discover how to practice the original teachings of Christianity which leads to the Kingdom of Heaven. $24.95   ISBN# 1-884564-05-4 size: 8½" X 11"

24. *THE STORY OF ASAR, ASET AND HERU:* An Ancient Egyptian Legend (For Children)   Now for the first time, the most ancient myth of Ancient Egypt comes alive for children. Inspired by the books *The Asarian Resurrection: The Ancient Egyptian Bible* and *The Mystical Teachings of The Asarian Resurrection, The Story of Asar, Aset and Heru* is an easy to understand and thrilling tale which inspired the children of Ancient Egypt to aspire to greatness and righteousness.   If you and your child have enjoyed stories like *The Lion King* and *Star Wars you will love The Story of Asar, Aset and Heru.* Also, if you know the story of Jesus and Krishna you will discover than Ancient Egypt had a similar myth and that this myth carries important spiritual teachings for living a fruitful and fulfilling life.   This book may be used along with *The Parents Guide To The Asarian Resurrection Myth: How to Teach Yourself and Your Child the Principles of Universal Mystical Religion.* The guide provides some background to the Asarian Resurrection myth and it also gives insight into the mystical teachings contained in it which you may introduce to your child. It is designed for parents who wish to grow spiritually with their children and it serves as an introduction for those who would like to study the Asarian Resurrection Myth in depth and to practice its teachings. 8.5" X 11"   ISBN: 1-884564-31-3 $12.95

25. *THE PARENTS GUIDE TO THE AUSARIAN RESURRECTION MYTH:*   How to Teach Yourself and Your Child the Principles of Universal Mystical Religion.   This insightful manual brings for the timeless wisdom of the ancient through the Ancient Egyptian myth of Asar, Aset and Heru and the mystical teachings contained in it for parents who want to guide their children to understand and practice the teachings of mystical spirituality. This manual may be used with the children's storybook *The Story of Asar, Aset and Heru* by Dr. Muata Abhaya Ashby.   ISBN: 1-884564-30-5 $16.95

26. *HEALING THE CRIMINAL HEART.* Introduction to Maat Philosophy, Yoga and Spiritual Redemption Through the Path of Virtue   Who is a criminal? Is there such a thing as a criminal heart? What is the source of evil and sinfulness and is there any way to rise above it? Is there redemption for those who have committed sins, even the worst crimes?   Ancient Egyptian mystical psychology holds important answers to these questions. Over ten thousand years ago mystical psychologists, the Sages of Ancient Egypt, studied and charted the human mind and spirit and laid out a path which will lead to spiritual redemption, prosperity and Enlightenment.   This introductory volume brings forth the teachings of the Asarian Resurrection, the most important myth of Ancient Egypt, with relation to the faults of human existence: anger, hatred, greed, lust, animosity, discontent, ignorance, egoism jealousy, bitterness, and a myriad of psycho-spiritual ailments which keep a human being in a state of negativity and adversity   ISBN: 1-884564-17-8 $15.95

27. *TEMPLE RITUAL OF THE ANCIENT EGYPTIAN MYSTERIES--THEATER & DRAMA OF THE ANCIENT EGYPTIAN MYSTERIES*: Details the practice of the mysteries and ritual program of the temple and the philosophy an practice of the ritual of the mysteries, its purpose and execution. Featuring the Ancient Egyptian stage play-"The Enlightenment of Hathor' Based on an Ancient Egyptian Drama, The original Theater -Mysticism of the Temple of Hetheru 1-884564-14-3 $19.95 By Dr. Muata Ashby

28. *GUIDE TO PRINT ON DEMAND: SELF-PUBLISH FOR PROFIT,* SPIRITUAL FULFILLMENT AND SERVICE TO HUMANITY Everyone asks us how we produced so many books in such a short time. Here are the secrets to writing and producing books that uplift humanity and how to get them printed for a fraction of the regular cost. Anyone can become an author even if they have limited funds. All that is necessary is the willingness to learn how the printing and book business work and the desire to follow the special instructions given here for preparing your manuscript format. Then you take your work directly to the non-traditional companies who can produce your books for less than the traditional book printer can. ISBN: 1-884564-40-2 $16.95 U. S.

29. *Egyptian Mysteries: Vol. 1,* Shetaut Neter What are the Mysteries? For thousands of years the spiritual tradition of Ancient Egypt, *Shetaut Neter,* "The Egyptian Mysteries," "The Secret Teachings," have fascinated, tantalized and amazed the world. At one time exalted and recognized as the highest culture of the world, by Africans, Europeans, Asiatics, Hindus, Buddhists and other cultures of the ancient world, in time it was shunned by the emerging orthodox world religions. Its temples desecrated, its philosophy maligned, its tradition spurned, its philosophy dormant in the mystical *Medu Neter,* the mysterious hieroglyphic texts which hold the secret symbolic meaning that has scarcely been discerned up to now.   What are the secrets of *Nehast* {spiritual awakening and emancipation, resurrection}. More than just a literal translation, this volume is for awakening to the secret code *Shetitu* of the teaching which was not deciphered by Egyptologists, nor could be understood by ordinary spiritualists. This book is a reinstatement of the original science made

available for our times, to the reincarnated followers of Ancient Egyptian culture and the prospect of spiritual freedom to break the bonds of *Khemn*, "ignorance," and slavery to evil forces: *Såaa* . ISBN: 1-884564-41-0 $19.99

30. *EGYPTIAN MYSTERIES VOL 2:* Dictionary of Gods and Goddesses This book is about the mystery of neteru, the gods and goddesses of Ancient Egypt (Kamit, Kemet). Neteru means "Gods and Goddesses." But the Neterian teaching of Neteru represents more than the usual limited modern day concept of "divinities" or "spirits." The Neteru of Kamit are also metaphors, cosmic principles and vehicles for the enlightening teachings of Shetaut Neter (Ancient Egyptian-African Religion). Actually they are the elements for one of the most advanced systems of spirituality ever conceived in human history. Understanding the concept of neteru provides a firm basis for spiritual evolution and the pathway for viable culture, peace on earth and a healthy human society.   Why is it important to have gods and goddesses in our lives? In order for spiritual evolution to be possible, once a human being has accepted that there is existence after death and there is a transcendental being who exists beyond time and space knowledge, human beings need a connection to that which transcends the ordinary experience of human life in time and space and a means to understand the transcendental reality beyond the mundane reality. ISBN: 1-884564-23-2 $21.95

31. *EGYPTIAN MYSTERIES VOL. 3* The Priests and Priestesses of Ancient Egypt This volume details the path of Neterian priesthood, the joys, challenges and rewards of advanced Neterian life, the teachings that allowed the priests and priestesses to manage the most long lived civilization in human history and how that path can be adopted today; for those who want to tread the path of the Clergy of Shetaut Neter. ISBN: 1-884564-53-4 $24.95

32. *The War of Heru and Set:* The Struggle of Good and Evil for Control of the World and The Human Soul This volume contains a novelized version of the Asarian Resurrection myth that is based on the actual scriptures presented in the Book Asarian Religion (old name –Resurrecting Osiris). This volume is prepared in the form of a screenplay and can be easily adapted to be used as a stage play. Spiritual seeking is a mythic journey that has many emotional highs and lows, ecstasies and depressions, victories and frustrations. This is the War of Life that is played out in the myth as the struggle of Heru and Set and those are mythic characters that represent the human Higher and Lower self. How to understand the war and emerge victorious in the journey o life? The ultimate victory and fulfillment can be experienced, which is not changeable or lost in time. The purpose of myth is to convey the wisdom of life through the story of divinities who show the way to overcome the challenges and foibles of life. In this volume the feelings and emotions of the characters of the myth have been highlighted to show the deeply rich texture of the Ancient Egyptian myth. This myth contains deep spiritual teachings and insights into the nature of self, of God and the mysteries of life and the means to discover the true meaning of life and thereby achieve the true purpose of life. To become victorious in the battle of life means to become the King (or Queen) of Egypt.Have you seen movies like The Lion King, Hamlet, The Odyssey, or The Little Buddha? These have been some of the most popular movies in modern times. The Sema Institute of Yoga is dedicated to researching and presenting the wisdom and culture of ancient Africa. The Script is designed to be produced as a motion picture but may be addapted for the theater as well. $21.95   copyright 1998 By Dr. Muata Ashby ISBN 1-8840564-44-5

33. *AFRICAN DIONYSUS: FROM EGYPT TO GREECE:* The Kamitan Origins of Greek Culture and Religion ISBN: 1-884564-47-X   FROM EGYPT TO GREECE This insightful manual is a reference to Ancient Egyptian mythology and philosophy and its correlation to what later became known as Greek and Rome mythology and philosophy. It outlines the basic tenets of the mythologies and shoes the ancient origins of Greek culture in Ancient Egypt. This volume also documents the origins of the Greek alphabet in Egypt as well as Greek religion, myth and philosophy of the gods and goddesses from Egypt from the myth of Atlantis and archaic period with the Minoans to the Classical period. This volume also acts as a resource for Colleges students who would like to set up fraternities and sororities based on the original Ancient Egyptian principles of Sheti and Maat philosophy. ISBN: 1-884564-47-X $22.95 U.S.

34. *THE FORTY TWO PRECEPTS OF MAAT, THE PHILOSOPHY OF RIGHTEOUS ACTION AND THE ANCIENT EGYPTIAN WISDOM TEXTS* <u>ADVANCED STUDIES</u> This manual is designed for use with the 1998 Maat Philosophy Class conducted by Dr. Muata Ashby. This is a detailed study of Maat Philosophy. It contains a compilation of the 42 laws or precepts of Maat and the corresponding principles which they represent along with the teachings of the ancient Egyptian Sages relating to each. Maat philosophy was the basis of Ancient Egyptian society and government as well as the heart of Ancient Egyptian myth and spirituality. Maat is at once a goddess, a cosmic force and a living social doctrine, which promotes social harmony and thereby paves the way for spiritual evolution in all levels of society. ISBN: 1-884564-48-8 $16.95 U.S.

35.   *THE SECRET LOTUS: Poetry of Enlightenment*
Discover the mystical sentiment of the Kemetic teaching as expressed through the poetry of Sebai Muata Ashby. The teaching of spiritual awakening is uniquely experienced when the poetic sensibility is present. This first volume contains the poems written between 1996 and 2003. **1-884564--16 -X $16.99**

36. The Ancient Egyptian Buddha: The Ancient Egyptian Origins of Buddhism
This book is a compilation of several sections of a larger work, a book by the name of African Origins of Civilization, Religion, Yoga Mysticism and Ethics Philosophy. It also contains some additional evidences not contained in the larger work that demonstrate the correlation between Ancient Egyptian Religion and Buddhism. This book is one of several compiled short volumes that has been compiled so as to facilitate access to specific subjects contained in the larger work which is over 680 pages long. These short and small volumes have been specifically designed to cover one subject in a brief and low cost format. This present volume, The Ancient Egyptian Buddha: The Ancient Egyptian Origins of Buddhism, formed one subject in the larger work; actually it was one chapter of the larger work. However, this volume has some new additional evidences and comparisons of Buddhist and Neterian (Ancient Egyptian) philosophies not previously discussed. It was felt that this subject needed to be discussed because even in the early 21st century, the idea persists that Buddhism originated only in India independently. Yet there is ample evidence from ancient writings and perhaps more importantly, iconographical evidences from the Ancient Egyptians and early Buddhists themselves that prove otherwise. This handy volume has been designed to be accessible to young adults and all others who would like to have an easy reference with documentation on this important subject. This is an important subject because the frame of reference with which we look at a culture depends strongly on our conceptions about its origins. in this case, if we look at the Buddhism as an Asiatic religion we would treat it and it's culture in one way. If we id as African [Ancient Egyptian] we not only would see it in a different light but we also must ascribe Africa with a glorious legacy that matches any other culture in human history and gave rise to one of the present day most important religious philosophies. We would also look at the culture and philosophies of the Ancient Egyptians as having African insights that offer us greater depth into the Buddhist philosophies. Those insights inform our knowledge about other African traditions and we can also begin to understand in a deeper way the effect of Ancient Egyptian culture on African culture and also on the Asiatic as well. We would also be able to discover the glorious and wondrous teaching of mystical philosophy that Ancient Egyptian Shetaut Neter religion offers, that is as powerful as any other mystic system of spiritual philosophy in the world today.

37. The Death of American Empire: Neo-conservatism, Theocracy, Economic Imperialism, Environmental Disaster and the Collapse of Civilization
This work is a collection of essays relating to social and economic, leadership, and ethics, ecological and religious issues that are facing the world today in order to understand the course of history that has led humanity to its present condition and then arrive at positive solutions that will lead to better outcomes for all humanity. It surveys the development and decline of major empires throughout history and focuses on the creation of American Empire along with the social, political and economic policies that led to the prominence of the United States of America as a Superpower including the rise of the political control of the neo-con political philosophy including militarism and the military industrial complex in American politics and the rise of the religious right into and American Theocracy movement. This volume details, through historical and current events, the psychology behind the dominance of western culture in world politics through the "Superpower Syndrome Mandatory Conflict Complex" that drives the Superpower culture to establish itself above all others and then act hubristically to dominate world culture through legitimate influences as well as coercion, media censorship and misinformation leading to international hegemony and world conflict. This volume also details the financial policies that gave rise to American prominence in the global economy, especially after World War II, and promoted American preeminence over the world economy through Globalization as well as the environmental policies, including the oil economy, that are promoting degradation of the world ecology and contribute to the decline of America as an Empire culture. This volume finally explores the factors pointing to the decline of the American Empire economy and imperial power and what to expect in the aftermath of American prominence and how to survive the decline while at the same time promoting policies and social-economic-religious-political changes that are needed in order to promote the emergence of a beneficial and sustainable culture.

38. The African Origins of Hatha Yoga: And its Ancient Mystical Teaching
The subject of this present volume, The Ancient Egyptian Origins of Yoga Postures, formed one subject in the larger works, African Origins of Civilization Religion, Yoga Mysticism and Ethics Philosophy and the Book Egypt and India is the section of the book African Origins of Civilization. Those works contain the collection of all correlations between Ancient Egypt and India. This volume also contains some additional information not contained in the previous work. It was felt that this subject needed to be discussed more

directly, being treated in one volume, as opposed to being contained in the larger work along with other subjects, because even in the early 21st century, the idea persists that the Yoga and specifically, Yoga Postures, were invented and developed only in India. The Ancient Egyptians were peoples originally from Africa who were, in ancient times, colonists in India. Therefore it is no surprise that many Indian traditions including religious and Yogic, would be found earlier in Ancient Egypt. Yet there is ample evidence from ancient writings and perhaps more importantly, iconographical evidences from the Ancient Egyptians themselves and the Indians themselves that prove the connection between Ancient Egypt and India as well as the existence of a discipline of Yoga Postures in Ancient Egypt long before its practice in India. This handy volume has been designed to be accessible to young adults and all others who would like to have an easy reference with documentation on this important subject. This is an important subject because the frame of reference with which we look at a culture depends strongly on our conceptions about its origins. In this case, if we look at the Ancient Egyptians as Asiatic peoples we would treat them and their culture in one way. If we see them as Africans we not only see them in a different light but we also must ascribe Africa with a glorious legacy that matches any other culture in human history. We would also look at the culture and philosophies of the Ancient Egyptians as having African insights instead of Asiatic ones. Those insights inform our knowledge bout other African traditions and we can also begin to understand in a deeper way the effect of Ancient Egyptian culture on African culture and also on the Asiatic as well. When we discover the deeper and more ancient practice of the postures system in Ancient Egypt that was called "Hatha Yoga" in India, we are able to find a new and expanded understanding of the practice that constitutes a discipline of spiritual practice that informs and revitalizes the Indian practices as well as all spiritual disciplines.

39. The Black Ancient Egyptians

This present volume, The Black Ancient Egyptians: The Black African Ancestry of the Ancient Egyptians, formed one subject in the larger work: The African Origins of Civilization, Religion, Yoga Mysticism and Ethics Philosophy. It was felt that this subject needed to be discussed because even in the early 21st century, the idea persists that the Ancient Egyptians were peoples originally from Asia Minor who came into North-East Africa. Yet there is ample evidence from ancient writings and perhaps more importantly, iconographical evidences from the Ancient Egyptians themselves that proves otherwise. This handy volume has been designed to be accessible to young adults and all others who would like to have an easy reference with documentation on this important subject. This is an important subject because the frame of reference with which we look at a culture depends strongly on our conceptions about its origins. in this case, if we look at the Ancient Egyptians as Asiatic peoples we would treat them and their culture in one way. If we see them as Africans we not only see them in a different light but we also must ascribe Africa with a glorious legacy that matches any other culture in human history. We would also look at the culture and philosophies of the Ancient Egyptians as having African insights instead of Asiatic ones. Those insights inform our knowledge bout other African traditions and we can also begin to understand in a deeper way the effect of Ancient Egyptian culture on African culture and also on the Asiatic as well.

40. The Limits of Faith: The Failure of Faith-based Religions and the Solution to the Meaning of Life

Is faith belief in something without proof? And if so is there never to be any proof or discovery? If so what is the need of intellect? If faith is trust in something that is real is that reality historical, literal or metaphorical or philosophical? If knowledge is an essential element in faith why should there by so much emphasis on believing and not on understanding in the modern practice of religion? This volume is a compilation of essays related to the nature of religious faith in the context of its inception in human history as well as its meaning for religious practice and relations between religions in modern times. Faith has come to be regarded as a virtuous goal in life. However, many people have asked how can it be that an endeavor that is supposed to be dedicated to spiritual upliftment has led to more conflict in human history than any other social factor?

41. <u>Redemption of The Criminal Heart Through Kemetic Spirituality and Maat Philosophy</u>

Special book dedicated to inmates, their families and members of the Law Enforcement community. ISBN: 1-884564-70-4
$5.00

42. COMPARATIVE MYTHOLOGY

What are Myth and Culture and what is their importance for understanding the development of societies, human evolution and the search for meaning? What is the purpose of culture and how do cultures evolve? What are the elements of a culture and how can those elements be broken down and the constituent parts of a culture understood and compared? How do cultures interact? How does enculturation occur and how do people interact with other cultures? How do the processes of acculturation and cooptation occur and what does this mean for the development of a society? How can

the study of myths and the elements of culture help in understanding the meaning of life and the means to promote understanding and peace in the world of human activity? This volume is the exposition of a method for studying and comparing cultures, myths and other social aspects of a society. It is an expansion on the Cultural Category Factor Correlation method for studying and comparing myths, cultures, religions and other aspects of human culture. It was originally introduced in the year 2002. This volume contains an expanded treatment as well as several refinements along with examples of the application of the method. the apparent. I hope you enjoy these art renditions as serene reflections of the mysteries of life. ISBN: 1-884564-72-0
Book price $21.95

43. CONVERSATION WITH GOD: Revelations of the Important Questions of Life
$24.99 U.S.   Inmate Price $17.00

   This volume contains a grouping of some of the questions that have been submitted to Sebai Dr. Muata Ashby. They are efforts by many aspirants to better understand and practice the teachings of mystical spirituality. It is said that when sages are asked spiritual questions they are relaying the wisdom of God, the Goddess, the Higher Self, etc. There is a very special quality about the Q & A process that does not occur during a regular lecture session. Certain points come out that would not come out otherwise due to the nature of the process which ideally occurs after a lecture. Having been to a certain degree enlightened by a lecture certain new questions arise and the answers to these have the effect of elevating the teaching of the lecture to even higher levels. Therefore, enjoy these exchanges and may they lead you to enlightenment, peace and prosperity.
Available Late Summer 2007 ISBN: 1-884564-68-2

44. MYSTIC ART PAINTINGS
(with Full Color images) This book contains a collection of the small number of paintings that I have created over the years. Some were used as early book covers and others were done simply to express certain spiritual feelings; some were created for no purpose except to express the joy of color and the feeling of relaxed freedom. All are to elicit mystical awakening in the viewer. Writing a book on philosophy is like sculpture, the more the work is rewritten the reflections and ideas become honed and take form and become clearer and imbued with intellectual beauty. Mystic music is like meditation, a world of its own that exists about 1 inch above ground wherein the musician does not touch the ground. Mystic Graphic Art is meditation in form, color, image and reflected image which opens the door to the reality behind the apparent. I hope you enjoy these art renditions and my reflections on them as serene reflections of the mysteries of life, as visual renditions of the philosophy I have written about over the years. ISBN 1-884564-69-0

45. Coming in Spring 2008
THE KEMETIC TREE OF LIFE
From the earliest teachings of Ancient Egypt
The Tree of Life is a roadmap of a journey which explains how Creation came into being and how it will end. It also explains what Creation is composed of and also what human beings are and what they are composed of. It also explains the process of Creation, how Creation develops, as well as who created Creation and where that entity may be found. It also explains how a human being may discover that entity and in so doing also discover the secrets of Creation, the meaning of life and the means to break free from the pathetic condition of human limitation and mortality in order to discover the higher realms of being by discovering the principles, the levels of existence that are beyond the simple physical and material aspects of life. This book contains color plates **ISBN: 1-884564-74-7**
$24.95 U.S.

AUDIO LECTURE SERIES
BY DR. MUATA ASHBY

All cassettes on Sale for only $ 9.99   Use the number
when ordering.

Learning the Serpent Power

4057 Class 57 – Maat and the Serpent Power Part 1 Audio Cassette
4058 Class 58 – Maat and the Serpent Power Part 2 Audio Cassette
7022 The 2 Goddesses and the Serpent Power V.11 Audio Cassette

VIDEO: Serpent Power Meditation Lesson 1
VIDEO: Serpent Power and the Egyptian Yoga Postures

Wisdom of Egyptian Yoga
100 Introduction to Egyptian Yoga, the paths of Yoga and Mystical Religion 9/15/97 $9.99
100A-100B Introduction to Egyptian Yoga, the paths of Yoga and Mystical Religion 2 tapes $14.99
102 What is Yoga and how can it transform your life? Radio Interview in LA - $4.99
103 Wisdom of Egyptian Yoga Part 1 $9.99 - 90min (103 & 104 - 2 tape set)
104 Wisdom of Egyptian Yoga Part 2 $9.99 - 90min (103 & 104 - 2 tape set)
105 Maat Workshop Part 1: How to Practice the Teachings - $9.99- 90min
106 Maat Workshop Part 2: How to Practice the Teachings -$9.99- 90min
107 Pert Em Heru: Introduction to the Book of Coming Forth By Day Part 1-$9.99
108 Pert Em Heru: Introduction to the Book of Coming Forth By Day Part 2-$9.99
109 Initiation Into Shetaut Aset Part 1: The Teachings of The Temple of Aset- $9.99
110 Initiation Into Shetaut Aset Part 2: The Teachings of The Temple of Aset - $9.99
111 The Cycles of Time - $14.99 - 2 hours
112 Race Relations in the light of Yoga Philosophy $9.99 - 90 min
113 Nature Of Embodiment
114 Seven Steps Of Maat
115 Cycles of Time – Study of History from the Mystical perspective.
116A Indus Kamit Kush Part 1
116B Indus Kamit Kush Part 2

The process of Initiation and the Initiatic Way of Life
200 Initiation Into Egyptian Yoga Part I- $9.99 (200 & 201 - 2 tape set) 90min
201 Initiation Into Egyptian Yoga Part II- $9.99 (200 & 201 - 2 tape set) 90 min.
209 Sheti Workshop Part 1
210 Sheti Workshop Part 2
211 The Initiatic Way Of Ed (Ohio) 2/9/97- $14.99 -Two hours

Initiation Series Class Lectures Based on the Book
203 CLASS 1 Initiation: How to be a Disciple of Yoga: - $9.99 - 90 min
204 CLASS 2 Initiation: The Ten Virtues of a Spiritual Aspirant Part 1 -$9.99- 60 min
(204 & 205 set)
205 CLASS 3 Initiation: The Ten Virtues of a Spiritual Aspirant Part 2 -$9.99 - 60 min
(204 & 205 set)
206 CLASS 4 Introduction to Meditation: The Art of Concentration $9.99 - 60 min
207 CLASS 5 Initiation: Health, Vegetarianism and Yoga $9.99 - 90 min
212 Good Association – The Importance of and how to conduct the Sheti Group Study
Meetings

Ausarian Resurrection Series 1997 Based on The Book Ausarian Resurrection: The
Ancient Egyptian Bible
300 Ausarian Resurrection, (Presentation) Part 1- $9.99
301 Ausarian Resurrection, (Presentation) Part 2- $9.99
302 CLASS 1 The Three Levels of Religion - $9.99 - 90 min.
303 CLASS 2 The Story of Hethor and Djehuti: The Three States of Consciousness - $9.99
- 90 min.
304 CLASS 3 The Story of Ra and Aset $9.99 - 90 min.
305 CLASS 4 Understanding the mind and how to transcend the Ego $9.99
306 CLASS 5 The Glory of Devotional Love, Part 1 - $9.99 - 90 min
307 CLASS 6 The Glory of Devotional Love, Part 2 - $9.99 - 90 min
308 CLASS 7 The Birth of Heru & the Meaning of Happiness - $9.99 - 90 min
309 CLASS 8 The Death of Heru: How Egoism Poisons Spiritual Aspiration $9.99 - 90
min
310 CLASS 9 The Glory of Listening to the Teachings - $9.99 - 90 min
311 CLASS 10 The Initiation of Heru $9.99 - 90 min
312 CLASS 11 How the soul becomes incarnated and trapped in the body $9.99 - 60 min
313 CLASS 12 How the soul operated through mind and senses and ego $9.99 - 90 min
314 CLASS 13 How externalized senses lead to suffering and how suffering leads to
enlightenment $9.99
315 CLASS 14 How Karma Works to Guide the Soul and How to overcome the warlike
mentality $9.99
316 Class 15 Lecture 1/25/98 Verse 71 The Initiation of Heru
316B Class 15B Verse 86 The Nature of Human Embodiment
317 Class 16 3/8/98, Verse 95-110
318 Class 17 3/15/98, Verse 111-119
319 Class 18 3/22/98, Verse 120
320 Class 19 3/29/98, Illusory Nature Of World
321 Class 20 4/4/98, Verse 130
322 Class 21 Illusion of Desires, Tantrism, Sexuality and Enlightenment 4/26/98.
323 Class 22 5/3/98, Verse 145 The challenge of the Lower Self against three
Higher Self
324-325 Class 23 Conclusion Two tape Set 5/10/98: Desperation, Sexuality,
Spiritual Victory -Verse 163 to conclusion.

Daily Worship, Chanting, Devotional Practice.
501 Ushet Morning Worship: Adorations to Ra-Khepera and Hethor $9.99 - approx. 30
min.
502 Ushet Morning Worship: Adorations to Amun - $9.99 - 60 min.
503 Morning Worship Led By Vijaya
504 Morning Worship To Khepra and Midday worship to Ra
900 Ushet Devotional Chanting of Hekau *Amma Su En Pa Neter* - $9.99 - 60 min.

901 Ushet Devotional Chanting of Divine Name Hekau: *Om Amun Ra Ptah* - $9.99 - 60 min.
902 Ushet Devotional Chanting of Divine Name Hekau: *Om Asar, Aset, Heru* - $9.99 - 60 min.

Physical Exercise Workout
600 The Egyptian Yoga Exercise Workout with Vijaya Level I- short session $9.99 45 min.
601 The Egyptian Yoga Exercise Workout with Vijaya Level II- long session $9.99 - 90 min
603 The Egyptian Yoga Exercise Workout and Meditation with Muata Level III - long session $9.99 - 90 min
604 The Egyptian Yoga Exercise Workout with Muata Short session $9.99   30 min

Meditation Practice Based on the Book
700 Meditation Lecture Series Part 1 (St. Louis)- $9.99 -60 min. (700, 701 & 702 - 3 tape set)
701 Meditation Lecture Series, Part 2 (St. Louis) - $9.99 - 60 min. (700, 701 & 702 - 3 tape set)
702 Meditation Lecture Series, Part 3 (St. Louis) - $9.99 - 60 min. (700, 701 & 702 - 3 tape set)
703 Guided Meditation Session $9.99
704 Lotus Meditation (Vijaya), 6/27/98
705 Concentration-meditation session 15 minutes for use with the Initiation Class lecture series.
706 Slowness Meditation Session
707 Meditation for Transcending Fear
800 Serpent Power Level I: Lecture, Music and Meditation -$9.99 - 90min
801 Serpent Power Level II: Lecture, Music and Meditation - $9.99 - 90min

Christian Yoga Based on the Book Christian Yoga
1000 Issues in Christian Yoga-Lecture at Unity Church in Los Angeles $9.99
1001-A Introduction to Christian Yoga: How to understand and Study the Book $9.99 (Part I)
1001-B Introduction to Christian Yoga: Questions and Answers about Christian Yoga (Part II)
1002 Orthodox Religion vs. Yoga Philosophy – resolving the conflict.

Advanced Teaching Series
2000 How To Teach yoga

Special Interest Lectures
3000 Mystic Poetry Readings by Dr. Ashby and students 3/15/98
3001 Creation of the Sema Institute of Yoga Temple 4/19/98
3002 Inspiration for Teenagers (dealing with anger, sex and discovering the purpose of life.)
3003 Inspiration for College students Set up Fraternities and Sororities based on original Egyptian Wisdom.
3004 Glory of Silence
3005-3008 Yoga and Mental Health Seminar (4 tapes)
3009-3010 Ancient Egyptian origins of Fraternities and Sorrorities and Western Culture and Philosophy (2 tapes)
3011 Spiritual Self-Publishing
3012 Dramatic Arts, Music and Enlightenment in Ancient Egyptian Theater

Maat Philosophy Series 1998 Lectures Maat, the 42 Laws, the Ancient Egyptian Wisdom Texts

4001 Class 1 - Introduction to Maat Philosophy
4002 Class 2 - Profound issues of Maat and its practice in life
4003 Class 3 - Profound issues and the Cycle of Vice
4004 Class 4 - Introduction to the Principle of Truth
4005 Class 5 - Principle of Truth Part 2
4006 Class 6 - Principle of Truth Part 3
4007 Class 7 - Principle of Truth part 4
4008 Class 8 - Introduction to the Principle of Non-violence
4009 Class 9 - Principle of Non-violence Part 2
4010 Class 10 - Principle of Non-violence Part 3
4011 Class 11 - Principle of Non-violence Part 4
4012 Class 12 – Principle of Non-stealing Part 1
4013 Class 13 – Principle of Non-stealing Part 2
4014 Class 14 – Principle of Non-stealing Part 3
4015 Class 15 – Principle of Selfless Service
4016 Class 16 – Principle of Right Action
4017 Class 17 – Principle of Right Speech Part 1
4018 Class 18 – Principle of Right Speech Part 2
4019 Class 19 – Principle of Right Speech Part 3
4020 Class 20 – Principle of Right Speech Part 4
4021 Class 21 – Principle of Right Worship Part 1
4022 Class 22 – Principle of Right Worship Part 2
4023 Class 23 – Principle of Right Worship Part 3
4024 Class 24 – Principle of Right Worship Part 4
4025 Class 25 – Principle of Right Worship Part 5
4026 Class 26 – Principle of Right Worship Part 6
4027 Class 25 – Principle of Right Thinking Part 1

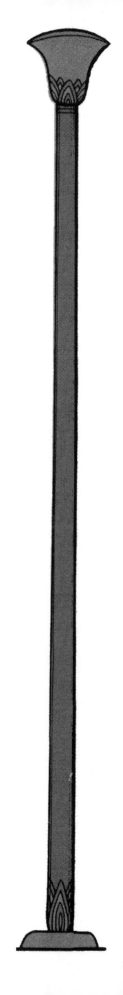

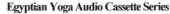

Egyptian Yoga Audio Cassette Series

Introduction to Egyptian Yoga Tape I $9.99, Tape II $9.99 Three hours

Maat Workshop I How to Practice the Teachings Tape I $9.99, Tape II $9.99 Three hours

The Serpent Power Lecture, Music and Meditation Tape I $9.99, Tape II $9.99 Three hours

Indus Kamit Kush - Yoga in Ancient Egypt and India $14.99 Two hours

The Egyptian Yoga Exercise Workout $9.99 One hour

The Inner Meaning of The Egyptian, Christian and Indian Trinity $14.99 -

Initiation Into Egyptian Yoga - $19.99 Two tapes

The Initiatic Way of Education - $14.99 Two hours

The Meditation and Chanting Workshop Series - Four Tapes 3 hours-40 minutes $30.00

Ushet I: Words of Power Chanting - Daily worship and Meditation $9.99 30 Minutes each side

Ushet II: Words of Power Chanting "Om-Amun-Ra-Ptah" - $9.99 30 Minutes each side

Ushet III: Words of Power Chanting "Amma Su en Pa Neter" - Give Thyself to God - $9.99 30 Minutes each side

Ushet IIII: Words of Power Chanting "Om-Asar_Aset-Heru" - $9.99 30 Minutes each side

Ushet IV: Words of Power Chanting "Haari Om" - $9..99 30 Minutes each side

Egyptian Yoga Audio Compact Disk Series

The Serpent Power I Lecture, Music and Meditation Disk I $19.99,

The Serpent Power II Lecture, Music and Meditation Disk II $19.99

Egyptian Yoga Video Cassette Series

Introduction to Egyptian Yoga $19.99

Indus - Kamit - Kush Yoga in Ancient Egypt and India $19.99

Thef Neteru: The Movement of The Gods and goddesses, The Egyptian Yoga Exercise Workout $19.99

The Inner Meaning of The Egyptian, Christian and Indian Trinity $19.99

Meditation and Chanting Workshop 3 hours-40 minutes $40.00

Initiation Into Egyptian Yoga Video with manual - Class 1 of the the Course in Yoga and Mystical Spirituality at Florida International University in Miami Florida $24.99

Music Based on the Prt M Hru and other Kamitic Texts

Available on Compact Disc $14.99 and Audio Cassette $9.99

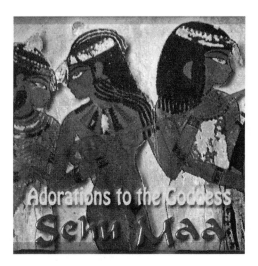

Adorations to the Goddess

Music for Worship of the Goddess

NEW Egyptian Yoga Music CD
by Sehu Maa
Ancient Egyptian Music CD
Instrumental Music played on reproductions of Ancient Egyptian Instruments–
Ideal for <u>meditation</u> and
reflection on the Divine and for the practice of spiritual programs and <u>Yoga</u>
<u>exercise sessions.</u>

©1999 By Muata Ashby
CD $14.99 –Cassette $10

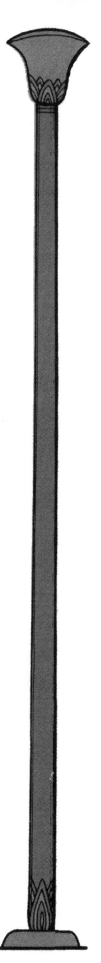

MERIT'S INSPIRATION
NEW Egyptian Yoga Music CD
by Sehu Maa
Ancient Egyptian Music CD
Instrumental Music played on
reproductions of Ancient Egyptian Instruments– Ideal for <u>meditation</u> and
reflection on the Divine and for the practice of spiritual programs and <u>Yoga</u>
<u>exercise sessions.</u>
©1999 By
Muata Ashby
CD $14.99 –Cassette $10
UPC# 761527100429

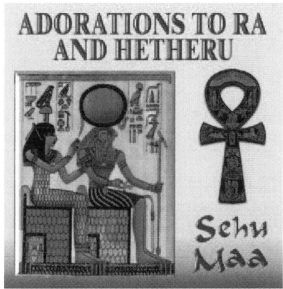

ANORATIONS TO RA AND HETHERU
NEW Egyptian Yoga Music CD
By Sehu Maa (Muata Ashby)
Based on the Words of Power of Ra and Hetheru
played on reproductions of Ancient Egyptian Instruments **Ancient Egyptian**
Instruments used: Voice, Clapping, Nefer Lute, Tar Drum, Sistrums,

Cymbals – The Chants, Devotions, Rhythms and Festive Songs Of the Neteru – Ideal for meditation, and devotional singing and dancing.
©1999 By Muata Ashby
CD $14.99 –Cassette $10
UPC# 761527100221

SONGS TO ASAR ASET AND HERU
NEW
Egyptian Yoga Music CD
By Sehu Maa
played on reproductions of Ancient Egyptian Instruments– The Chants, Devotions, Rhythms and Festive Songs Of the Neteru - Ideal for meditation, and devotional singing and dancing.
Based on the Words of Power of Asar (Asar), Aset (Aset) and Heru (Heru) Om Asar Aset Heru is the third in a series of musical explorations of the Kamitic (Ancient Egyptian) tradition of music. Its ideas are based on the Ancient Egyptian Religion of Asar, Aset and Heru and it is designed for listening, meditation and worship. ©1999 By Muata Ashby

CD $14.99 –Cassette $10
UPC# 761527100122

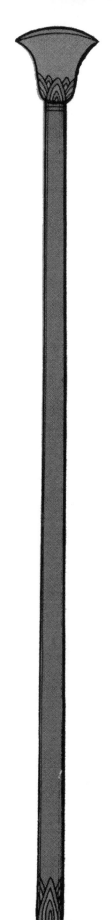

HAARI OM: ANCIENT EGYPT MEETS INDIA IN MUSIC
NEW Music CD
By Sehu Maa

The Chants, Devotions, Rhythms and
Festive Songs Of the Ancient Egypt and India, harmonized and played on reproductions of ancient instruments along with modern instruments and beats. Ideal for meditation, and devotional singing and dancing.

Haari Om is the fourth in a series of musical explorations of the Kamitic (Ancient Egyptian) and Indian traditions of music, chanting and devotional spiritual practice. Its ideas are based on the Ancient Egyptian Yoga spirituality and Indian Yoga spirituality.

©1999 By Muata Ashby
CD $14.99 –Cassette $10
UPC# 761527100528

RA AKHU: THE GLORIOUS LIGHT
NEW
Egyptian Yoga Music CD
By Sehu Maa

The fifth collection of original music compositions based on the Teachings and Words of The Trinity, the God Asar and the Goddess Nebethet, the Divinity Aten, the God Heru, and the Special Meditation Hekau or Words of Power of Ra from the Ancient Egyptian Tomb of Seti I and more...

played on reproductions of Ancient Egyptian Instruments and modern instruments - **Ancient Egyptian Instruments used: Voice, Clapping, Nefer Lute, Tar Drum, Sistrums, Cymbals**

— The Chants, Devotions, Rhythms and Festive Songs Of the Neteru – Ideal for meditation, and devotional singing and dancing.

©1999 By Muata Ashby

CD $14.99 –Cassette $10

UPC# 761527100825

GLORIES OF THE DIVINE MOTHER

Based on the hieroglyphic text of the worship of Goddess Net.

The Glories of The Great Mother

©2000 **Muata Ashby**

CD $14.99 UPC# 761527101129

SEMA UNIVERSITY www.SemaUniversity.org

The Sema University School of Kemetic Culture and Ancient Egyptian Mysteries offers online studies leading to Associate and Bachelor degrees.

ASSOCIATE DEGREE

You may earn an Associate degree in Kemetic studies by completing 5 courses over a period of 1-1/4 years. Those who complete the Associate Degree are granted a certificate with the title of Teacher of Kemetic Culture

BACHELOR DEGREE

You may earn an Bachelor degree in Kemetic religion or philosophy within 2 years by concentrating in specific areas of study like:

	Degree Concentration area	Degree Concentration area	Degree Concentration area	Degree Concentration area	Degree Concentration area
Degree title	*Kamitan African Theology* *33 credit*	*Sema (Yoga) & Health Practitioner* *30 credit*	*Kamitan African Philosophy of Religion and Ethics* *27 credit*	*Comparative Religion and World Religion* *24 credit*	*Interdisciplinary Kamitan Studies* (Student may combine electives to create a program of their choice with approval of their mentor.) *24 credit*
FOCUS OF THE DEGREE PROGRAM 	Understanding the nature of Kamitan religion and its special concept of theism the nature of the Divine and its relationship to the Self as well as the main religious Kamitan paths to spiritual enlightenment.	Understanding the nature of Kamitan disciplines of SEMA or Yoga the sciences for attaining spiritual enlightenment through cultivation of body mind and soul.	Understanding the nature of Kamitan philosophy psycho-mythology and wisdom for transforming and enlightening the mind to attain higher consciousness.	Understanding the nature of world religion and its dept to Kamitan religion as well as discovering the true meaning of religion and how to get to the source and true purpose of religion: Spiritual enlightenment and human peace.	Student must complete the core courses and then choose at least 5 electives from the other degree programs

Those who complete the Bachelor degree program receive a Diploma and the title of Basu (instructor, teacher) in their chosen area of concentration.

ONLINE: The program is delivered online and via correspondence. The student receives lesson plans and interactive contact via the internet and can communicate with Sebai Dr. Muata Ashby, mentors and other students.

ACCESS TO STUDENT ONLY AREAS of the Sema University Web site containing special lectures, access to online conferences on philosophy, meditative practice, and more.

Begin your studies at any time of the year and start your path of self-discovery, learn how to promote the Kemetic path in your community and promote the upliftment of humanity through Ancient Egyptian Spirituality

www.SemaUniversity.org

Order Form

Telephone orders: Call Toll Free: 1(305) 378-6253. Have your AMEX, Optima, Visa or MasterCard ready.

Fax orders: 1-(305) 378-6253   E-MAIL ADDRESS: Semayoga@aol.com

Postal Orders: Sema Institute of Yoga, P.O. Box 570459, Miami, Fl. 33257. USA.

Please send the following books and / or tapes.

ITEM

_____ Cost $_____

_____ Cost $_____

_____ Cost $_____

_____ Cost $_____

_____ Cost $_____

Total $_____

Name:_____

Physical Address:_____

City:_____ State:_____ Zip:_____

Sales tax: Please add 6.5% for books shipped to Florida addresses

_____ Shipping: $4.50 for first book and .50¢ for each additional

_____ Shipping: Outside US $5.00 for first book and $3.00 for each additional

_____ Payment:_____

_____ Check -Include Driver License #:

_____

_____ Credit card: _____ Visa, _____ MasterCard, _____ Optima, _____ AMEX.

Card number:_____

Name on card:_____ Exp. date:_____/_____

Printed in Poland
by Amazon Fulfillment
Poland Sp. z o.o., Wrocław